MARXISM MAOISM AND UTOPIANISM

MARXISM MAOISM AND UTOPIANISM

Eight Essays

Maurice Meisner

THE UNIVERSITY OF WISCONSIN PRESS

Published 1982

The University of Wisconsin Press
114 North Murray Street
Madison, Wisconsin 53715

The University of Wisconsin Press, Ltd.
1 Gower Street
London WC1E 6HA, England

First printing

Printed in the United States of America

For LC CIP information see the colophon

ISBN 0-299-08420-5

Chapter 2, "Utopian Socialist Themes in Maoism," was originally published in *Peasant Rebellion and Communist Revolution in Asia*, John Wilson Lewis, ed. (Stanford, Calif.: Stanford University Press, 1974), pp. 207–52, 340–45 reprinted with the permission of the publishers, Stanford University Press; © 1974 by the Board of Trustees of the Leland Stanford Junior University; Chapter 3, "Leninism and Maoism: Some Populist Perspectives on Marxism-Leninism in China," in *The China Quarterly* 45 (January–March, 1971): 2–36; Chapter 4, "Utopian Goals and Ascetic Values in Chinese Communist Ideology," in *The Journal of Asian Studies* 28.1 (November 1968): 101–10; Chapter 5, "Images of the Paris Commune in Contemporary Chinese Marxist Thought," in *The Massachusetts Review* 12.3 (1971): 479–97 © 1971 The Massachusetts Review, Inc.; and Chapter 7, "Utopian and Dystopian Elements in the Maoist Vision of the Future," in *Radical Visions of the Future*, Seweryn Bialer and Sophia Sluzar, eds. (Boulder, Colo.: Westview Press, 1977), pp. 85–126, 188–92 © 1977 The Research Institute on International Change, Columbia University.

For Jeff

Contents

Preface

Is Communism only the piling of brick on brick?
—Mao Tse-tung, 1965

On 27 June 1981, on occasion of the sixtieth anniversary of the founding of the Chinese Communist Party, the post-Maoist leaders of the People's Republic of China announced their long-delayed assessment of the place of Mao Tse-tung in the history of the Chinese Revolution. The lengthy resolution issued by the Communist Party of China, while concluding that Mao's "contributions to the Chinese Revolution far outweigh his mistakes," nevertheless sets forth a rather harsh indictment of the final two decades of the late Chairman's rule. The resolution enumerates a long list of "leftist" errors committed by Mao from the time of the Great Leap Forward campaign to the "catastrophe" of the Cultural Revolution and its "feudal-fascist" aftermath. Particularly prominent among the aging Mao's mistakes, according to his official assessors, were political and ideological proclivities that Marxists conventionally have labelled "utopian" and therefore "unscientific." Mao, it is charged, "overestimated the role of man's subjective will and efforts," he indulged in forms of thinking and practice "divorced from reality," and he raised entirely unrealistic expectations of the advent of a communist utopia. Having thereby violated the presumably "objective laws" of historical development, Mao Tse-tung, from the orthodox Marxist-Leninist perspectives of the current Peking leadership, stands censured for his "utopian" heresies.

In condemning Maoist utopianism, China's present political and ideological leaders were long preceded by Western students of contemporary Chinese history. Since the time of the Great Leap Forward campaign of 1958, most foreign scholars viewed Mao's ideas and policies as recklessly utopian, wildly irrational, and wholly incongruous with presumably universal and necessary processes of modern economic and political development. And many other Western observers who found so many virtues in Maoism during the Maoist era have now come to see the errors of their ways (now that the errors have been officially revealed in Peking) and join in the general celebration of the new course followed by Mao's successors. Peking and most Western students of the People's Republic stand on unaccustomed common ground in praising the "pragmatism" of China's new leaders and their sober pursuit of the "Four Modernizations."

Consigning Maoist utopianism to the "dustbin of history," as is currently fashionable among Peking's leaders and their foreign observers, is of course very much in accord with the general temper of the times. For we live in an age when utopian visions of a future good society have all but vanished in both the industrialized capitalist world and the ostensibly "socialist" world. The advanced capitalist countries, should they not be crushed under the social weight of their own technologies, suffer from a cruel paradox, which has been acutely diagnosed by Frank and Fritzie Manuel:

> Just when magnificent new scientific powers have become available to us, we are faced with a paucity of invention in utopian modalities. . . . Scientists tell us that they can now outline with a fair degree of accuracy the procedures necessary to establish a space colony in a hollowed comet or asteroid. But when it comes to describing what people will do there, the men most active in the field merely reconstruct suburbia—garden clubs and all—in a new weightless environment.

The Manuels have good and more than sufficient reason to lament "the discrepancy between the piling up of technological and scientific instrumentalities for making all things possible, and the pitiable poverty of goals."[1]

No less pitiful is the impoverishment of goals in Communist-ruled lands. Socialist revolutions, which in decades past seemed to many the hope of the future, clearly have failed to produce socialist societies. Marxist visions of a communist utopia have given way to the

1. Frank E. Manuel and Fritzie P. Manuel, *Utopian Thought in the Western World* (Cambridge, Mass.: Harvard University Press, 1979), p. 811.

goals of modern economic development—and official Marxist-Leninist doctrines, correspondingly, have degenerated into little more than ideologies of modernization, their wearisome ideological rhetoric barely disguising the banal nationalist aims of their bureaucratic authors. The "socialist" countries, all latecomers on the world industrial scene, mimic their capitalist predecessors in "the piling up of technological instrumentalities," playing out a historical parody in tattered Marxian garb.

Our time is one when Communist and capitalist lands alike suffer from a pitiable poverty of goals and an appalling lack of vision. And for those who envision a future for mankind that embraces more than the assumed "rationality" of modern industrial society, it is perhaps not the time to hasten to applaud the demise of utopianism in China or elsewhere. The Maoist brand of utopianism may no longer be of any political relevance, but it does have a historical significance, and its significance deserves to be understood in terms that are historically and humanly comprehensible. To dismiss the utopianism of Mao Tse-tung as an unfortunate historical aberration—whether the dismissing is done by orthodox Marxist-Leninists or by orthodox theorists of "the modernization process"—does little to further the understanding of the past, nor does it yield such guidance as the past might have to offer for those who still hope and strive for a new and better future.

This book is an inquiry—or more precisely, an interrelated series of inquiries proceeding from different intellectual and historical points of departure—into the utopian aspects of the Maoist mentality. It is primarily a study in the intellectual history of Maoism, confined to (and limited by), it should be emphasized, the pursuit of themes and issues directly relevant to the utopian side of Mao Tse-tung's thought. There are, of course, many other sides of Mao, but it is not the aim of the present inquiry to discuss Maoist theory as a whole or the political practice which flowed from it. Yet the utopian side of Mao is not historically inconsequential, and this volume, it is hoped, is not simply a study in the history of ideas. For it was precisely Mao's "utopian" departures from Marxist and Leninist orthodoxies, it is argued in the chapters that follow, which were essential in transforming the inherited body of Marxist theory into a doctrine relevant to the needs of revolution in the modern Chinese historical environment. And, it is further argued, it was Mao's visionary utopianism in the years after 1949 which had a great deal to do with molding much of what has been distinctive about the postrevolutionary history of the People's Republic. Maoist utopianism is not an exotic intellectual curiosity but a historical phenomenon intimately related to the social and political history of modern and contemporary China.

It is not the purpose of this volume to assess the historical results of the Maoist era. In an earlier book, I offered the views I hold on the Maoist attempt to construct a socialist society in an economically backward land—and concluded that while the attempt was historically remarkable it was found wanting in the end.[2] Mao Tse-tung, like most revolutionaries—and perhaps more ardently than most—strove to attain what was historically impossible in his time in order to attain what was attainable. But whatever historical judgments one wishes to make about Mao Tse-tung and the Maoist era (and no historical judgment is ever final), that era will be recorded as one of the great utopian episodes in world history, and the history of Maoism will remain relevant for those who seek to understand the fate of Marxism and the role of utopianism in the modern world, whatever their political persuasions. In an age which suffers from a paucity of utopian imagination, it is perhaps a history worth recalling.

Five of the eight chapters of this book appeared earlier in the form of essays, and I am grateful to their original publishers for permission to include them in the present volume. These five essays (from which Chapters 2, 3, 4, 5, and 7 are derived) were written during the period of the Cultural Revolution, an era now condemned in Peking as "the ten lost years," and no doubt they bear the marks and blemishes of their time. Yet since the nature of Maoism appears essentially the same to me now as it did then, I have not attempted to rewrite these chapters with the sometimes dubious benefits of historical hindsight. Save for stylistic changes, they remain, in substance and interpretation, as they originally were written; they have not been retailored to fit current fashion. Three chapters (1, 6, and 8) were prepared specifically for this book.

2. *Mao's China: A History of the People's Republic* (New York: The Free Press, 1977).

I am grateful to the Research Committee of the University of Wisconsin Graduate School and the Social Science Research Council, who provided me with the free time during which much of this book was written. I owe a very special debt to Lynn Lubkeman, whose ideas and insights contributed enormously to the content of the volume, and who did much of the work necessary in preparing it for publication. I am also grateful to Elizabeth Steinberg, Chief Editor of the University of Wisconsin Press, a constant source of intellectual stimulation and moral encouragement. This book is affectionately dedicated to my son Jeff, who combines an appreciation of the benefits of modern technology with a social vision of a new and better world.

M. M.

Madison, Wisconsin
August 1981

MARXISM
MAOISM AND
UTOPIANISM

1

Marxism and Utopianism

I. History and Utopia

The term "utopia," Lewis Mumford once observed, can be taken to mean either the ultimate in human hope or the ultimate in human folly. Mumford also noted that Sir Thomas More, whose celebrated work introduced the term to modern political discourse, was aware of both meanings of the word when he pointed to its divergent Greek origins: *eutopia*, which means the good place; and *outopia*, which means no place.[1]

The ambiguity of "utopia"—at once suggesting the grandeur of striving to reach "the good place" and the futility of searching for "no place"—reflects the ambiguity inherent in utopian modes of thought and their ambiguous relationship to history. For utopias are the products of trans-historical moral ideals, and the relationship between moral demands and historical realities is a most tenuous and uncertain one. Utopia, the perfect future that men wish for, and history, the imperfect future that men are in the process of creating, do not correspond. And it is the consciousness of that lack of correspondence which gives utopian thought its sense of moral pathos and its historical ambiguity. Morally, utopia may be "the good place," but historically it may be "no place."

Yet the ambiguity of utopia is its virtue, not its vice. For it is

1. Lewis Mumford, *The Story of Utopias* (New York: Viking Press, 1962), p. 1.

precisely because utopia has not been realized in history—and indeed is something historically unlikely and perhaps impossible—that provides utopian thought with its continuing intellectual and historical vitality. The historical significance and utility of utopian visions frequently has been noted. Utopian conceptions of the world as it should be clash with the world as it is to generate a sense of tension between what Max Weber termed "the actually existent and the ideal," and at the same time generate a sense of hope for the future, thereby producing the essential preconditions for human actions which aim to transform the world in accordance with an image of what it should be.[2] It is the *striving* for utopia, not its accomplishment, that is the dynamic force in history—and indeed a historically necessary one. As Weber once observed, "Man would not have attained the possible unless time and again he had reached out for the impossible."[3] And as Karl Mannheim warned: "With the relinquishment of utopias, man would lose his will to shape history and therewith his ability to understand it."[4] But the historical process can never be fully shaped into a utopian mold without relinquishing both history and utopia. If utopia was ever realized it would lose its historical significance, for history (an imperfect state of affairs) implies process and change, whereas utopia (a perfect state) would be static, immobile, lifeless, and boring. Utopia, if it ever arrived, would mark the end of history.

The ambiguous relationship between utopia and history was not a problem, or at least not recognized as a problem, before the Enlightenment introduced the idea of history as progress—and utopian thinking thereby became infused with historical optimism. Prior to the late eighteenth century, the long tradition of Western secular utopian thought neither implied historical hopefulness nor demanded political activism. From Plato to Sir Thomas More and his imitators, as Judith Shklar has pointed out, utopia was a trans-historical model

2. Max Weber, *The Sociology of Religion* (Boston: Beacon Press, 1963), p. 144.

3. Hans Gerth and C. Wright Mills, eds., *From Max Weber: Essays in Sociology* (New York: Oxford University Press, 1958), p. 128.

4. Karl Mannheim, *Ideology and Utopia* (New York: Harcourt Brace, 1952), p. 236.

which invited contemplation, not activity; it was a standard of moral judgment in the present, not a prescription for the future.[5] The classical utopias were of course "historical" in the sense that they reflected the historical conditions of their producers and often offered, at least implicitly, radical critiques of the evils of existing social orders. Karl Kautsky, who viewed (perhaps mistakenly) Thomas More as "the father of Utopian Socialism,"[6] was probably correct in interpreting the detailed picture of the ideal society depicted in More's *Utopia* as "the exact opposite" of sixteenth-century England.[7] Yet if More envisioned the island of Utopia as the perfect order, he was less than sanguine that the ideal would ever be realized. The Commonwealth of Utopia, More plaintively remarks, is what "I wish rather than expect to see followed."[8] Nor did he issue any calls for political action to refashion England in accordance with the ideal society he so painstakingly outlined.

The absence of both historical optimism and political activism are also characteristic of utopian strains in the Chinese tradition—at least prior to the disintegration of traditional Chinese civiilzation under the impact of foreign imperialism and the Chinese adoption of modern Western ideas and ideologies. The celebrated Confucian concept of *Ta-t'ung* (the realm of Great Harmony) resided in the misty regions of an idealized and irretrievable antiquity; and the very fact that it was regarded as irretrievable made *Ta-t'ung* a notion that reinforced, rather than undermined, the Confucian desire to accommodate to the world as it was. The heterodox *Kung-yang* strain in Confucianism lay intellectually and politically dormant over two millennia until it was reinterpreted in utopian fashion at the end of the nineteenth century in light of modern Western ideas and doctrines of progress. Moreover, secular Taoist utopias (as distinct from popular religious Taoism, which, on occasion, was fashioned into mes-

5. Judith Shklar, "The Political Theory of Utopia: From Melancholy to Nostalgia," in Frank E. Manuel, ed., *Utopias and Utopian Thought* (Boston: Beacon Press, 1967), p. 105.

6. Karl Kautsky, *Thomas More and His Utopia* (New York: International Publishers, 1927), p. 249.

7. Ibid., p. 243.

8. Sir Thomas More, *Utopia* (New York: Appleton-Century-Crofts, 1949), p. 83.

sianic ideologies connected with peasant rebellions), such as Chuang Tzu's "state of established virtue," never broke away from the Taoist injunction to minimize social and political activity, nor from the Taoist condemnation of history as an estrangement from the state of nature and the natural state of man.[9]

Before a historically significant secular utopianism was to appear in China, it was to make its appearance in the Western world. But it was not until the triple impact of modern capitalism, the Enlightenment, and the French Revolution connected utopia with the idea of historical progress that secular utopianism became a potent historical force. It was a fusion that received its most powerful expression in the ideas of Karl Marx.

II. Marxism and Utopianism

Marxism at once conveys the most powerful of utopian visions of the future and presents the most devastating critique of "utopianism." On the one hand, Marxist theory prophesies mankind's leap from "the realm of necessity" to "the realm of freedom," a leap that is to mark the dramatic passage from "pre-history" to a "truly human history" which is to be made under communism. Despite Marx's well-known reluctance to draw detailed blueprints of the future, he did set forth a vision of a future communist society "where the free development of each is the condition for the free development of all,"[10] a society which could inscribe on its banners the principle of "from each according to his abilities, to each according to his needs."[11]

9. For an interpretation which stresses the modern persistence of traditional Chinese utopian-type impulses and conceptions, and their merging with the Maoist version of Marxism, see Wolfgang Bauer's impressive and intriguing study *China and the Search for Happiness* (New York: The Seabury Press, 1976), esp. pp. 371–420.

10. Karl Marx and Friedrich Engels, "Manifesto of the Communist Party," in Karl Marx and Friedrich Engels, *Selected Works* (Moscow: Foreign Languages Publishing House, 1950), vol. 1, p. 51.

11. Karl Marx, "Critique of the Gotha Program," in Karl Marx and Friedrich Engels, *Selected Works* (Moscow: Foreign Languages Publishing House, 1949), vol. 2, p. 23. The full passage, perhaps Marx's most eloquent statement of his vision of the future, reads: "In a higher phase of communist society, after the enslaving subordination of the individual to the division of labour, and therewith

And he offered other glimpses of the communist utopia he envisioned, as when he described the realm of freedom that would reign with the abolition of the tyranny of the division of labor:

> . . . in communist society, where nobody has one exclusive sphere of activity but each can become accomplished in any branch he wishes, society regulates the general production and thus makes it possible for me to do one thing to-day and another to-morrow, to hunt in the morning, fish in the afternoon, rear cattle in the evening, criticize after dinner, just as I have a mind, without ever becoming hunter, fisherman, shepherd or critic.[12]

Such utopian images of the future communist society, however scattered and fragmentary in the writings of Marx and Engels, form an essential component of Marxist theory—and one that is essential for understanding the appeals of Marxism in the modern world. Although one can hardly imagine a more idyllic utopian vision than Marx's picture of the "all-round" communist man creatively and cooperatively realizing his fully human potentialities "just as [he has] a mind," Marx nevertheless condemned as "utopian" the visions of future ideal societies set forth in other socialist theories, so that the term "utopian" acquired highly pejorative connotations in the Marxist tradition. That which is "utopian" in the Marxist vocabulary refers at best to idle and empty fantasizing about the future, and more often than not, to reactionary ideologies opposed to the progressive demands of history and the necessity of class struggle.

How was it that Marx projected a vision of the future communist utopia yet condemned as "utopian" (and thus reactionary) similar socialist and communist visions? It was not that Marx necessarily objected to the social ideals portrayed in the writings of the utopian

---

also the antithesis between mental and physical labour, has vanished; after labour has become not only a means of life but life's prime want; after productive forces have also increased with the all-round development of the individual, and all the springs of cooperative wealth flow more abundantly—only then can the narrow horizon of bourgeois right be crossed in its entirety and society inscribe on its banners: From each according to his ability, to each according to his needs!"

12. Karl Marx and Friedrich Engels, *The German Ideology* (New York: International Publishers, 1960), p. 22.

socialists of his time, although there were some schemes he regarded as fantastic and bizarre. Nor did Marx reject their utopian visions as impossible in principle. Indeed, Marx and Engels often praised the socially critical role of the works of utopian visionaries. The utopias of More and Campanella were viewed as the first "theoretical enunciations" of the early revolutionary strivings of the embryonic proletariat.[13] And the writings of Saint-Simon, Fourier, and Owen were praised because they "attack every principle of existing society. Hence they are full of the most valuable materials for the enlightenment of the working class."[14]

But if the utopians had been socially critical and historically progressive in their times, their time now had passed. With the emergence of mature capitalism and a mature modern proletariat—and with the appearance of Marxian "scientific socialism" as the "theoretical expression of the proletarian movement"—the persistence of the utopian socialist mode of thought had become a barrier to the working class movement and its socialist mission. As Marx put it: ". . . although the originators of these [utopian socialist] systems were, in many respects, revolutionary, their disciples have, in every case, formed reactionary sects. They hold fast by the original views of their masters, in opposition to the progressive historical development of the proletariat."[15] It was not the ends the utopian socialists sought that made them "utopian" in the Marxist sense, but rather the inadequacy of the means proposed to achieve those ends. This incongruity between means and ends in utopian socialist ideologies, according to Marx, was a function of history, or more precisely, a reflection of the conditions of historical underdevelopment which originally gave rise to those ideologies. Indeed, the Marxist critique of utopian socialism is essentially a criticism of the failure of the utopians to understand the workings of modern history, neither recognizing the restraints that history imposes nor appreciating the potentialities that history offers.

The utopian socialist mode of thought which Marx condemned

13. Engels, "Socialism: Utopian and Scientific," in Marx and Engels, *Selected Works*, vol. 2, pp. 108–9.

14. Marx and Engels, "Manifesto," p. 59.

15. Ibid.

was characterized not by a faith in history but rather by a faith (inherited from the eighteenth-century French *philosophes*) in an eternal realm of Reason which, once properly understood, it was confidently assumed, would reshape sociohistorical reality in accordance with the utopian ideal and thus make the world conform to the demands of Reason. The utopians, consequently, placed an extraordinary emphasis on human will and especially on the timely appearance of men of genius who were the bearers of truth and reason—and whose ideas and deeds would naturally appeal to a naturally good human nature by virtue of moral example and through the appeal of social models fashioned according to the dictates of Reason. These notions reflected an inability to conceive of history as an objective process and a failure to establish any coherent relationship between moral ideals and historical events. As Engels diagnosed the utopian socialist mentality:

> If pure reason and justice have not, hitherto, ruled the world, this has been the case only because men have not rightly understood them. What was wanted was the individual man of genius, who has now arisen and who understands the truth. That he has now arisen, that the truth has now been clearly understood, is not an inevitable event, following of necessity in the chain of historical development, but a mere happy accident. He might just as well have been born 500 years earlier, and might then have spared humanity 500 years of error, strife, and suffering.[16]

Socialism, for the utopian socialists, thus was not the product of history but rather the more or less fortuitous expression of absolute truth—and such truth, as Engels noted, is "independent of time, space, and of the historical development of man, it is a mere accident when and where it is discovered."[17] The arrival of utopia, in the utopian socialist conception, is at the disposal of man's free will, the exercise of which is unrestrained by objective historical conditions. In Marxist theory, by contrast, it is precisely historical conditions which define and delimit the powers of the human will and ideas to change the world, and the achievement of socialism is therefore

16. Engels, "Socialism: Utopian and Scientific," p. 109.
17. Ibid., p. 117.

dependent on the stage of socio-historical development which human beings have created. In Marx's classic formulation, "Men make their own history, but they do not make it just as they please; they do not make it under circumstances chosen by themselves, but under circumstances directly encountered, given and transmitted from the past."[18]

Marx and Engels did not condemn the original utopian socialists for believing as they did, for believing that those who were armed with truth and inspired by the proper will could create a new and perfect order "just as they please." For the thought of the early socialists could not go beyond the limits imposed upon them by their time. And their time was one when modern industrialism was still embryonic and the modern proletariat yet in its infancy. The ahistorical and "utopian" character of early socialist thought quite naturally reflected these undeveloped conditions of capitalism as it existed at the end of the eighteenth century. As Engels summarized the Marxist judgment:

> To the crude conditions of capitalistic production and the crude class conditions corresponded crude theories. The solution of the social problems, which as yet lay hidden in undeveloped economic conditions, the Utopians [i.e., Saint-Simon, Fourier, Owen] attempted to evolve out of the human brain. Society presented nothing but wrongs; to remove these was the task of reason. It was necessary, then, to discover a new and more perfect system of social order and impose this upon society from without by propaganda, and, wherever it was possible, by the example of model experiments. These new social systems were foredoomed as Utopian; the more completely they were worked out in detail, the more they could not avoid drifting off into pure phantasies.[19]

Yet however far their ideas were divorced from historical realities, however fantastic their visions of the future often were, the utopians were still to be praised as historically progressive for their time, and indeed praised as "the founders of Socialism." "For ourselves," Engels remarks, "we delight in the stupendously grand thoughts and

18. Marx, "The Eighteenth Brumaire of Louis Bonaparte," in Marx and Engels, *Selected Works*, vol. 1, p. 225.

19. Engels, "Socialism: Utopian and Scientific," p. 111.

germs of thought that everywhere break out through their phantastic covering."[20]

What Marx and Engels condemned, then, was not the utopian striving for a socialist future but rather the persistence of the utopian mode of thought into an era when a well-developed modern capitalism and its social product, the modern proletariat, had come to dominate the historical stage. Whereas the original utopians failed to recognize the restraints that history imposed on the realization of the future socialist utopia, their successors failed more seriously in not recognizing the socialist potentialities that the modern capitalist historical epoch now offered. The nature of capitalism, and the solution for the social evils it brought, previously hidden, were now apparent—and fully revealed by the scientific light of Marxism. Modern capitalism, Marx taught, was laying the material basis for socialism and, at the same time, had produced the revolutionary class which would construct the future socialist society—the modern proletariat which was historically destined to be the agent of universal human emancipation. But contemporary utopian socialists understood neither the historical significance of capitalism nor the revolutionary role of the proletariat. In capitalism, the utopians saw only the social evils it perpetrated, not the socialist potentialities it offered. And in the proletariat they saw only the most exploited segment of society, not the potentially creative revolutionary class destined to be the bearer of the socialist future. For the utopian socialists, Marx observed, the proletariat offers only "the spectacle of a class without any historical initiative or any independence of political movement. . . . Only from the point of view of being the most suffering class does the proletariat exist for them."[21]

It was from the failure to take into account what Marxist theory defined as the real historical basis for socialism—primarily, the proposition that capitalism is the essential precondition for socialism, and the thesis that the proletariat is the revolutionary class whose historical mission is to transform the socialist potentialities of capitalism into a universal socialist reality—that the term "utopian" acquires its pejorative meaning in the Marxist vocabulary. The rejection of

20. Ibid., p. 112.
21. Marx and Engels, "Manifesto," p. 58.

these two fundamental Marxist premises was logically accompanied by several other features characteristic of the utopian socialist mentality: the belief that the thought and will of men of genius is the decisive factor in refashioning sociohistorical reality; the faith that socialism could be achieved by means of ethical example, through the building of experimental model communities and by moral appeals to society at large; and the proclivity to paint detailed pictures of the future socialist utopia. From the Marxist point of view, the utopian socialist enterprise, divorced from modern historical realities, was at best a futile search for "no place." At worst, utopian socialism, in the modern industrial age, had degenerated into a reactionary ideology that served only to deaden the class struggle and thus impede what Marx called "the march of modern history."[22]

If the Marxist critique of utopianism centers, in large measure, on the utopian socialist disposition to rely on the power of ideas rather than on the forces of history, it was not because Marx and Engels denied a role to ideas and ideals in the making of history. The very fact that the founding fathers of Marxism went to such great lengths to criticize the utopian mentality is itself testimony to the importance they attached to ideas in the realization of socialism. Indeed, Marxist theory itself is by no means immune to the ambiguity of utopia—the tension between the moral ideal of what should be and the historical imperative of what is. For it may safely be assumed that Marx arrived at the moral desirability of communism before he proclaimed its historical inevitability. But it was precisely by linking what was morally desirable with what was plausibly argued to be historically inevitable that Marx made utopianism so potent a force in modern history. Far from undermining the utopian vision of a perfect future order, Marxism reinforced it by making the socialist future seem the logical and necessary outcome of objective historical processes at work in the present. The communist utopia was no longer merely a dream of what might be historically "no place," but rather the "good place" located in a future guaranteed by history—or at least a future

22. The harshest Marxist condemnation of utopian socialism appears in Part III of the Communist Manifesto, entitled "Socialist and Communist Literature" (see Marx and Engels, *Selected Works*, vol. 1 pp. 51–60). Lenin was later to level a similar critique against the Populists, the main carriers of utopian socialist ideas in late nineteenth–century Russia. On the latter, see Chapter 3 below.

guaranteed if people acted on the potentialities history offered them. For Marx, communism was "the real movement which abolishes the present state of things. The conditions of this movement result from the premises now in existence."[23]

The relationship between Marxism and utopianism is thus twofold. On the one hand, Marxism projects a utopian vision of a communist future that is seen as immanent in the history of the present. On the other hand, Marxist theory condemns as "utopian" socialist ideas and visions which it associates with the early stages of capitalism, which it identifies as crude ideological reflections of the backward conditions of preindustrial society, and which it regards as divorced from "the real movement" of modern history.

The term "utopianism," as it appears in the chapters which follow, is used in both its positive and negative Marxist senses, for both are relevant to understanding the subject of the present inquiry—the thought of Mao Tse-tung. For the Chinese variant of Marxism that came to be known in the Western world as "Maoism" (or, as it was officially canonized in China, "Mao Tsetung Thought") retained—and in some ways transformed—the positive Marxist vision of a future communist utopia, and, at the same time, is a doctrine that bears many of the characteristics which Marx and Engels pejoratively labelled "utopian."

Yet there are other issues involved in interpreting the role of utopianism in modern history than those suggested in Marxist theory. And it might be well to briefly consider some of these broader historical questions before beginning our inquiry into the utopian features of Maoism.

III. Utopianism and Contemporary Social Theory

"Utopia," both "the good place" and "no place." For the most part, Western scholars prefer the latter meaning and ignore the former. That which is "utopian," as the term is commonly used, is that which is unrealizable in principle. And it therefore follows that those who strive to achieve "the impossible" are, at best, hopeless daydreamers in search of "no place," or, more often than not, dangerous

23. Marx and Engels, *The German Ideology,* p. 26.

fanatics driven to irrational actions. It is very much in the mainstream of contemporary Western thought and scholarship to contrast (and condemn) the "utopian" mode of thinking against that celebrated as "rational," "realistic," "sober," "empirical," and "pragmatic." Thus we are constantly warned to beware of the danger of utopian visions and messianic prophecies intruding into the practical and secular realm of politics, and we are encouraged to applaud the demise of utopian aspirations and ideologies, and to deplore their survivals and revivals. The widespread acceptance of the profoundly antiutopian writings of J. L. Talmon, Norman Cohn, Hannah Arendt, Karl Popper, Adam Ulam, and those associated with the school of thought which proclaimed (prematurely, it would seem) "the end of ideology," testifies to the dominant Western scholarly view that utopian strivings are not only futile endeavors to reach "no place," but also politically dangerous and historically pernicious.

We are of course confronted here with more than the semantic problem of determining what the term "utopianism" means. The meanings that are attributed to utopianism and the varying ways the term is understood and utilized in interpreting human historical experience reflect profoundly different perceptions of historical change, differing views about how and where history is (or should be) moving, and, most importantly, differences about the role of revolution in modern world history. For if revolutions are inspired by utopian hopes and expectations, then it is only logical that those who find utopianism distasteful should also condemn revolution. Thus Norman Cohn finds in the "revolutionary messianism" of medieval Europe the source of most revolutionary movements since the seventeenth century, the "prologue to the vast revolutionary upheavals of the present century," and the harbinger of modern totalitarianism.[24] J. L. Talmon is convinced that it was the "political messianism" of the French Enlightenment which gave birth to both the "Jacobin and Marxist conceptions of Utopia," releasing a "revolutionary spirit" of "totalitarian democracy" which eventually spent itself in Western Europe but was destined to "spread eastwards until it found its

24. Norman Cohn, *The Pursuit of the Millennium* (New York: Harper & Row, 1961), pp. 308–9.

natural home in Russia."[25] And one can move further east with Adam Ulam who argues that in the modern West "the utopian character of much of socialist thinking represented . . . a kind of rearguard action which withdrawing radicalism conducted against the triumphant march of industrialism and liberalism."[26] The revolutionary utopian menace now comes from the vast non-Western areas of the world where radical utopianism has "withdrawn" and where modern industrialism and liberalism have yet to triumph. For, as Ulam candidly and rhetorically queries, is not "all utopian thinking and much of socialist thought but a critique of the values and traditions of the West?"[27]

There is no need to catalogue the long list of recent and contemporary Western writers who condemn both utopianism and revolution, particularly as the threat of "revolutionary utopianism" is perceived as lurking in non-Western lands. It is perhaps sufficient to note that, though modern biases against revolution (and against the utopian impulses which inspire revolution) long have been prominent in Western social thought—indeed, as long as the history of modern revolutions—the bias has become increasingly widespread and more strident in recent decades as the epicenter of revolution has moved in the twentieth century from the advanced industrialized countries of the West to the economically backward lands of Asia, Africa, and Latin America. As G. Pettee has observed:

> From the time of the American and French Revolutions to about 1940 it would seem fair to say that the general opinion in the West was that revolution is good when needed, and that the conditions in which it is needed can occur fairly often. There were voices to the contrary, of course, but they were at least seemingly outnumbered. From about 1940 on, there has been slowly increasing doubt of this belief. . . . The supporters of revolution are now little heard in the advanced West. The great concern is with countermeasures to revolution as an instrument of power politics, and with the means by which states and governments may be

25. J. L. Talmon, *The Origins of Totalitarian Democracy* (New York: Praeger, 1965), pp. 252–53.
26. Adam Ulam, "Socialism and Utopia," *Daedalus* 94.2 (Spring 1965):392.
27. Ibid., p. 399.

brought along most quickly and effectively to make revolution unnecessary. There is a strong emphasis on military strength as the immediate means of defending existing regimes; and also considerable awareness that this may be overemphasis. But there is much agreement that revolution should be prevented or forestalled.[28]

The conventional wisdom that flows from conventionally conservative Western scholarly minds, as E. H. Carr has summarized the temper of our Western times, is a warning "to mistrust radical and far-reaching ideas, to shun anything that savours of revolution, and to advance—if advance we must—as slowly and cautiously as we can."[29] The same advice is, of course, gratuitously offered to the non-Western world. If economically backward lands must advance, then they should do so preferably without revolution, and certainly without revolutionary utopian fervors, for it is typically assumed that there is a "basic contradiction between the goals of utopia and modernity."[30] Should revolution take place, however, the proposed cure is that revolutionaries who become rulers will be sobered by the responsibilities of power, recognize the contradiction, and opt for "modernization."

There is, to be sure, a rich and continuing Western scholarly tradition that treats utopianism in more historically understandable and humanly sympathetic terms. But the insights offered in this body of scholarly literature largely have been confined to understanding Western historical experience and seem to have had little impact on those who write on contemporary non-Western revolutions and societies.[31] Most of what has been written on modern Chinese rev-

28. Cited in Carl Friedrich, ed., *Revolution* (New York: Atherton Press, 1967), pp. 29–30.

29. Edward Hallett Carr, *What Is History?* (New York: Vintage, 1967), p. 208. The terms "utopianism" and "messianism," as Carr observes, "have become the current terms of opprobrium for far-reaching radical ideas on the future of society" (p. 205).

30. Richard Lowenthal, "Development vs. Utopia in Communist Policy," in Chalmers Johnson, ed., *Change in Communist Systems* (Stanford, Calif.: Stanford University Press, 1970), p. 51.

31. The editor of one of the best recent books on utopianism, for example, acknowledges that "the representation (in this volume) is exclusively from the Atlantic community, which may account for its undisguised provinciality. The

olutionary history and politics, it seems fair to say, reflects the anti-utopian and antirevolutionary proclivities dominant in Western scholarly thought in general, placing a high normative value on "stability" and "equilibrium." For contemporary China in particular, the preference and prescription is for the assumed virtues of "bureaucratic professionalism" and "instrumental rationality" in political and economic life—and for processes of routinization and institutionalization in general. (Unfortunately, the question of what is being, or what should be, institutionalized is rarely raised.) Thus when encountering such terms as "Maoist utopianism" or "Mao's vision" in most of the literature, the reader is usually being told that some element of politically abnormal or economically irrational behavior has intruded on the historical scene.

IV. Utopianism and Totalitarianism

More ominous (for antiutopians) than utopianism's association with revolution, and its alleged incompatibility with "modernity," is the common assumption that some sort of causal relationship exists between utopian thought and totalitarian politics. The usual and widely influential argument is that any ideology which sets forth a highly utopian vision of the future is in part responsible for, and is an essential feature of, modern totalitarianism in general—and, in the form of a messianic commitment to Marxist utopian goals, for Communist totalitarianism in particular.[32] As Talmon has so forcefully

---

utopian traditions of China and the Muslim world perforce stand neglected; the Western tradition has been difficult enough to assimilate." Frank E. Manuel, ed., *Utopias and Utopian Thought* (Boston, Beacon Press, 1967), p. xv. The same acknowledgment might be made for the excellent and humanly sympathetic volume by Frank E. Manuel and Fritzie P. Manuel, *Utopian Thought in the Western World* (Cambridge, Mass.: Harvard University Press, 1979).

32. The general argument is not exclusively applied to modern history, but has been extended back to antiquity. The writings of Plato, for example, are regarded by some scholars as totalitarian in nature because his philosophy aimed at remolding the social and political orders in accordance with a vision of "the Good." As Sheldon Wolin has pointed out, Plato's reputation as a totalitarian is undeserved. See Sheldon S. Wolin, *Politics and Vision* (Boston: Little, Brown and Co., 1960), Chapter 2.

argued, at the root of modern totalitarian tyranny is a special messianic temperament which postulates the inevitable coming of "a perfect scheme of things."[33] According to this view, the most repressive features of contemporary Communist states can be explained, in large measure, in terms of the apocalyptic acceptance of the utopian Marxist promise of the universal advent of a totally egalitarian society; totalitarian domination in the present is not only justified, but also essentially determined, by a belief in necessary laws of historical development inevitably leading to worldwide salvation. Thus Communist totalitarianism, as Waldemar Gurian has characterized it, is essentially a "secularized sociopolitical religion" based on the "utopian eschatology" of Karl Marx.[34] This notion is of course similar to one of the central assumptions of the widely accepted "totalitarian model" of Communism. It might be recalled that the first of the five essential features which Carl Friedrich, the principal builder of that model, attributes to "all totalitarian societies" is "an official ideology . . . characteristically focused in terms of chiliastic claims as to the 'perfect' final society of mankind."[35]

Here we encounter not merely the view that utopianism is the ultimate in human folly and that utopia is a search for "no place" (although that too is assumed), but also the perception of utopianism as a most darkly sinister force in modern history. We also are presented, in part, with what Michael Walzer has incisively noted to be "that easy and false equation of radicalism and totalitarianism which has become so common among historians, sociologists and political scientists."[36] It is precisely because it is so easy, and thus so common, to assume that radical utopianism necessarily has sinister political implications that it is so difficult to consider the historical role

33. Talmon, *Origins of Totalitarian Democracy,* passim.

34. Waldemar Gurian, "Totalitarianism as Political Religion," in Carl J. Friedrich, ed., *Totalitarianism* (New York: Grosset & Dunlap, 1964), pp. 119–37. The argument is presented in more elaborate fashion by Gurian in *Bolshevism: An Introduction to Soviet Communism* (Notre Dame, Ind.: University of Notre Dame Press, 1952).

35. Carl J. Friedrich, "The Unique Character of Totalitarian Society," in Friedrich, ed., *Totalitarianism,* p. 52.

36. Michael Walzer, *The Revolution of the Saints* (Cambridge, Mass.: Harvard University Press, 1965), pp. viii–ix.

of utopianism without condemning it from the beginning. It is an easy assumption because there is some apparent general truth in the proposition that historical actors seized by utopian visions of a perfect future order—and who are determined to bring about that future—are likely to feel morally free to employ the most immoral means to reach the desired and presumably inevitable end. Yet to accept this seeming truism as a universally valid generalization risks distorting one's historical perspectives on utopianism from the outset.

The notion that there is in all cases a necessary causal relationship between utopianism and totalitarianism is not one that will stand the test of serious historical scrutiny. Both in modern and premodern times, totalitarian regimes and societies have appeared unaccompanied by utopian ideologies and messianic expectations.[37] Obviously many historical conditions and forces tend to produce totalitarian states, ranging from external threats and wars to various economic and other internal crises, and it is altogether too simplistic to believe that the crucial factor always lurking in the background is a special messianic or utopian temperament. Here is might suffice to take brief note of two modern historical examples.

In the case of modern Chinese history, the pronounced totalitarian character of the Kuomintang regime (both on the Chinese mainland before 1949 and in Taiwan since 1949) clearly was never associated with any utopian ideology—nor, for that matter, even with any serious program for social change. Perhaps more pertinent for the present discussion is the case of the Soviet Union. It is instructive to recall that the Marxian utopian promises and imagery which Lenin invoked on the eve of the Bolshevik Revolution (most notably in

37. Arguing that totalitarianism cannot wholly be attributed to industrialism or identified with the industrial age, Barrington Moore has examined three historical cases of premodern totalitarian-type regimes: Ch'in China (third century B.C.), the Maurya dynasty in India (ca. fourth century B.C.), and Calvin's Geneva. Of the three, only the latter was associated with what might vaguely be described as a utopian ideology. The Legalist doctrine of the Ch'in state was marked by "a strictly amoral and technically rational attitude toward political behavior," as was the case with Maurya India. See "Totalitarian Elements in Pre-Industrial Societies," in Barrington Moore, *Political Power and Social Theory* (New York: Harper & Row, 1965), pp. 30–88.

State and Revolution) and during the early days of the new Soviet regime tended to vanish from his speeches and writing after mid-1918, precisely at the time the Soviet state was becoming increasingly despotic and oppressively bureaucratic. It might further be observed that Stalinist Russia (the major historical case for the entire totalitarian model) is a classic historical case not of utopianism run amok but rather of the *ritualization* of utopian goals and aspirations. The manner in which Stalin "postponed" Marxist goals, turned them into empty rituals, and then cynically manipulated those ritualized Marxian symbols and goals to ideologically rationalize the policies and practices of a brutal bureaucratic-totalitarian state is a history too well known to need retelling here.[38] What makes the common association between utopianism and totalitarianism so questionable is precisely the common failure to distinguish between genuine utopianism and the ritualization of utopia. Yet that distinction is essential for any serious analysis of the sociohistorical significance of utopianism, and especially for understanding the nature and role of the Maoist utopian mentality.

V. The Utility of Utopia

One need not ignore the ambiguities of utopianism, nor its potential dangers, to appreciate the historical truism (as George Lichtheim, who certainly was no utopian revolutionary, once put it) that "civilizations are founded upon utopian and messianic promises which are never fulfilled, but without which there would have been no progress."[39] Utopia may not be "the truth of tomorrow," as Victor Hugo optimistically exclaimed, but the capacity of people to conceive a better tomorrow is essential for meaningful efforts to change what exists today. For people must hope before they can act, and their hopes must be lodged in a vision of a better future if their

38. Symptomatic of Stalinist antiutopianism was Stalin's abrupt suppression, during the cultural cataclysm of 1929–32, of all the utopian social and cultural experiments that marked the first decade of Soviet history. See Richard Stites, "Utopia and Experiment in the Russian Revolution" (colloquium paper, Kennan Institute for Advanced Russian Studies, Woodrow Wilson International Center for Scholars, Washington, D.C., May, 1981).

39. *New York Review of Books*, 16 September 1965, p. 14.

actions are not to be blind and devoid of purpose. Indeed, it is an inherent and unique attribute of mankind that human actions are both purposive and future oriented. In this respect, the utility of utopias is obvious. Utopian visions of the future not only serve as critiques of existing social orders but offer alternatives to it, and thus serve not only to make people aware of the imperfections of the present but also move them to transform it in accordance with the utopian ideal. The historical significance of utopianism has been expressed in particularly insightful fashion by Frederick Polak in his analysis of the role of "images of the future" in historical development:

> First and most important is man's emerging time-schizophrenia, his dualistic mental capacity to imagine another and radically different world and time. An elite of spiritual leaders and visionary messengers enter on the scene. They create positive images of a future better than the present. Certain of these images, which happen to combine intellectual insights and esthetic appeal in such a way as to strike emotional resonance with the social and mental needs of the time, arouse great enthusiasm in the masses. Society is then fired by the force of these dominating visions which draw men toward that other and better future. The promises inhering in the visions burst through the historical past-present and break open the hidden present-future. In the process, some of them are seized upon and, as it were, "chosen" by society out of a great many possible futures and harnessed to the present. These images of the future have formed one of the main driving forces of cultural dynamics and have been playing a preponderent role, through their alternating strength and weakness, in the rise and fall of civilization.[40]

The unique human capacity to imagine "another and radically different world and time" is clearly essential for historical progress. For if people make history, and are not simply passive instruments in the hands of impersonal and immutable "forces of history," then the making of history presupposes the human ability to conceive of a different world located in the future. Such "images of the future" bear upon one of the enduring features of human historical experience—the tension between the imperfections of the world as it is and

40. Frederik L. Polak, "Utopia and Cultural Renewal," in Manuel, ed., *Utopias and Utopian Thought*, p. 288.

a vision of the world as it should be. This sense of tension between the real and the ideal lies at the root of the utopian mentality, and it is an essential and universal feature of both religious and secular utopianism. Yet such tension, however acute, does not necessarily lead to historically significant forms of action. It may well result (perhaps more often than not) in attempts to withdraw from the sordid world in a search for individual salvation, or dissipate itself in salvationist religious ideologies which promise relief and the good life in the hereafter. In order for the tensions generated by utopian aspirations to become dynamic forces of change, they must find a place in a comprehensive world view which aims at what Weber termed "a collective revolutionary transformation of the world in the direction of a more ethical status."[41] At the same time, it must be a world view which sanctions values freed from tradition and which thus orients human conduct in an innovative fashion toward the achievement of utopian goals in the here and now. Moreover, utopian world views become reality-transcending forces only when they fulfill, and become identified with, the socioeconomic and psychological needs of oppressed and disprivileged social groups;[42] ideologies which set forth a utopian vision of the future, but which counsel patience with the present, simply serve as ideological justifications for the existing state of affairs. What is therefore crucial for understanding the sociohistorical significance of utopianism is not only the character of the "visionary messenger" and the content of his prophecy but also the mass response to them. Prophetic messages and utopian appeals are of little historical interest if no one is listening. It is "the nature of the values held by the mass of the followers," Peter Worsley has observed, that is of primary importance for understanding how utopian leaders "are able to mobilize support readily, or, in some cases, even have support thrust upon them."[43] Thus, however important and interesting the personality of the prophet, the

41. Weber, *Sociology of Religion*, p. 125.

42. As Weber points out, ". . . classes with high social and economic privilege will scarcely be prone to evolve the idea of salvation. Rather, they assign to religion the primary function of legitimizing their own life pattern and situation in the world" (ibid., p. 107).

43. Peter Worsley, *The Trumpet Shall Sound*, 2nd ed. (New York: Shocken Books, 1968), p. xiii.

focus of attention must also extend to the nature of the relationship between leader and followers, and to the question of how and why "followers with possibly utopian or at least diffuse and unrealized aspirations cleave to an appropriate leader because he articulates and consolidates their aspirations."[44] In somewhat different terms, the problem is determining the circumstances, as Reinhard Bendix has formulated it, under which "the inspirations of the few become the convictions of the many."[45] It is only those rare historical moments when the messages of utopian visionaries strike responsive chords among the masses which permit, although by no means guarantee, the revolutionary breakthroughs and the radical ruptures with the past that the critics of utopia find so distressing—and the partisans of utopia find so essential for historical progress.[46]

It might be noted that no distinction is made here between religious and secular forms of utopianism. Though a clear line of demarcation may exist in typological terms, there are few meaningful

44. Ibid., p. xiv. For an enlightening discussion of this and related theoretical problems which cannot be considered adequately here, see Worsley's Introduction, pp. ix–lxix.

45. Reinhard Bendix, *Max Weber: An Intellectual Portrait* (Garden City, N.Y.: Doubleday, 1962), p. 259. Worsley perhaps defines the problem more precisely and treats it more clearly than did Weber, but his criticism that Weber concentrated on the personality of the prophet to the neglect of the more crucial questions of the relationship between leaders and followers, and to the neglect of the content of the leader's message, are charges better directed at some of Weber's disciples than Weber himself. Indeed, the problem of how "the inspirations of a few become the convictions of the many" is one of the principal problems raised and treated by Weber. Whether "Weberians" have dealt with the question in adequate fashion is quite another matter.

46. It must be acknowledged that the injunction set forth in this paragraph is not heeded in this volume. The chapters which follow focus on the nature of the Maoist utopian mentality but regrettably pay relatively little attention to the question of the relationship between Mao Tse-tung and the masses who were his followers, partly due to the limitations of available historical source materials and partly because of the limitations of the author. Yet even a cursory review of such massive movements as the agricultural collectivization campaign (1955–56), the Great Leap Forward (1958–60), and the Cultural Revolution (1966–69) suggest, in abundant measure, that the Maoist message struck deeply responsive chords in Chinese society and that Mao did in fact articulate the aspirations of the masses at many critical historical junctures.

historical distinctions to be drawn—at least insofar as utopian or messianic religious ideologies demand human action in the here and now, and do not prescribe resignation in the present while awaiting a heavenly utopia located in an afterlife. Indeed, through most of human history the most profound transformations of secular life have been wrought by religious utopian doctrines promising the advent of the Kingdom of God on Earth. The Christian-inspired revolutionary (or protorevolutionary) peasant movements of medieval Europe and the Islamic revolutions of the contemporary era are but two items in a long historical record. Moreover, it is impossible to ignore the strongly religious overtones in even the most secular of modern revolutionary and utopian movements, and it is well to keep in mind that millennarian cults often become transformed into secular political movements.[47] The conventional distinction between religious and secular utopias, though no doubt important, perhaps does more to obscure than to clarify the historical role of utopianism.

Far more significant than the distinction between the religious and the secular, at least for the purposes of the present discussion, is that between activist and passivist forms of utopianism. Passivist utopianism, often taking the form of essentially literary descriptions of the good society, is part of a long tradition of utopian thought which (in its secular and Western form) goes back to Plato, constantly reappears as an enduring strain throughout the Middle Ages, finds renewed expression in Thomas More's famous work, and reemerges in the various nature utopias of the eighteenth century and in the flood of utopian socialist schemes which came with the early industrial era. In various forms, both old and new, it is a tradition which continues to the present day, even though one may lament the paucity of the utopian imagination in the contemporary era.[48] Literary de-

47. Millenarian beliefs, as Worsley demonstrates, "form an integral part of that stream of thought which refused to accept the rule of a superordinate class, or a foreign power, or some combination of both, as in Taiping China. This anti-authoritarian attitude is expressed not only in the form of direct political resistance, but also through the rejection of the ideology of the ruling authority. . . . It is therefore natural that millenarian doctrines often become openly revolutionary and lead to violent conflict between rulers and ruled." *The Trumpet Shall Sound*, pp. 225–26.

48. As do Frank E. Manuel and Fritzie P. Manuel, who note "the discrepancy

scriptions of utopia, to be sure, are not without historical significance, at least not insofar as they lay bare the evils of the present and open minds to new potentialities. But certainly of far greater historical significance—and clearly more relevant to the present inquiry—is the activist form of utopianism, which not only sets forth a vision of the future society but also combines that vision with the expectation that its advent is more or less imminent, or at least in the process of becoming; it is a utopianism which carries the conviction that people can create the new and perfect order by their own actions in the present; and it is thus a utopianism which demands collective political action to transform society in accordance with the vision of what it should be. Such an activistic utopian mentality, at least in its secular form, is a distinctively modern product of the modern industrial age, and, as suggested earlier, one which found particularly powerful expression in nineteenth-century Marxist theory.

Yet Marxism is a doctrine amenable both to political activism and to political passivity. Whereas Marx enjoined that the task was to change the world and not merely understand it, the world was not changed according to the Marxist image in the advanced industrialized countries, where Marx assumed socialist revolutions would first take place. In the deterministic reading of Marx that characterized the dominant "orthodox Marxism" of Kautsky and Plekhanov, and which promoted the reformist political practice of Marxian Social-Democratic parties, it was assumed that the future socialist utopia would be the more or less automatic outcome of objective and impersonal historical forces and laws. It was an interpretation of Marxism which counseled a reliance on the workings of History, and one which purged Marxism of its activistic and utopian impulses. There was little place in "scientific" Marxist theory to think in terms of "what should be," for it was believed that it was only necessary to await what inevitably would be. "The Social Democrat swims with the streams of History," Plekhanov proclaimed, and the forces of historical progress, he added, "have nothing to do with human will

---

between the piling up of technological and scientific instrumentalities for making all things possible, and the pitiable poverty of goals." *Utopian Thought in the Western World,* p. 811.

and consciousness."[49] The vision of a communist utopia remained, but the realization of that vision was made dependent on objective processes of historical development that were conceived in essentially evolutionary terms. And an evolutionary conception of history, as Wilbert Moore has observed, "is poorly designed to include purpose. Chance rather than design is the principal feature of evolutionary change. . . . Were some utopian social order to emerge from processes of evolution, it would be a long time coming, and essentially accidental."[50]

As Marxism moved eastward from its Western European homeland, to the economically backward and underdeveloped lands, the doctrine tended to become increasingly infused with political activism and utopian purpose. A voluntaristic approach to historical change and a chiliastic utopian expectation were the necessary ingredients for Marxism to find meaningful political expression in economically backward lands, and not remain an exotic intellectual curiosity. These ingredients were present in Leninism, and even more so in the Chinese variant of Marxism that came to be known as Maoism. If the Marxian-defined material prerequisites for socialism were absent, Lenin came to teach (and Mao reemphasized the lesson), then it was necessary to harness human wills and energies to create those very prerequisites in the here and now, and to begin the work of constructing the future socialist society in the process.

Without a utopian reading of Marx, and the voluntarist and politically activist impulses that such a reading sanctions, Marxism would have been politically impotent and historically irrelevant in the nonindustrialized countries of the world. And without the survival of a vital utopian vision of the socialist future, Marxism, in the economically backward lands where successful Marxist-led revolutions have occurred, becomes little more than an ideology of modernization. Such has been the fate of Marxism in the Soviet Union and else-

49. G. Plekhanov, *Izbrannye filosofskie proizvendeniya* (Moscow, 1956), vol. 4, p. 86, as quoted in A. Walicki, *The Controversy Over Capitalism* (Oxford: Clarendon Press, 1969), p. 159.

50. Wilbert E. Moore, "The Utility of Utopias," *American Sociological Review* 31 (1966):767. In his later writings, Engels unwittingly may have contributed to the emergence of an evolutionary interpretation of the Marxist theory of history by his tendency to equate the laws of nature and the laws of history.

where, and it offers historical evidence for Adam Ulam's prediction that "socialism, once it assumes power, has as its mission the fullest development of the productive resources of society," that the socialist state "will in no wise proceed differently from the capitalist," and that "socialism continues and intensifies all the main characteristics of capitalism."[51]

An activist utopianism is essential to the vitality of Marxism as a revolutionary theory. In the absence of that utopian spirit, Marxism in the advanced industrialized countries of the West tends to become an ideology that adapts itself to the social reformism of the capitalist welfare state. And in postrevolutionary "socialist" societies it degenerates into vacuous revolutionary rhetoric which only thinly disguises the mundane modernizing and banal nationalist aims of the rulers of autonomous bureaucracies.

Certainly the most striking departure from these familiar processes of the deradicalization of Marxism is to be found in the history of Maoism, for the body of ideas officially canonized as "Marxism-Leninism-Mao Tsetung Thought" (at least during the Maoist era) is the most significant historical case of Marxism as a utopian ideology. Mao Tse-tung has now passed from the historical scene, and with him perhaps "Maoism" as well. But the intellectual history of the Maoist era in China will remain relevant for those who seek to understand the fate of Marxism and the role of utopianism in the modern world. It is a history which perhaps enables us to better appreciate Mannheim's warning that "with the relinquishment of utopias, man would lose his will to shape history" and Weber's belief that "man would not have attained the possible unless time and again he had reached out for the impossible."

51. Adam Ulam, *The Unfinished Revolution* (New York: Random House, 1960), p. 45.

2

Utopian Socialist Themes in Maoism: The Relationship Between Town and Countryside

Modern history, Karl Marx once wrote, "is the urbanisation of the countryside, not, as among the ancients, the ruralisation of the city."[1] Mao Tse-tung, seemingly, was intent on reversing the direction of the modern historic process. In Maoist theory and practice, modern revolutionary history was made by peasants in the countryside, who culminated their revolutionary efforts by overwhelming the presumably conservative inhabitants of the cities. And in the postrevolutionary era, Mao's "ruralism" reflected itself in an emphasis on socioeconomic development of the rural areas, a perception that the true sources for socialist reconstruction reside in the countryside, and the notion that urban dwellers can acquire "proletarian" revolutionary virtues by going to the villages and living and working with peasants.

Yet before concluding that Mao stood Marx completely on his head, it should be noted that although Marx celebrated as historically progressive the modern dominance of the city over the countryside, he was ultimately concerned with the historic separation between town and countryside, a phenomenon produced by the tyranny of the social division of labor in mankind's alienated "pre-history." For Marx, moreover, the resolution of the problem was not the urbanization of the countryside in the capitalist present, but the abolition

1. Karl Marx, *Grundrisse*, in Karl Marx, *Pre-Capitalist Economic Formations* (New York: International Publishers, 1965), p. 78.

of the distinction between town and country in the socialist and communist future.

Mao fully shared the utopian goal that Marx prophesied; indeed, there is no feature of the original Marxist vision of future communist society that occupies so prominent a place in Maoist theoretical writings. And the theoretical concern expressed not only a utopian hope, but also a preoccupation with immediate practical problems of development. In China, as in other predominantly agrarian countries, no social question is more critical than the gap between the modern cities and the backward countryside. It is a gap that is political and cultural, as well as economic, and the manner in which the problem is perceived has crucial implications for virtually every aspect of public policy. For those seeking egalitarian socialist ends, the Marxist historical analysis of the separation between town and country is a matter of special theoretical and practical relevance, and the Marxist goal of abolishing that separation is especially attractive.

Although Mao shared the utopian goal Marx proclaimed, he differed significantly in his historical understanding of the problem, and the means by which he strove to resolve it are profoundly different from anything Marx or Lenin might have conceived. In examining the question of the relationship between town and countryside in the history of Maoist thought and action, one is struck by a more general phenomenon—the appearance in Maoism of conceptions and notions similar to those characteristic of a variety of nineteenth-century Western non-Marxist socialist theories, especially those pejoratively labelled "utopian" by Marx and Lenin.

It should hardly be surprising—and especially not to Marxists—that where Marxist theory has taken root in underdeveloped lands it should take on certain characteristics of earlier "pre-Marxian" socialist ideologies. Whereas Marxism presupposed the existence and development of modern industrial capitalism, utopian socialist theories had their intellectual origins in an earlier era of modern economic development; like Marxism, they were protests against the injustices of early industrialism, but, unlike Marxism, they did not accept or take into account the historical and social consequences of modern capitalism. If there is a casual relationship between sociohistorical environments and modes of thought, as one may assume to be the general historical case, then it seems not illogical that ideas appropriate to a preindustrial or early industrial culture should appear (however implicitly and unconsciously) in the revolutionary Marxist ideologies that today flourish in the economically backward areas of the world.

This chapter will attempt to identify certain of the "utopian socialist" strains in Maoist thought, particularly as they are revealed in the Maoist conception of the relationship between town and countryside in modern history and in the making of modern revolutions, and to assess their theoretical implications and sociohistorical functions. This will necessitate not only a comparison between original Marxism and the later Maoist variant of the theory, but also, to begin with, an inquiry into some of the theoretical and historical differences between Marxism and other nineteenth-century Western socialist ideologies.

I. Marxism

All history, according to Marxist theory, is marked by a "constant war" between town and countryside. One of the distinguishing features of "civilization" (as opposed to primitive communalism), Engels wrote, is the "fixation of the contrast between town and country as the basis of the entire division of social labour."[2] This perennial antagonism between urban and rural areas is a phenomenon of central importance in Marxist historical theory. As Marx formulated the matter in *Capital:* "The foundation of every division of labor that is well developed, and brought about by the exchange of commodities, is the separation between town and country. It may be said that the

2. Friedrich Engels, "The Origins of the Family, Private Property and the State," in Karl Marx and Friedrich Engels, *Selected Works* (Moscow: Foreign Languages Publishing House, 1949), vol. 2, p. 294. Marx's best-known statement on the matter appears in *The German Ideology:* "The greatest division of material and mental labour is the separation of town and country. The antagonism between town and country begins with the transition from barbarism to civilization, from tribe to State, from locality to nation, and runs through the whole history of civilization to the present day." Karl Marx and Friedrich Engels, *The German Ideology* (New York: International Publishers, 1960), p. 43. However, his most interesting and detailed discussions of the problem are to be found in less well-known writings, especially the *Grundrisse*.

whole economical history of society is summed up in the movement of this antithesis."[3]

Although a universal historical phenomenon, the distinction between town and countryside became a dynamic antithesis only in the Western line of historical evolution leading from classical antiquity to modern capitalism. As Marx described the process, town and countryside have existed in a continuous and antagonistic relationship, alternately providing the basis of successive historical stages. The salient feature of the Marxist analysis is that historical progress is identified with the supremacy of the city, whereas the dominance of rural areas is associated with periods of historical stagnation or regression. Marx, for example, explained the decline of Greek and Roman antiquity and the rise of feudalism as follows:

> If antiquity started out from the town and its territory, the Middle Ages started out from the country. This different starting point was determined by the sparseness of the population at that time. . . . In contrast to Greece and Rome, feudal development therefore extends over a much wider field. . . . The last centuries of the declining Roman Empire and its conquest by the barbarians destroyed a number of productive forces; agriculture had declined, industry had decayed for want of a market, trade had died out or been violently suspended, the rural and urban population had decreased. From these conditions and the mode of organisation of the conquest determined by them, feudal property developed under the influence of the Germanic military constitution.[4]

It is noteworthy that Marx attributed the emergence of the new rural-centered feudal order not to any underlying process of economic development, but rather primarily to a fortuitous political factor, i.e., the barbarian conquests and their retrogressive effects on population and production. Nowhere is it suggested that feudalism was the inevitable or historically logical result of the "ancient" mode of production. Nor is there any implication that feudalism was a stage in a process of progressive historical evolution. To the contrary, the rural-based feudal system is described as a retrogressive devel-

3. Karl Marx, *Capital* (Chicago: Kerr, 1906), vol. 1, p. 387.
4. Marx and Engels, *The German Ideology*, pp. 11–12.

opment, resulting from a decline in productive forces and population.

The major Marxist concern, however, is not with the origins of feudalism, but with the question of the transition from feudalism to capitalism. Here the gradual emergence of commercial towns on the fringes of feudal society—with the consequent conflict between the burgher towns and the feudal countryside—becomes crucial in the Marxist explanation of the genesis of modern capitalism. With the growth of large-scale trade in the late medieval era, the accumulation of commercial capital, the specialization of urban craft industries, and the influx of a surplus rural population, the towns became increasingly separated from the countryside—a division that reflected the separation between capital and landed property and intensified the "constant war of the country against the town." It was a war that the towns were bound to win, though now the changing relationship between town and countryside is attributed to economic factors—in contrast to the political-military origins of feudalism and the earlier dominance of the countryside. The rapid extension of the division of labor in the towns (especially the development of modern manufactures) led to the disintegration of feudalism and the triumph of the modern bourgeoisie, a class that tended to absorb all earlier possessing classes while turning the majority of the population of the emergent towns into a new oppressed class, the modern urban proletariat. For Marx, the rise of capitalism was not only inseparable from the dominance of town over countryside, it also foreshadowed the dominance of urbanized industrial nations over rural peasant countries—for the permanence of the productive forces of capitalism could be assured only if capitalism achieved worldwide dominion.[5] Marx had little doubt that this universal triumph of the capitalist mode of production was immanent in the modern historic process. As the "Manifesto of the Communist Party" proclaimed:

> The bourgeoisie has subjected the country to the rule of the towns. It has created enormous cities, has greatly increased the urban population as compared with the rural, and has thus rescued a considerable part of the population from the idiocy of rural life. Just as it has made the country

5. Ibid., pp. 43–49.

dependent on the towns, so it has made barbarian and semi-barbarian countries dependent on the civilized ones, nations of peasants on nations of bourgeois, the East on the West.[6]

Despite this celebration of the supremacy of the modern capitalist city over the internal and external "countryside" as historically progressive, Marx morally condemned the separation between cities and rural areas: "The antagonism of town and country can only exist as a result of private property. It is the most crass expression of the subjection of the individual under the division of labour, under a definite activity forced upon him—a subjection which makes one man into a restricted town-animal, the other into a restricted country-animal, and daily creates anew the conflict between their interests."[7] Thus the abolition of the distinction between town and countryside was a precondition for achieving the "truly human life" the socialist revolution promised. Among the measures Marx proposed for the transition to a communist society once the proletariat achieved political supremacy was the "combination of agriculture with manufacturing industry" accompanied by the "gradual abolition of the distinction between town and country, by a more equable distribution of the population over the country."[8]

Yet the Marxist conception of the revolutionary process that would eventually abolish the antagonism between cities and rural areas was firmly centered on the modern industrialized city. Capitalist forces of production had led to the definitive economic and political dominance of town over countryside and at the same time had established the essential (and urban-based) material and social conditions for the future socialist transformation of society—large-scale industry and the modern proletariat. For Marx, the modern historical stage was the city, and its principal actors were the two urban classes into which capitalist forces of production inevitably were dividing society as a whole: the bourgeoisie and the industrial proletariat. In this

6. Karl Marx and Friedrich Engels, "Manifesto of the Communist Party," in Karl Marx and Friedrich Engels, *Selected Works* (Moscow: Foreign Languages Publishing House, 1950) vol. 1, p. 37.

7. Marx and Engels, *The German Ideology*, p. 44.

8. Marx and Engels, "Manifesto," p. 51.

conception of modern history, the countryside and its inhabitants had a minimal role to play at best, and possibly a retrogressive one. It was assumed that a substantial portion of the peasantry would be thrown into the ranks of the urban proletariat, and the remainder would be transformed into rural proletarians, working as wage-laborers in large agricultural enterprises organized on a capitalist basis of production. As Engels typically put the Marxist position on the matter: "Our small peasant, like every other survival of a past mode of production, is hopelessly doomed. He is a future proletarian."[9]

Thus it was assumed that the peasantry *qua* peasantry would largely disappear from the historical scene. And insofar as it did not, Marx viewed the persisting peasant population either as politically irrelevant in the making of modern history or, in a more sinister light, as a potentially reactionary force that might serve as the social basis for historically retrogressive Caesarist-type dictatorships and Bonapartist cults—a possible development that raised the specter of the resurgence of the reactionary social forces of the countryside over the progressive social forces of the modern city.[10]

It is noteworthy that neither in the Marxist analysis of the transition from feudalism to capitalism nor in the Marxist conception of the forthcoming socialist revolution does one find any place for the peasantry as an independent or creative force in modern history. Although peasants are the main victims of exploitation in feudal society, it is the urban bourgeoisie that plays the historically progressive role in overthrowing feudal socioeconomic and political relationships. The peasants are largely passive victims of the transformation. To be sure, Marx and Engels did not wholly preclude the possibility that the peasants might make some positive contribution to the final class struggle between urban workers and capitalists. But they would be able to do so only as "auxiliaries" of the proletariat and only insofar as they accepted the ideological and political lead-

9. Friedrich Engels, "The Peasant Question in France and Germany," in Marx and Engels, *Selected Works*, vol. 2, p. 384.

10. This possibility is discussed by Marx, with reference to French peasant support for the dictatorship and the cult of Napoleon III, in *The Eighteenth Brumaire of Louis Bonaparte* (Chicago: Kerr, 1919), especially pp. 144–46. On the relationship between the Chinese peasantry and the cult of Mao Tse-tung, see Chapter 6.

ership of the working class of the cities. As Marx succinctly put the matter in his analysis of the Paris Commune of 1871 (a document enshrined as the Marxian model of proletarian revolution and the dictatorship of the proletariat despite the abortiveness of the historical event itself), the Communal Constitution of the Parisian proletariat "brought the rural producers under the intellectual lead of the central towns of their districts, and there secured to them, in the workingmen, the natural trustees of their interests."[11] In original Marxism, in short, the sources of historical progress and the creative forces of revolution resided in the cities; and modern history, insofar as it was to be modern and progressive, was indeed no less than the "urbanization of the countryside."

Furthermore, Marx placed a positive value on the forms of political and economic centralization that industrialism entailed. The large-scale organization of both industry and agriculture and the increasing specialization of the division of labor based on an ever more complex technology were seen as creating the necessary conditions of economic abundance on which the future socialist society must rest. Not only did Marx and Engels champion the superiority of centrally directed, large-scale economic enterprises, they also saw as historically progressive (and a prophetic pointer to the socialist revolution) the modern, centralized bourgeois state. In describing the revolutionary accomplishments of capitalism as the prelude for socialism, Marx observed: "The bourgeoisie keeps more and more doing away with the scattered state of the population, of the means of production, and has concentrated property in a few hands. The necessary consequence of this was political centralization."[12] Although the centralized bourgeois state apparatus was to be "smashed" (and not merely taken over) in the socialist revolution, the ensuing "transition period" would temporarily intensify centralized political and economic control. "The proletariat," Marx predicted, "will use its political supremacy to wrest, by degrees, all capital from the bourgeoisie, to centralize all instruments of production in the hands of the State."[13]

11. Karl Marx, *The Civil War in France* (New York: Labor News Co., 1965), p. 77.

12. Marx and Engels, "Manifesto," p. 37.

13. Ibid., p. 50.

Moreover, among the specific measures proposed following the success of proletarian revolution were "centralization of credit" and "centralization of the means of communication and transport in the hands of the State."[14]

Needless to say, the processes of political and economic centralization that Marx saw as historically progressive in both capitalism and the early phase of socialism presupposed urbanization; they were processes that fortified the dominance of town over countryside, as modern historical progress demanded. Marx was not unaware of the social costs of centralization and urbanization. He wrote with great sympathy about the tragic human price involved in uprooting peasants from the land and from their old social world of sanctified custom and tradition, as well as the dehumanization of the growing proletariat in large factories and overcrowded cities. But, in the Marxist view, this was the price of historical progress, and the price had to be paid. It was precisely a "dehumanized" proletariat, after all, that was to be the agent of a universal process of human liberation, and it was a large-scale industrialization that was creating the economic prerequisites for the birth of the new society. Just as the abolition of the state had to be preceded by its centralization, so the eventual abolition of the distinction between town and countryside had to be preceded by the complete dominance of the cities over the rural areas.

Moreover, there could be no retreat from the course that history dictated, and there was no hope of "bypassing" the social consequences of urbanization and industrialization. To those who hoped to do so, Marx replied that "the country that is more developed industrially only shows, to the less developed, the image of its own future."[15] Indeed, a "premature" social revolution—one that took place before capitalist productive forces were fully developed—would be futile at best and possibly historically retrogressive:

> If the proletariat destroys the political rule of the bourgeoisie [Marx argued], that will only be a temporary victory, only an element in the service of the bourgeois revolution itself, as in 1794, so long as in the

14. Ibid., pp. 50–51.
15. Marx, *Capital*, vol. 1, Preface, p. 13.

course of history, in its "movement," the material conditions are not yet created which make necessary the abolition of the bourgeois mode of production. . . . Men do not build themselves a new world out of the fruits of the earth, as vulgar superstition believes, but out of the historical accomplishments of their declining civilization. They must, in the course of their development, begin by themselves producing the material conditions of a new society, and no effort of mind or will can free them from this destiny.[16]

More ominous was the potential for regression in any attempt to force the pace of history. Marx and Engels raised this possibility in responding to Russian Populist proposals to "skip over" the capitalist stage and thus avoid the evils of industrialization and urbanization. Engels summed up the general Marxist position on the matter in 1875:

Only at a certain level of development of the productive forces of society, an even very high level for our modern conditions, does it become possible to raise production to such an extent that the abolition of class distinctions can be a real progress, *can be lasting without bringing about stagnation or even decline* [emphasis added] in the mode of social production. But the productive forces have reached this level of development only in the hands of the bourgeoisie. The bourgeoisie, therefore, in this respect is just as necessary a precondition of the socialist revolution as the proletariat itself. Hence a man who will say that this revolution can be more easily carried out in a country, because, *although* it has no proletariat, it has no bourgeoisie *either,* only proves that he has still to learn the ABC of Socialism.[17]

Marx's characterization of modern history as "the urbanization of the countryside" was thus no mere rhetorical turn of phrase; the proposition is central to his analysis of the modern historical process and its socialist outcome. For Marx the city was the symbol of historical progress, for it was in the cities that the prerequisites for

16. Karl Marx, "Die moralisierende Kritik und die kritisierende Moral," in Karl Marx, *Selected Writings in Sociology and Social Philosophy* (London: Watts, 1956), p. 240.

17. Friedrich Engels, "On Social Relations in Russia," in Marx and Engels, *Selected Works,* vol. 2, pp. 46–47.

socialism resided. The social evils of urbanization and industrialization—the degradation and dehumanization of workers in modern factories and in large cities, their increasing enslavement to an ever more complex and specialized technology and division of labor, their further alienation under the unbearable weight of gigantic forms of economic and political organization—were the historical costs that mankind had to pay for its eventual liberation. The new society could only be built on the material accomplishments of the past and would bear the burdens of the past. Socialism could only be the product of capitalism, and thus "in every respect" socialist society would be "still stamped with the birthmarks of the old society from whose womb it emerges."[18] For Marx the historical process had to be carried to its modern breaking point before mankind could break away from its alienated "pre-history." Just as man's total alienation in modern capitalist society was the precondition for his total liberation, so the total dominance of town over countryside was the necessary price and prelude for achieving the abolition of the separation between town and countryside.

II. Marxism and Utopian Socialism

Utopian visions of a future egalitarian social order are as old as the history of social thought, recurring throughout the ages in the histories of all major civilizations. But socialism, although not unrelated to this older tradition, is a distinctively modern intellectual response to early industrial capitalism in Western Europe. More precisely, the emergence of socialist theories must be seen as the specific response of workers and intellectuals to the twin upheavals of the French Revolution and the industrial revolution, not simply (and simplistically) as an ageless quest for freedom and social justice.

Marxism is but one socialist response to the traumatic social and political transformations wrought by Western European industrial capitalism. It is neither an eternal truth, as some of its adherents present it, nor a modern expression of the ancient Judeo-Christian

18. Karl Marx, "Critique of the Gotha Program," ibid., p. 21.

prophetic tradition, as some critics would have us believe.[19] What distinguishes Marxism from its nineteenth-century rivals, from those socialist doctrines which Marx and Engels pejoratively characterized as "utopian," are, broadly put, three major issues: first, the acceptance of modern industrial capitalism as a necessary and progressive stage in sociohistorical development; second, the belief that the urban industrial proletariat is the truly creative revolutionary class historically destined to transcend the bourgeois order and usher in the new classless society; and, third, a belief in an objective historical process amenable to a scientific analysis that reveals the potentials men can seize upon to realize what is immanent in history itself—as opposed to any reliance on moral examples or the innate goodness of human nature.

These are perspectives not present in the various utopian socialisms of Fourier, Saint-Simon, Owen, and others—however much else Marx shared with them and derived from them. Nor were they present in similar "utopian" views found in the anarchist and populist socialist ideologies (of which Rousseau and Proudhon were the intellectual forerunners) that flourished in the less economically advanced European countries. Although the utopian socialists were no less vigorous than the Marxists in condemning the social evils of capitalist industrialism, their critiques tended to be based more on moral judgments of the injustices of the new economic order than on any historical analysis of the nature and function of the system. As Engels noted: "The socialism of earlier days certainly criticized the existing capitalistic mode of production and its consequences. But it could not explain them, and, therefore, could not get mastery of them. It could only simply reject them as bad."[20] Moreover, as George Lichtheim observed, the utopian socialists were inclined "to

19. Perhaps the most vulgar expression of this widely held, but highly misleading, notion is to be found in Toynbee: "Marx has taken the goddess 'Historical Necessity' in place of Yahweh for his deity, and the internal proletariat of the Western World in place of Jewry for his chosen people, and the Messianic Kingdom is conceived of as a Dictatorship of the Proletariat; but the salient features of the Jewish Apocalypse protrude through his threadbare disguise." *A Study of History* (New York: Oxford University Press, 1947), p. 400.

20. Friedrich Engels, "Socialism: Utopian and Scientific," ibid., p. 124.

identify the critique of capitalism as a system of production with the rejection of industrialism as such."[21]

Quite naturally accompanying this ambiguous attitude toward modern industrialism were ambiguous and uncertain solutions for the social problems it produced. In utopian socialist writings, the proletariat appears as the object of exploitation but not as the subject in any future process of emancipation. Rather the solution is to be found through means of education and by force of moral example, through the appeal of ideal social models fashioned by those who have grasped reason and understand social truth. As Marx acutely put the matter: "In the formation of their plans they [the utopian socialists] are conscious of caring chiefly for the interests of the working class, as being the most suffering class. Only from the point of view of being the most suffering class does the proletariat exist for them." While recognizing the existence of social class divisions, they nonetheless "consider themselves far superior to all class antagonisms," Marx further observed. "They want to improve the condition of every member of society. . . . Hence, they habitually appeal to society at large. . . . For how can people, when once they understand their system, fail to see in it the best possible plan of the best possible state of society?"[22]

What is striking about utopian socialist ideas in this respect are their highly elitist political implications. Although utopian socialist theorists rose in protest against the social injustices of capitalist industrialization, they did not assign to the proletariat—the principal victims of capitalism—the main role in removing those injustices and transforming society. Rather, they appealed to man in general, assuming the fundamental goodness of an essentially unchanging human nature. But despite this faith in the powers of reason and the moral goodness of man, the ultimate bearers of the new and perfect social order remain the Social Planners themselves; in the end the

21. George Lichtheim, *The Origins of Socialism* (New York: Praeger, 1969), p. 5. Although Lichtheim's statement is generally true, there are some obvious exceptions, most notably Saint-Simon, the champion of modern industrialism and the "father of technocracy."

22. Marx and Engels, "Manifesto," pp. 58–59.

historical initiative rests with those supraclass men of genius who alone possess truth and reason.

Utopian socialism can thus be seen as an essentially "precapitalist" rejection of capitalism, as a general mode of thought that had its greatest appeal to social groups threatened by the early phases of modern capitalist development (artisans and peasants, along with their self-appointed intellectual spokesmen), and thus as an ideology that tended to find roots in the less economically advanced countries of Europe in the nineteenth century. Marxism, on the other hand, was an intellectual product of a more mature phase of capitalist development and found its natural home among the intellectuals and urban workers of the economically advanced countries, for it was a theory that accepted modern capitalism and all its social consequences. It is in the light of these general historical and theoretical differences that one must understand the very different conceptions of the relationship between town and countryside in Marxism and non-Marxian socialist ideologies.

For the purposes of the present inquiry no attempt will be made to distinguish between the many different socialist predecessors and contemporaries whom Marx and Engels condemned as "utopian." Nor, for the time being, will we be particularly concerned with the differences between the utopian socialist theories that arose in the Western European countries in the first half of the nineteenth century and the Populist theories that flourished in Russia during the second half of the century. (Russian Populism, as a form of utopian socialism, and its relationship to Marxism and Maoism, will be discussed in Chapter 3.) The concern here will be to characterize in broad outline a general mode of thought that underlies a wide variety of non-Marxian responses to the social consequences of early capitalist industrialism. Indeed, in large measure, it is only in contrast to the Marxist analysis of capitalism that "utopian socialism" becomes a historically definable intellectual-political tradition.

One general and fundamental feature of utopian socialist thought is a perception of history as basically a struggle between "natural" and "unnatural" forces of development. Like Rousseau, the nineteenth-century utopian socialists attributed social evils to unnatural institutions that had imposed themselves on society and tended to pervert a basically good human nature. Thus the solution of social problems was seen in terms of removing unnatural institutions (or preventing their further development); an ideal social order would then emerge as a result of the release of natural human desires. The achievement of the task was based on a profound faith in the powers of human consciousness, a faith that the moral suasion and social examples of "enlightened" men would naturally appeal to the instincts of all men to do away with false institutions.

From this rationalist, unhistorical perspective, capitalism and its social forms and consequences were seen as unnatural as well as morally evil phenomena, and the modern city—the symbol and center of capitalist industrialism—as the principal source of social corruption and dehumanization. The condemnation of the bourgeois city, accompanied by a strongly agrarian orientation, appears in the Babouvist doctrine[23] that grew out of the French Revolution, a doctrine that marks the earliest expression of modern socialist and communist ideas. Philippe Michel Buonarroti, the major ideologist of Babouvism, advocated that the urban masses should go "back to the land" to achieve an egalitarian order: "Agriculture and the arts of first necessity, being the true nutritive supports of society, it is to the scene of these occupations that men are called by nature to live, whether it be to till the soil or furnish the agriculturalists with commodities and recreations."[24] Buonarroti, as J. L. Talmon observed, "saw in the great cities and capitals 'symptoms of public malady, an infallible forerunner of civil convulsions.' The evils of the old regime were to him indissolubly interwoven with the huge cities, which have condemned one portion of the people to overwhelming toil, and the other to demoralizing inaction. The countryside has been

23. Babouvism, as Lichtheim noted, "enters history as an abortive rising of the nascent urban proletariat against a bourgeois regime. . . . The importance of Babouvism lies in the fact that it foreshadowed the themes of the later communist movement, after an industrial working class had come into being" (*Origins of Socialism*, p. 21). For a discussion of the relationship between the early socialist and communist theories of the French Revolution and the "utopian socialism" of the early nineteenth century, ibid. pp 17–38.

24. Quoted in J. L. Talmon, *The Origins of Totalitarian Democracy* (New York: Praeger, 1965), p. 244.

crushed, the cities overcrowded. The latter became seats of 'voluptuous pleasure' of the rich, the source and manifestation of most glaring inequality, greed, envy, and unrest. Agriculture should be restored to its ancient primacy and glory." Thus to realize the ideal society, the large cities had to be broken up, "by scattering their inhabitants over the country to live in healthy smiling villages."[25]

The antiurban biases expressed in the first crude stirrings of modern communist egalitarianism became one of the major themes of utopian socialist thought. The assumption was that the modern division between town and countryside was not (as in Marxism) a logical historical development, but rather an unnatural phenomenon that separated men from each other and dehumanized them. Just as capitalism in general was unnatural, so the modern bourgeois city was an external intrusion that forced men to live in a manner alien to their "true" human needs. This assumption is reflected in the utopian socialist solution to the social evils wrought by capitalism and industrialism: the creation of a network of small rural-based socialistic communities which, by moral appeal and social example, would spread to undermine the urban-based capitalist system.[26]

What is particularly striking is the strongly agrarian character of the ideal communities the utopian socialists envisioned and attempted to establish. Their self-sufficient socialistic communes were to be set up in relatively remote areas of the countryside as much out of preference as necessity—not simply because they had to grow and function independently of capitalist socioeconomic relationships and

25. Ibid.

26. There is an interesting similarity between the utopian socialist conception of how socialism would come into being and the generally accepted view of the process of the transition from feudalism to capitalism. In the latter case, bourgeois towns developed outside the feudal system and eventually undermined and overwhelmed it. The utopian socialist communes, which were to be established beyond the confines of capitalist society, presumably were to function in a similar manner. In the Marxist view, of course, the transition to socialism presupposed a qualitatively different historical process: socialism could emerge only on the basis of the material and social foundations of capitalism and only through the working out of the contradictions within the capitalist mode of production itself. In addition to producing the necessary economic conditions for socialism, capitalism also produced the modern proletariat, the agent of socialist historical redemption. In short, as Marx put it in the "Manifesto," the bourgeoisie creates "its own gravediggers."

political control (and thus serve as alternative models of social development), but also because of what were perceived to be the social virtues of rural life in general. Fourier's famed phalansteries, for example, were to be voluntary associations of 1,600 persons cultivating some 5,000 acres of land. Generally hostile to modern large-scale industry and technology, the Fourierists believed that agriculture was the natural occupation of men and celebrated the virtues of agrarian simplicity.[27]

Even those utopians who recognized the potential social benefits of modern industry and technology, and thus wished to bring them under the collective social control of the producers, envisioned ideal communities in which the cultivation of the soil occupied a prominent and honored place. Étienne Cabet, perhaps more properly characterized as a "utopian communist" than as a "utopian socialist," was an ardent advocate of industrialization. Yet, deeply tied to the eighteenth-century tradition of Natural Law ethics, he believed, as Lichtheim noted, "that there are certain universally true propositions about human nature which, once understood, can lead only to one conclusion: that by going back to 'nature' (i.e., to the precapitalist order of things) men will go back to their own 'true' nature."[28] In Cabet's visionary description of the completely egalitarian Icaria, one finds the majority of the inhabitants engaging in agriculture, albeit with the assistance of modern technology.[29] Even Robert Owen, himself a wealthy industrialist with a profound faith in the powers of science and industry to yield unlimited economic abundance, eventually proposed that the restructuring of society should be brought about by the establishment of model agrarian-based socialist com-

27. For Fourier's conception of the phalanstery, see *Selections from the Works of Fourier*, Julia Franklin, trans. (London: Swan Sonnenschein, 1901), especially pp. 137–54. Although Fourier did not totally reject modern industry, it was to occupy a subordinate place to agriculture in a new rural setting. "Factories," he wrote, "instead of being, as today, concentrated in cities where swarms of wretched people are huddled together, will be scattered over all the fields and phalanxes of the globe, in order that man, while applying himself to factory labour, should never deviate from the paths of attraction, which tends to make use of factories as accessories to agriculture and a change from it, not as the chief occupation, either for a district or for any of its individuals" (ibid., p. 119).

28. Lichtheim, *Origins of Socialism*, p. 29.

29. Étienne Cabet, *Voyage en Icarie* (Paris: Au bureau du Populaire, 1846).

munities—the more or less self-sufficient "Villages of Cooperation."[30]

Although the utopian socialists' attitudes toward modern industry and technology were highly diverse, ranging from Luddite-type hostilities to celebrations of the social benefits their proper use would yield, they stood on common ground (for the most part) in rejecting the modern industrial city as the starting point for socialist transformation. Rather, they saw the model socialistic communities, operating outside the capitalist system in the more remote areas of the countryside yet untouched by modern capitalism, as the agency of transformation. And these models, as a general rule, pictured the ideal society as one where agriculture and industry were combined (in varying fashions and degrees) in a new rural setting. This ideal, which implicitly rejects the modern industrialized city, became a cornerstone of utopian socialism. More explicitly advocated later by Proudhon and especially by the Russian Populists, it remains the cornerstone of the contemporary utopian socialist tradition. "The union of agriculture, industry and handicraft in a modern village community," according to Martin Buber (the most eloquent twentieth-century spokesman for utopian socialism), is the ideal social arrangement and the means by which the socialist society is to be achieved.[31]

The generally antiurban thrust of utopian socialist thought is reflected in a variety of characteristic beliefs that negate the features associated with the modern city. One of the most prominent themes in early socialist literature is a profound distrust of all forms of large-scale organization. This hostility to centralization—represented in the political realm by the modern bureaucratic state and in the economic realm by modern capitalist forms of industrial organization—appears most explicitly and forcefully in the writings of Proudhon. "The prime cause of all the disorders that visit society, of the oppression of the citizens and the decay of nations," he wrote, "lies in the single and hierarchical centralization of authority. . . . We need to

30. The literature by and on Owen is, of course, voluminous. For a succinct survey of his ideas, see G. D. H. Cole, *A History of Socialist Thought* (London: Macmillan, 1953), vol. 1, pp. 86–101.

31. Martin Buber, *Paths in Utopia* (Boston: Beacon Press, 1958), passim.

make an end of this monstrous parasitism as soon as possible."[32] His remedy for the problem (in accord with the general utopian socialist solution) was a free federation of autonomous communal units unfettered by centralized, bureaucratic entanglements. "The dispersion of the masses and their redistribution is beginning," he optimistically proclaimed, and thus the center of social life was moving from the overpopulated cities to "the new agricultural and industrial groupings."[33]

Closely associated with this hostility to modern large-scale and centralized organization was a distaste for occupational specialization. The inhabitants of Fourier's ideal phalansteries, for example, were to engage in various occupations and activities and switch from one to another every two hours. The ideal was the well-rounded individual, a person who would combine many different kinds of physical labor with a wide variety of cultural and intellectual pursuits, thus satisfying a natural human desire for diversity and self-fulfillment. This bias against specialization was also a source of anti-intellectualism. In this ideal society, there would be no need for formal institutions of education, for the young would educate themselves spontaneously in a natural social setting based on the unity of living and working;[34] and there would be no place for university-educated intellectuals, whose specialized training necessarily created a sharp separation between mental and manual labor incongruous with the new order. This notion was later to be emphasized by Kropotkin in his anarchist-populist variant of the utopian socialist tradition; Kropotkin advocated the wholesale abolition of institutions of higher education in favor of "school-workshops" that would integrate study with work, thus eliminating the distinction between

32. Quoted by Buber, ibid., p. 27.

33. Quoted by Buber, ibid., p. 34.

34. Fourier, as Cole observed (*History of Socialist Thought*, vol. 1, p. 65), "wanted the children to follow their natural bents, and to learn a variety of trades by attaching themselves freely to their elders in a sort of manifold apprenticeship. . . . He held that the best way to learn was to do, and that the way to make children want to learn was to give them the chance of doing. Given free choice, he said, they would pick up easily enough the kinds of knowledge towards which they had a natural attraction." For Fourier's own words on what he termed "harmonic education," see *Selections from Fourier*, pp. 67–75.

mental and manual labor.[35] Among the earlier utopians, anti-intellectualism—in the form of a Rousseauist distrust of intellectuals in general—is particularly marked in the writings of Proudhon and Wilhelm Weitling, the most noted German exponent of French utopian socialist ideas.[36]

Other prominent (though not universal) themes in utopian socialist thought are asceticism and complete egalitarianism. As opposed to the opulence and extravagance that marked urban bourgeois life, the utopians advocated the virtues of a simple and spartan life style; in reaction to the gross inequalities and rigid social stratification of the modern industrial city, there arose demands for wholesale and immediate social leveling. For Marx, by contrast, asceticism in general reflected total human self-alienation, and egalitarian social leveling a crudely premature (and, for its time, reactionary) ideological demand that flowed from a still underdeveloped industrial capitalism and a still immature proletariat.[37]

The forces of centralization and specialization which the utopian socialists so strongly condemned were of course identified with the modern city. It was in the cities that large-scale industry developed and where its horrendous social consequences were most evident; it was in the cities that the human personality was fragmented by an increasingly complex and specialized division of labor; it was in the cities that the bureaucratic state power resided; it was in the cities that university-trained specialists and intellectual elites were produced and resided. And it was to be by going *outside* of the cities that the utopian socialists hoped to negate all of the evils and in-

35. A. Walicki, *The Controversy Over Capitalism: Studies in the Social Philosophy of the Russian Populists* (Oxford: Clarendon Press, 1969), pp. 88–90.

36. For a brief summary of Weitling's ideas, see Cole, *History of Socialist Thought*, vol. 1, pp. 226–28.

37. Marx generally viewed utopian socialism as ideological expression of the first futile strivings of the emergent proletariat, strivings that "necessarily failed, owing to the then underdeveloped state of the proletariat, as well as to the absence of the economic conditions for its emancipation, conditions that had yet to be produced, and could be produced by the impending bourgeois epoch alone. The revolutionary literature that accompanied these first movements of the proletariat had necessarily a reactionary character. *It inculcated universal asceticism and social leveling in its crudest form.*" (Emphasis added.) In Marx and Engels, "Manifesto," p. 58.

equities associated with urban capitalism, including the unnatural division between town and countryside.

In utopian socialist thought, the city was thus perceived as the site and source of the principal evils that afflicted society—modern capitalism, the modern centralized state, and modern industrialism in its bourgeois form. But the forces of urban industrialism that the utopian socialists perceived as alien were of course the very ones that Marxist theory celebrated as the historically natural and necessary road to the socialist future. And no Marxist celebrated more ardently the historically progressive character of modern capitalist industrialism than did Lenin.

III. Leninism, Stalinism, and the Soviet Experience

The history of Marxism in Russia is, in one sense, the history of the triumph of town over countryside. The ascendancy of Marxism over Populism (the dominant form that the Western European utopian socialist tradition assumed in Russia), a development which coincided with a period of rapid industrial growth in the last decade of the nineteenth century, marked the ideological dominance of town over countryside in the history of the Russian revolutionary intelligentsia. The Bolshevik victory of 1917 proved to be the political triumph of the city over the countryside. Stalinist industrialization culminated the process, basing the economic dominance of the city on the exploitation of the rural areas.

Russian Marxism arose as an ideology that explicitly rejected the Populist faith in a noncapitalist, agrarian road to socialism. In denying (and condemning as "utopian") the possibility of bypassing the capitalist phase of development and by reaffirming (and universalizing) the original Marxist analysis of the dominance of town over countryside, Plekhanov and Lenin proved to be more "orthodox" Marxists than Marx—and on this point, Lenin was no less orthodox than his Marxist mentor Plekhanov. Both Plekhanov and Lenin characterized Russian Populism as a form of utopian socialism, and their lengthy polemical critiques of the Narodniki were similar to those Marx and Engels had leveled against earlier utopian socialist ideologies in the West. Lenin argued that modern capitalist forces of production had already achieved dominance in Russia, that the collectivist features of traditional agrarian institutions had been undermined by modern economic forces and class divisions, and that the inevitable development of urban industrialization and the consequent emergence of a modern urban proletariat had transferred the revolutionary arena from the countryside to the cities.[38] For Lenin, "no historical peculiarities of our country will free it from the action of universal social laws."[39] Those laws dictated a capitalist future with all of its social consequences, including the complete domination of town over countryside. "The separation of town from country," Lenin insisted, "their oppositeness, and the exploitation of the countryside by the town" are the "universal concomitants of developing capitalism. . . . Therefore, the predominance of the town over the countryside (economically, politically, intellectually, and in all other respects) is a universal and inevitable thing in all countries where there is commodity production and capitalism, including Russia: only sentimental romanticists can bewail this. Scientific theory, on the contrary, points to the progressive aspect given to this contradiction by large-scale industrial capital."[40]

Those who refused to recognize the progressive character and potential of modern capitalism, and instead based their hopes for a socialist future on an atavistic idealization of the "primitive" forms of traditional agrarian life, were condemned to historical oblivion by the same universal and immutable forces of modern socioeconomic development that had already destroyed the precapitalist social relationships they romanticized. Although the Populists had been progressive in their time by first posing the problem of capitalism, they now had become "utopian reactionaries" still "dreaming about 'different paths for the fatherland,' "[41] the carriers of a reactionary petty-bourgeois ideology that represented the interests of the doomed

38. With a wealth of economic data, the argument is pursued at tedious length in Lenin's 1899 work *The Development of Capitalism in Russia*. See V. I. Lenin, *Collected Works* (Moscow: Foreign Languages Publishing House, 1960), vol. 3, pp. 23–607.

39. George Plekhanov, "Our Differences," in Plekhanov, *Selected Philosophical Works* (Moscow: Foreign Languages Publishing House, n.d.), vol. 1, p. 326.

40. V. I. Lenin, "A Characterisation of Economic Romanticism," in Lenin, *Collected Works*, vol. 2, p. 229.

41. V. I. Lenin, "The Economic Content of Narodism," ibid., vol. 1, p. 445.

small producer and promoted "stagnation and Asiatic backwardness."[42]

When Lenin turned to the peasantry as a potential revolutionary ally after 1900, he did so essentially for immediate tactical political reasons, not because of any newfound faith in the socialist potentialities of the countryside. The peasantry found a place in Leninist revolutionary strategy only because the Russian bourgeoisie had compromised with Tsarist autocracy and thus had failed to play its appointed political role in the bourgeois-democratic revolution. Without entering into all the complexities of Lenin's views on the revolutionary role of the peasantry, the essence of the matter is that the peasantry was to serve, in the "democratic" phase of the revolution, as the political surrogate for the liberal bourgeoisie of the cities, who had proved politically useless.

Whatever the implications of this revised strategy for original Marxist theory, Lenin retained his basic Marxist faith that the genuinely progressive economic, social, and intellectual forces in modern history resided in the cities. Nor did this strategy dispel his basic distrust of the peasantry and the backward countryside or in any way mitigate his hostility to Populist ideology, which he continued to regard as a basically "utopian" and reactionary expression of the interests of a still petty-bourgeois peasantry. The alliance of the proletariat and peasantry was simply one of political expediency confined to the bourgeois-democratic phase of the revolution, a means by which to hasten history on its proper course in the absence of a revolutionary bourgeoisie; when the revolution reached its socialist phase it was assumed that the union would prove untenable. Moreover, even in performing the necessary bourgeois-democratic tasks, the peasantry was the junior partner in this unorthodox alliance; the proletariat was not merely to ally itself with the peasantry, but was to "lead" it. Further, Lenin took it for granted that the proletariat and the peasantry would be represented by two different political parties, one "socialist" (i.e., the Bolsheviks), and the other "democratic." The Bolsheviks remained an urban-based party and acquired no roots in the countryside; the latter was left to the Socialist Revolutionaries, whom the Bolsheviks took to be the political representatives of the "democratic" peasantry.

42. V. I. Lenin, "The Heritage We Renounce," ibid., vol. 2, p. 516.

The political formula for this unorthodox version of a bourgeois-democratic revolution was to be a "democratic dictatorship of the proletariat and peasantry." There is no need to discuss here the ambiguities involved in this curious notion or its ambiguous history in Leninist theory and practice except to note that it became irrelevant to political realities with the Bolshevik triumph. State power rested in the hands of an urban-based party that claimed to embody "proletarian consciousness." The suppression of the Socialist Revolutionaries in 1918 destroyed even the pretense of peasant political participation. Further, the traditional peasant distrust of the towns and of the state was intensified by the extension of Bolshevik political power to the countryside and the dispatch of urban Communists to the rural areas to requisition grain from an increasingly hostile peasantry.

With the failure of the anticipated socialist revolutions in the advanced industrialized countries, the Bolsheviks were confronted with the problem of what to do with a successful anticapitalist revolution in an economically backward land—a country not only isolated in a hostile international arena but also one that contained a vast and largely hostile peasantry. Their response to this problem, a problem unanticipated in Leninist theory, was largely determined by orthodox Marxist perspectives, most notably on the question of the relationship between town and countryside. However unorthodox Lenin may have been in other areas and however unorthodox the revolution he led, he and his followers were wedded to the Marxist assumption that the cities held the progressive forces of modern history and the countryside the forces of stagnation and potential regression.

To be sure, Lenin had the gravest doubts about attempting to build a socialist society in an economically and culturally backward land. Indeed, in his last years, he was plagued by a profound sense of guilt about the moral and historical validity of the Bolshevik Revolution. The brutalities and irrationalities of Stalinism were in no sense inherent in Leninism. But insofar as Lenin confronted the problem that Stalin later formulated as "socialism in one country," the general thrust of his views and policies foreshadowed the "revolution from above" over which Stalin was to preside. Lenin concluded that the Bolshevik Revolution, if it remained confined to backward Russia, could be no more than a bourgeois revolution, whose first and most pressing priority was to carry out the unfulfilled tasks of capitalist economic development, albeit under socialist political auspices. This meant, above all, urban industrialization, which required a strong state apparatus that could impose its political control over the countryside and extract from agricultural production the capital necessary for the industrial development of the cities. Lenin's preoccupation with the need for rapid economic development (which he stressed increasingly after mid-1918) was reinforced by his "technocratic bias" (epitomized by his striking formula that "electrification plus Soviets" equals socialism, his slogan "learn from the capitalists," his fascination with the economic efficiency of "Taylorism," and his emphasis on heavy industry); his unqualified acceptance of the virtues of centralization; his persisting antirural sentiments; and his distrust of all forms of "spontaneity." Such were the Leninist ideological points of departure for the Stalinist strategy of urban industrialization based on forced rural collectivization, the nature and social consequences of which are all too well known. It is sufficient to observe that although Stalinism, in its particular fashion, has perhaps confirmed Marx's original characterization of modern history as the "urbanization of the countryside," it has contributed nothing to the realization of Marx's goal of abolishing the distinction between town and countryside. Indeed, if anything, the Soviet model of industrialization—and the urban elites it spawned—has widened the gap between the modern cities and the backward rural areas.

IV. Maoism

It is one of the great ironies of modern history that Marxism, a theory addressed to the urban working class of advanced industrialized nations, should have become the dominant ideology of anticapitalist revolutionary movements in the "backward" peasant countries. And it is one of the ironies of the history of Marxism that many contemporary versions of the theory incorporate socialist ideas and conceptions Marx and Lenin condemned as "utopian" and "reactionary."

The crucial factor in the emergence of "utopian"-type conceptions within contemporary Marxist-Leninist ideologies is the manner in which modern capitalism is perceived. Utopian socialist theories assumed that capitalism was an unnatural and alien phenomenon—

and thus unnecessary to the achievement of a new socialist order. Marxist theory, by contrast, holds that the full development of capitalist forces of production (with all of their consequences) is historically necessary to create the social and material prerequisites for socialism. Lenin, despite all his unorthodoxies in the realm of revolutionary strategy, never abandoned the fundamental Marxist premise that socialism presupposes capitalism.

The modern Chinese historical situation was hardly conducive to the acceptance of this Marxist faith in the progressive nature of capitalism. Modern capitalist industrialism was not an indigenous development, but one that came to China under the aegis of foreign imperialism. Insofar as industrial capitalism developed in twentieth-century China, it not only created all the social evils associated with early industrialism in the West (and in more extreme form), but also developed mainly in areas of the country under foreign domination, primarily the treaty ports. If a perception of capitalism as alien and evil is a general response to the effects of early industrialization, it was a perception that the modern Chinese historical experience served to intensify. Although some of the more Western-oriented Chinese Marxists attempted to adhere to orthodox Marxist-Leninist views, the Chinese situation did not encourage holding to a faith in the socialist potential of a capitalism so alien in origin and so distorted in form. The general tendency, as it found expression in Maoism, was to identify capitalism with imperialism, to see both as external impingements, and to look elsewhere for the socialist regeneration of Chinese society.

On the intellectual level, Chinese Marxist rejections of the Marxist historical analysis of capitalism were facilitated by the absence of competing socialist ideologies—in striking contrast to both original Marxist theory and Russian Marxism, both of which developed in opposition to various utopian socialist ideologies that failed to appreciate the sociohistorical significance of new capitalist forces of production. Chinese Marxists, never seriously confronted with the ideological-political opposition of non-Marxian socialist theories, had less need to defend or affirm (as did Lenin) the Marxist view that socialism presupposes capitalism, a proposition that many viewed as incongruous both with Chinese historical reality and with their own socialist hopes. Moreover, Chinese converts to Communism were politically committed to the Marxist-Leninist program of revolution long before they became intellectually committed to Marxist theory; in a country that lacked a Marxian social-democratic tradition, Chinese Communists were much less firmly tied to Marxist theoretical concepts than their Western and Russian counterparts. Thus, many Chinese Marxists (and most notably, Mao Tse-tung) found it relatively easy to ignore or reinterpret the Marxist view that capitalism was a historically progressive phenomenon, much less an essential condition for socialism.

There are many ambiguities in the treatment of capitalism in Maoist theory, and much that is obscured by the ideological need to conform to Marxist-Leninist orthodoxy and by tactical political concerns. Leaving aside such ideological and tactical considerations, two major themes dominated this realm of Maoist thought. First, capitalism in China was seen as insolubly bound up with foreign imperialism. Second, the Chinese revolution (both in its bourgeois-democratic phase, as that term was radically redefined in Maoist theory, and in its socialist stage) was conceived as part of a worldwide struggle of the forces of socialism against those of capitalist imperialism, with China appearing (at least implicitly) as the vanguard nation in a global revolutionary process. Both propositions served the larger Maoist need to deny that China's socialist future rested on the social and material results of modern capitalist forces of production—or that the relative absence of such forces constituted a barrier to the pursuit of revolutionary socialist goals.

The identification of capitalism with imperialism—one of the most prominent themes in Maoist theoretical literature—is intimately related to the manner in which the relationship between town and countryside was conceived in both the Maoist strategy of revolution and the Maoist strategy of postrevolutionary development. The theme appeared in Mao's earliest writings as a Marxist,[43] and was later theoretically formulated in the notion that the "principal contradiction" in Chinese society (and thus the principal impetus for revolution) was between "imperialism and the Chinese nation."[44]

43. Most notably in the unrevised versions of "Analysis of the Classes in Chinese Society" of 1926 and the "Hunan Report" of early 1927. We shall return to these shortly.

44. Mao Tse-tung, *The Chinese Revolution and the Chinese Communist Party* (1939; Peking: Foreign Languages Press, 1954).

Excluded from membership in the nation were classes and groups "in league with imperialism," as Mao put it in 1926,[45] namely, warlords, landlords, and the comprador big bourgeoisie and their intellectual representatives. These, in effect, were regarded as internal foreigners—groups dependent on an alien capitalism imposed on the Chinese nation from without, and socially, economically, and above all (for Mao) ideologically tied to the external capitalist-imperialist order. Potentially excludable from the nation and potentially alien was the remainder of the bourgeoisie, politically wavering groups who stood on a precarious middle ground. Mao's distrust of the bourgeoisie in general was expressed in its most pristine form in the original version of his 1926 "Analysis of the Classes in Chinese Society," a seminal document in which he undertook to define the attitudes of social groups toward a revolution whose aim was "to overthrow world capitalist imperialism":

> As to the vacillating middle bourgeoisie, its right wing must be considered our enemy; even if it is not already, it will soon become so. Its left wing may become our friend, but it is not a true friend. . . . How many are our true friends? There are 395 million of them. How many are our true enemies? There are a million of them. How many are there of these people in the middle, who may be either our friends or our enemies? There are four million of them. Even if we consider these four million as enemies, this only adds up to a bloc of barely five million, and a sneeze from 395 million would certainly suffice to blow them down.[46]

Despite Mao's oft-repeated distinction between a reactionary comprador bourgeoisie and a presumably progressive national bourgeoisie, the latter did not in fact loom large in the Maoist revolutionary scheme of things. Indeed, Chinese capitalism in general was viewed as potentially reactionary and alien. "National capitalism," Mao wrote in 1939, "has developed to a certain extent and played a considerable part in China's political and cultural life, but it has not

45. Mao Tse-tung, "Analysis of the Classes in Chinese Society." The official *Selected Works* rendition bears little resemblance to the remarkable original document, and the quotations here are from the extracts from the original translated in Stuart R. Schram, *Political Thought of Mao Tse-tung* (New York: Praeger, 1969), pp. 210–14.

46. Ibid., p. 214.

become the principal socioeconomic form in China; quite feeble in strength, it is mostly tied in varying degrees to both foreign imperialism and domestic feudalism."[47] Moreover, the perceived alien character of even national capitalism was reinforced by the general Maoist analysis of Chinese history. In applying (perhaps halfheartedly) the standard Marxist periodization of Western historical development to China, Mao observed that although China had "a rich revolutionary tradition and a splendid historical heritage," it nonetheless "remained sluggish in her economic, political and cultural development after her transition from slave system into feudal society."[48] Chinese feudalism lasted some three thousand years, Mao noted, and "it was not until the middle of the nineteenth century that great internal changes took place in China as a result of the penetration of foreign capitalism." It was this foreign intrusion that undermined the traditional feudal economy and "created certain objective conditions and possibilities for the development of China's capitalist production," possibilities that were partially realized in the emergence of a "national capitalism . . . in a rudimentary form."[49]

Thus, like the comprador capitalism of the big bourgeoisie, the national capitalism of the national bourgeoisie owed its origins to foreign imperialism and therefore had an alien character. Although national capitalism had certain interests opposed to imperialism, nevertheless, as Mao constantly emphasized, it remained strongly tied to the external force that gave birth to it.

One cannot escape the impression that in the Maoist mentality capitalism and a bourgeoisie in whatever forms were seen as somehow alien to China. Chinese Communist theory takes as universally valid Marx's periodization of Western history;[50] Mao thus felt compelled to argue that "China's feudal society . . . carried within itself the embryo of capitalism," and that "China would of herself have developed slowly into a capitalist society even if there had been no

47. Mao, *The Chinese Revolution*, p. 22.

48. Ibid., p. 5

49. Ibid., pp. 11–14.

50. The whole notion of a universal, unilinear scheme of historical evolution is a distinctively Stalinist invention, foreign to Leninism as well as to original Marxism.

influence of foreign capitalism."[51] Yet Mao's strangely non-Marxian analysis of China's embryonic capitalism raises doubts about whether even an indigenous bourgeois development was seen as desirable. In Marx's analysis of the transition from feudalism to capitalism in the West, the dynamic historical force is the development of a capitalist mode of production in cities, operating at first *outside* the confines of feudal society, and the major class struggle is between the newly arisen bourgeoisie and the old feudal aristocracy; the peasants, though victims of the historical transition, are not major historical actors in the process. According to Maoist theory, by contrast, in Chinese feudal society the main contradiction was between peasants and landlords, not between a bourgeoisie and the feudal classes. This thesis is accompanied by the wholly non-Marxist proposition that the class struggles of the peasantry "alone formed the real motive force of historical development in China's feudal society."[52] The implication that capitalism is historically natural in the West but not necessarily in China is also suggested in the historical examples Mao offered to distinguish between "perceptual" and "rational" knowledge in his essay "On Practice." In the West, he observed, the proletariat arrived at a true knowledge of the world from its experiences with modern capitalism and, through the scientific summation of those experiences in Marxist theory, "came to understand the essence of capitalist society." In China, however, "the Chinese people arrived at rational knowledge when they saw the internal and external contradictions of imperialism, as well as the essence of the oppression and exploitation of China's broad masses by imperialism in alliance with China's compradors and feudal class; such knowledge began only about the time of the May 4 Movement of 1919."[53] Thus, whereas "capitalism" and the "proletariat" are the appropriate categories for analyzing the prospects for socialist revolutions in the West, the appropriate categories for the Chinese road to socialism are "imperialism" and "the Chinese people."

However one wishes to interpret Mao's view of the "sprouts"

51. Mao, *The Chinese Revolution*, p. 13.

52. Ibid., pp. 7, 11.

53. Mao Tse-tung, "On Practice," in Mao Tse-tung, *The Selected Works of Mao Tse-tung* (London: Lawrence and Wishart, 1954), vol. 1, pp. 288–89.

(*meng-ya*) of an indigenous capitalism in traditional China that proved abortive, he quite clearly viewed modern capitalist relationships introduced by imperialism, if not as an unnatural phenomenon, then certainly as an alien one—and in no sense the historical prerequisite for socialism. From the beginning Maoism looked not to the Marxist-defined socialist potentials of capitalist forces of production, but rather to "the Chinese people" for the sources of a socialist future. And "the people," of course, are basically the vast peasant masses, the overwhelming majority of that organic entity of 395 million identified in 1926 as the true friends of revolution. It is significant that in his "Analysis of the Classes in Chinese Society," Mao employed an almost wholly numerical criterion in assessing the revolutionary potential of social classes.[54] If the 4 million members of the potentially reactionary "middle bourgeoisie" were expendable, so also, implicitly, were the members of the urban proletariat, who when all is said and done constituted only a tiny percentage of the 395 million. Even more noteworthy is the famous "Hunan Report" of early 1927, where Mao was drawn exclusively to the spontaneity of peasant revolt, that creative and elemental tornado-like force "so extraordinarily swift and violent that no power, however great, will be able to suppress it."[55] In this lengthy document, which expresses the Maoist vision of revolution in its most pristine form, neither capitalism nor the modern social classes it produced are even mentioned in passing.

Later, in the early 1960s, Mao formulated his ideas on the relationship between capitalism and socialism more explicitly and elaborately, arguing that socialism was easier to achieve in China than in the advanced industrialized countries of the West precisely because China was less "poisoned" by modern capitalist forces of economic development and bourgeois ideology.[56]

54. This point is noted by Schram in his commentary on the original version of the article, *Political Thought of Mao*, p. 203.

55. Mao Tse-tung, "Report on an Investigation of the Peasant Movement in Hunan," in Mao, *Selected Works*, vol. 1, p. 22. (Hereafter cited as "Hunan Report.")

56. "Reading Notes on the Soviet Union's 'Political Economy' " *Mao Tse-tung Ssu-hsiang Wan-sui* [Long live the thought of Mao Tse-tung] (Taipei: n.p., 1969), p. 333. This lengthy and remarkable treatise is perceptively analyzed by Richard Levy in "New Light on Mao," *The China Quarterly* 61 (March 1975): 95–117.

Logically flowing from the Maoist rejection of the Marxist proposition that socialism presupposes capitalism was a relative lack of concern with the bourgeoisie and the proletariat, the two Marxian-defined revolutionary classes in modern history. Just as the national bourgeoisie was unnecessary in the "national" or "bourgeois-democratic" phase of the revolution, so the proletariat was unnecessary in its proletarian-socialist phase. There is no need to dwell here on the well-known abandonment of the urban proletariat in Maoist practice even if not in formal theory. The "leadership of the proletariat," of course, meant no more than the leadership of the Communist Party, or more precisely, revolutionary activists deemed to possess the appropriate proletarian socialist consciousness; whatever institutional form this consciousness might take, there was no need for any organic or organizational tie with the actual proletariat. And though Maoist theory makes a formal distinction between the bourgeois-democratic and socialist stages of the revolution, the distinction all but vanished in the Maoist redefinition of a bourgeois-democratic revolution. Without entering into the tortuous argument that converted "a bourgeois-democratic revolution of the general, old type" into "a democratic revolution of a special, new type," it is sufficient to note that the aim of this "new-democratic revolution" was to "steer away from a capitalist future and head towards the realization of socialism," and that the leadership of the revolutionary process in general "rests on the shoulders of the party of the Chinese proletariat, the Chinese Communist Party, for without its leadership no revolution can succeed."[57]

The utopian socialist character of Maoism is nowhere more apparent than in the rejection of the fundamental Marxist premise that socialism presupposes capitalism and the historical activity of the classes directly involved in modern capitalist relations of production. The Maoist tendency was to find the sources of socialism in those areas of society least influenced by capitalism—in a peasantry relatively uninvolved with capitalist socioeconomic relationships and in an intelligentsia uncorrupted by bourgeois ideas. As in utopian socialist theories, capitalism and its modern social and material products were not seen to be the preconditions for the socialist reorganization of

57. Mao, *The Chinese Revolution*, pp. 53–55.

society. Whereas Marx was concerned with the bourgeoisie and the proletariat as the dynamic classes in modern history, Mao was concerned with the relationship between peasants and intellectuals.

Other Maoist affinities with utopian socialist theories also logically accompany these departures from Marxism. In Maoism, as in utopian socialism, economic backwardness was not seen as an obstacle to the achievement of socialist goals but rather was converted into a socialist advantage. It was thus that Mao proclaimed the special Chinese revolutionary virtues of being "poor and blank" and saw preindustrial China pioneering the way to a universal socialist and communist future.

To celebrate the "advantages of backwardness" is to abandon the Marxist faith in the objective determining forces of history, to deny, in a word, that socialism is immanent in the progressive movement of history itself. Rather the historical outcome turns on "subjective factors"—the consciousness, the moral values, and the actions of dedicated men. Maoism shares with the utopian socialist tradition the view that socialism rests, not on the development of material productive forces, but rather on the moral virtues of "new men" who can and must impose their socialist consciousness on historical reality. There is nothing non-Maoist (although much that is non-Marxist) in Buber's utopian socialist formulation that the realization of socialism "depends not on the technological state of things" but rather "on people and their spirit."[58]

One also finds in Maoism a hostility to the organizational and institutional forms identified with modern economic development, similar to that found in the nineteenth-century utopian socialist ideologies. The bias against occupational specialization, the antipathy to large-scale and centralized forms of political and economic organization, the deep aversion to all manifestations of bureaucracy, and the distrust of formal higher education are aspects of the Maoist mentality too well known to require elaboration here. Like the utopian socialists, Mao was unwilling to accept the consequences of "modernity" as the necessary price of historical progress. And not merely because the price was regarded as too high. For if there is no objective historical process culminating in socialism, there is no

58. Buber, *Paths in Utopia*, pp. 46–47.

assurance that paying the price will lead to the predicted socialist end.

In sum, on the basis of the three broad questions that generally distinguish Marxism from utopian socialism, Maoism is clearly more akin to the latter than the former. First, Maoism rejects the Marxist premise that modern industrial capitalism is a necessary and progressive stage in historical development and a prerequisite for socialism. Second, Maoism denies (implicitly in theory and most explicitly in practice) the Marxist belief that the industrial proletariat is the bearer of the socialist future. Third, Maoism replaces the Marxist belief in objective laws of history with a voluntaristic faith in the consciousness and the moral potentialities of men as the decisive factor in sociohistorical development.

These departures from Marxism bear directly on the Maoist conception of the relationship between town and countryside in modern history. Just as the Maoist attitude toward capitalism in China was fundamentally conditioned by its imperialist origins and implications, so the Maoist attitude toward the relationship between town and countryside was molded by the foreign domination of modern Chinese cities. For Mao the city was not the modern revolutionary stage, as Marx believed, but a foreign-dominated stage. This was a perception that bred powerful antiurban biases and, correspondingly, a strong agrarian orientation; the city came to be identified with alien influences, and the countryside with the nation. Such a perception gave rise to a more general suspicion of the city as the site and source of foreign bourgeois ideological, moral, and social corruptions, a suspicion that lingered on after 1949, long after the foreigners were removed from the cities. And this suspicion tended to foster a rejection of the orthodox Marxist assumption that industrialization implies urbanization in favor of an alternative nonurban (and thus nonalien) path to modern economic development. The Marxist ideal of eliminating the distinction between town and countryside became particularly appealing because it was seen as not only a desirable social goal but a desirable national one as well.

There may well be traditional Chinese precedents for this modern antiurban impulse. As Rhoads Murphey has observed, the traditional Chinese admiration for nature expressed itself in a Confucian tendency to find wisdom and truth in the virtues of rural life, whereas "in the cities where man disregarded nature, truth was clouded [and] virtue weakened."[59] There is no need here to speculate on whether traditional antiurban views survived to influence modern Chinese attitudes. Whatever the influence of the Confucian gentry's preference for the rural virtues (or the possible influence of old peasant resentments against the parasitic administrative-based town in traditional China),[60] certainly the most important factor in molding modern perceptions was the modern imperialist impingement, which did in fact make cities foreign enclaves and the symbols of foreign domination. An early modern precedent might be noted in passing. During the Opium War, as Frederic Wakeman has pointed out, the British intrusion stimulated antiurban as well as antiforeign sentiments among the gentry and peasantry of Kwangtung province; the rural inhabitants saw the city of Canton as filled with "traitors" (*han-chien*), urban merchants, and corrupt Imperial officials who were collaborating with the foreign intruders.[61]

This "prenationalist" image of the city as infested with internal foreigners became a much more prominent theme in twentieth-century Chinese nationalism. As modern Chinese cities developed in a Western mold, thus widening the cultural as well as the socioeconomic gap between town and countryside, one nationalist response was to look to the rural areas (relatively uncorrupted by foreign influences)

59. Rhoads Murphey, "City and Countryside as Ideological Issues: India and China," *Comparative Studies in Society and History* 14.3 (June 1972): 253–54. For a fuller discussion of this strand in traditional Chinese thought, see Murphey, "Man and Nature in China," *Modern Asian Studies* 1.1 (January 1967): 313–33.

60. On the parasitic relationship of the traditional Chinese city, or "garrison town" (the seat of bureaucratic authority and the residence of wealthy gentry), to the countryside, see Fei Hsiao-t'ung, *China's Gentry* (Chicago: University of Chicago Press, 1953), especially pp. 91–107. As Fei characterizes traditional urban-rural relations: "Economic activity in these fortified centers of administration . . . was based not on an exchange of goods between producers but on the purchasing power of consumers who gained their wealth largely from exploitative relationships with the country" (ibid., p. 98). Whether Chinese peasants generally perceived the town as parasitic and whether, if they did, this generated any significant antiurban tradition among them are matters that the literature on traditional China does little to clarify.

61. Frederic Wakeman, *Strangers at the Gate* (Berkeley and Los Angeles: University of California Press, 1966), pp. 48–51.

for the true sources of national regeneration. It is by no means fortuitous that the most nationalistic of the early Chinese Communists (such as Li Ta-chao and Mao) were among the first and most ardent advocates of a peasant-based revolution and were willing, and indeed eager, to abandon the cities which they viewed as alien bastions of conservatism and moral corruption—as opposed to those Chinese Communists who accepted Marxist-Leninist theory in its more or less orthodox Western form as an international revolutionary message and who placed their socialist hopes in the development of urban industry and in the revolutionary potential of an urban proletariat formed in a Western image. Ruralism and nationalism are closely related phenomena in modern world history, and this is nowhere more dramatically demonstrated than in modern Chinese history, where a revolution based on an agrarian modification of Marxism-Leninism necessarily assumed the character of a war of the Chinese countryside against the foreign-infected cities.

Mao's antiurban bias was not simply the product of what became a rural-based revolution. It is apparent in his early writings and most strikingly in the "Hunan Report." Quite apart from relegating the city to a minor role in the revolutionary process, we find here (among other remarkable things, for a Marxist) the view that the foreign knowledge and culture of the Westernized urban intelligentsia are not only unsuited to the needs of the peasantry, but inferior to what the peasants can acquire on their own:

> In my student days, I used to stand up for the "foreign-style schools" when, upon returning to my native place, I found the peasants objecting to them. I was myself identified with the "foreign-style students" and "foreign-style teachers," and always felt that the peasants were somehow wrong. It was during my six months in the countryside in 1925, when I was already a Communist and adopted the Marxist viewpoint, that I realized I was mistaken and that the peasants' views were right. The teaching materials used in the rural primary schools all dealt with city matters and were in no way adapted to the needs of the rural areas. . . . Now the peasants are energetically organizing evening classes, calling them peasant schools. . . . As a result of the growth of the peasant movement, the cultural level of the peasants has risen rapidly. Before long there will be tens of thousands of schools sprouting in the rural areas throughout the whole province, and that will be something quite different

from the futile clamour of the intelligentsia and so-called "educators" for "popular education."[62]

In the same document, moreover, Mao suggested that revolutionaries who remained in the cities were likely to become ideologically corrupted and politically conservative. When news of "the revolt of the peasants in the countryside" reached Changsha, "there was not a single person who did not summarize the whole thing in one phrase: 'An awful mess!' Even quite revolutionary people, carried away by the opinion of the 'awful mess' school which prevailed like a storm over the whole city, became down-hearted at the very thought of the conditions in the countryside, and could not deny the word 'mess.' "[63] The remedy, of course, was for potentially "revolutionary people" to leave the corrupting life of the cities for the countryside, where revolutionary creativity resided. In vastly different political and historical circumstances, it was to remain the Maoist remedy after 1949.

Mao's early hostility to the city persisted to govern the Maoist conception of the relationship between town and countryside in both the revolutionary and postrevolutionary eras. Implicit in Maoist theory (and quite apparent in Maoist practice) was the identification of the city with what is foreign and reactionary and the countryside with what is truly national and revolutionary. Consider, for example, one of Mao's "antagonistic contradictions": that between town and countryside. We are told that whereas in Western capitalist society "the town under bourgeois rule ruthlessly exploits the countryside," in modern Chinese society it is *"the town under the rule of foreign imperialism* and the native big comprador bourgeoisie [that] most savagely exploits the countryside," thus creating an antagonism between the two of a particularly extreme character.[64]

No doubt the Maoist suspicion of the city was greatly fortified by the whole Chinese Communist revolutionary experience, in which peasant revolutionaries did in fact "surround and overwhelm" the

62. Mao, "Hunan Report," pp. 56–57.

63. Ibid., pp. 24–25.

64. Mao Tse-tung, "On Contradiction," in *Selected Works*, vol. 1, p. 336. My emphasis.

cities. But the unique political strategy that led to that outcome was itself determined in part by a preexisting faith in the revolutionary potential of the countryside and a negative perception of the city. Long before that strategy was formulated, much less proven in practice, Mao already viewed the cities as strongholds of a reactionary bourgeoisie who were seen as agents (or potential allies) of foreign imperialism, and the breeding places for alien social influences and ideological corruption in general. To be sure, the cities also held the urban proletariat, but however much one might sympathize with its plight, it was not, for Mao, a class that held much revolutionary potential. Numerically speaking—and Mao often spoke in numerical terms—it was but a tiny percentage of "the revolutionary people."

These views on the place of town and countryside in the revolutionary process flowed from Mao's larger (and strikingly non-Marxian) conception that a socialist-oriented revolution need not be dependent on modern industrial capitalism or its product, the urban proletariat, and need not proceed according to any Marxist-defined laws of objective historical development. Rather, revolutionary success depended on the vast peasant masses and "deurbanized" intellectuals who were willing and able to "unite" with the peasants and guide them along the correct path.

Both early ideological impulses and the concrete experience of the Chinese revolution contributed to the dichotomy between the revolutionary countryside and the conservative cities. The notion became deeply ingrained in the Maoist mentality, and it was to have profound implications for the domestic history of postrevolutionary China, as well as eventually to be projected into a global vision of a worldwide revolutionary process in which the "revolutionary countryside" of the economically backward lands would triumph over the "cities" of Europe and North America. Whereas Marx believed that modern history made the countryside dependent on the towns and "nations of peasants on nations of bourgeois," Mao believed that modern revolutionary history dictated the victory of the countryside over the town and the victory of peasant nations over bourgeois nations.

Although the Chinese Communist Revolution was rural-based (and its Maoist leaders rural-oriented as well), the "ultimate target" of the revolution, as John Lewis has pointed out, "was always the cities."[65] As early as 1939 Mao called for more attention to "work in the cities," for though the revolution would necessarily take the form of "a peasant guerrilla war" and would "triumph first in the rural districts," the "capture of the cities now serving as the enemy's main bases is the final objective of the revolution."[66] And in March of 1949, when the cities were falling to the Red Army in the last phase of the civil war, Mao announced that "the center of gravity of the Party's work has shifted from the village to the city."[67]

Yet the Communist capture of the cities in 1949 was the rather anticlimactic consummation of a revolution in which the decisive battles had been fought by rural people in the countryside. Communist control of the cities did not involve revolutionary political action but rather assumed the form of a military occupation of the urban centers by a largely peasant army. The Maoist suspicion of the cities and their inhabitants (who had contributed so little to the revolutionary victory) remained, and was later to reemerge in confronting new problems in vastly different historical circumstances. Indeed, in the same report in which Mao announced the inauguration of the period of "the city leading the village," he warned that revolutionaries might be susceptible to urban bourgeois corruptions—to "sugar-coated bullets"—and that the rural style of "plain living and hard struggle" might give way to the "love of pleasure and distaste for continued hard living" that city life encouraged.[68]

Nonetheless, in the early 1950s, it was Mao who promoted the urban-centered policies of postrevolutionary development, the social consequences of which he later was to condemn. Shortly before the formal establishment of the People's Republic, in the essay "On the

65. John Lewis, ed., *The City in Communist China* (Stanford, Calif.: Stanford University Press, 1970), p. 1. See also Lewis, "Political Aspects of Mobility in China's Urban Development," *American Political Science Review* 60.4 (December 1966): 899–912.

66. Mao, *The Chinese Revolution*, pp. 30–32.

67. Mao Tse-tung, "Report to the Second Plenary Session of the Seventh Central Committee of the Communist Party of China," in Mao Tse-tung, *The Selected Works of Mao Tse-tung* (Peking: Foreign Languages Press, 1961), vol. 4, pp. 363–64.

68. Ibid., p. 374.

People's Democratic Dictatorship," Mao postponed Marxist utopian goals to some indefinite time in the future in favor of the "immediate tasks" of building a strong state power and promoting rapid economic development.[69] With the city established as the new "center of gravity," the "immediate tasks" were pursued in accordance with the Soviet model of development which emphasized the rapid development of urban heavy industry and the establishment of centralized (and urban-based) political and economic bureaucracies. The social and political results of the First Five Year Plan of 1953–57 are well known: the growth of increasingly oppressive bureaucratic structures and practices; the emergence of new forms of social inequality, which manifested themselves especially in the appearance of privileged political-administrative and technological-intellectual elites in the cities; urban economic development to the detriment of the agricultural sector; processes of ideological decay (most notably, the tendency for Marxian socialist goals to become ritualized, and the abandonment, in practice if not in rhetoric, of the egalitarian rural revolutionary values of "plain living" and "hard work"); and a growing political, economic, and cultural gulf between the modernizing cities and the backward countryside.

In the Maoist response to this familiar pattern of postrevolutionary institutionalization, the Marxist goal of eliminating the distinction between town and countryside came to assume a special prominence, and Maoist affinities with utopian socialist ideas emerged with particular clarity, especially in the rural communization movement of the Great Leap Forward campaign and the accompanying theoretical literature on "the transition from socialism to communism." The Maoist remedy for the social consequences of urban industrialization was to industrialize the countryside, to move the political as well as the socioeconomic center of gravity from the cities to the new rural communes. The people's communes were to serve not only as the main agencies for economic development but also as the basic social units for China's "leap" to a communist utopia. Although it is by no means the most utopian document of the times, the chiliastic expec-

69. Mao Tse-tung, "On the People's Democratic Dictatorship," ibid., pp. 411–24.

tations of the era were conveyed in the official Party resolution of 10 December 1958, which defined the nature and sociohistorical function of the communes.

In 1958, a new social organization appeared fresh as the morning sun above the broad horizon of East Asia. This was the large-scale people's commune in the rural areas of our country which combines industry, agriculture, trade, education and military affairs and in which government administration and commune management are integrated. . . . The development of the system of rural people's communes . . . has shown the people of our country the way to the gradual transition from collective ownership to ownership by the whole people in agriculture, the way to the gradual transition from the socialist principle of "each according to his work" to the Communist principle of "to each according to his needs," the way to the gradual diminution and final elimination of the differences between rural and urban areas, between worker and peasant and between mental and manual labor, and the way to the gradual diminution and final elimination of the domestic functions of the state. . . . It can also be foreseen that in the future Communist society, the people's commune will remain the basic unit of social structure.[70]

These are some of the themes elaborated on *in extenso* in the voluminous Great Leap literature on the communes and their assigned role in "the transition from socialism to communism." Two aspects of this Maoist vision of the Chinese road to socialism are particularly noteworthy for the present discussion: first, the decidedly antiurban implications of the communization movement; and second, the extraordinary emphasis placed on the role of human consciousness and moral qualities in achieving ultimate Marxist goals.

The whole Great Leap Forward vision of decentralizing economic and political life in relatively autonomous and self-sufficient rural communes marked a drastic reversal of the Soviet-borrowed pattern of postrevolutionary development, in favor of policies that were intended, in part, to undermine the power and prestige of the new

70. "Resolution on Questions Concerning People's Communes," Sixth plenary session of the Eighth Central Committee of the CCP, 10 December 1958. New China News Agency, Peking, 18 December 1958. See *Current Background*, no. 542: 7–22.

urban elites. The emphasis on the "industrialization of the countryside" and the much-heralded scheme of combining industrial with agricultural production meant a radical deemphasis on the role of the cities and their inhabitants in achieving economic growth and revolutionary social change. Similarly, new educational policies based on the combination of education with productive labor (through "red and expert universities" and various "half-work, half-study" programs) devaluated urban-centered and urban-oriented institutions of higher education. The new rural schools, it was envisioned, would produce "new peasants" who combined a socialist consciousness with scientific expertise; the masses themselves, it was proclaimed, were to become the masters of science and technology. Moreover, the communes were to be not only the primary socioeconomic units, but also organs of revolutionary political power; indeed, the people's commune became the model Maoist instrument for carrying out all the socially revolutionary measures Marxist theory assigns to the era of "proletarian dictatorship," including the abolition of the distinction between town and countryside.

The radical policies pursued during the abortive Great Leap Forward campaign reflected longstanding Maoist hostilities to social and political forms generally associated with urban industrialism: occupational specialization, bureaucratic rationality, large-scale centralized organization, and formal higher education. And they posed a grave threat not only to the new urban elites, but to urban-based state and Party bureaucracies in general.[71]

The antiurban thrust of the communization movement was accentuated by a general celebration of the virtues of rural life and an assault on "decadent" urban lifestyles. Cadres were called on to practice and glorify the rural revolutionary tradition of "the fine work style of leading a hard and plain life" and to condemn those corrupted by city life who indulged in extravagance and waste and adopted the "bureaucratic airs" of lethargy, conceit, and effeminacy. The way to correct these vices was for city dwellers to live and work with the peasants in the countryside and there acquire true proletarian revolutionary virtues. It is noteworthy that the official Party resolu-

71. For a discussion of the political implications of the communes, see Chapter 5, pp. 141–145.

tion on the communes (of December 1958), while calling for the transformation "of the old cities" into "new socialist cities," observed that the communization of the cities would be more difficult and lengthy than the communization of the countryside, not only because of the greater complexity of urban life, but also because of the persistence of bourgeois ideology in the cities.[72]

Another striking feature of Maoist ideology during the Great Leap era was the enormous emphasis placed on the role of human consciousness and the spiritual transformation of the people. The utopian social goals of the movement were to be realized in the here and now; one had only to rely on the "enthusiasm and creativity of the masses," believe that the people would respond as enthusiastically to moral and ideological appeals as to purely monetary incentives, recognize that "man is the decisive factor," and trust in the emergence of "new men" of "all-round ability," whose consciousness and actions would bring about the new society.[73] This celebration of "the people's creativity" took on a strongly rural orientation, for revolutionary creativity and the potential to achieve the appropriate morality and consciousness were attributed essentially to "the pioneering peasants."[74] Those who argued that China lacked the objective economic basis for communization and the transition to communism were accused of holding to the heretical "productive force theory," refusing to recognize "the great role and revolutionary enthusiasm of more than five hundred million peasants." They were reminded of Chairman Mao's words, "Poverty inclines one to change, action and revolution," which meant that "under all circumstances attention should be given to the full display of the subjective activity of the masses."[75]

Although the utopian elements in Maoism received their fullest

72. "Resolution on Questions Concerning People's Communes," p. 8.

73. For a typical example of this emphasis, see Ch'en Po-ta, "Under the Banner of Comrade Mao Tse-tung," *Hung-ch'i* [Red flag], 16 July 1958, in *Selections from China Mainland Magazines,* 138: 5–17.

74. Ibid., p. 16.

75. Ch'en Cheng-liang, "The People's Commune Is a Necessary Product of China's Political and Economic Development," *Hsin chien-she* [New construction], 7 November 1959, in *Selections from China Mainland Magazines,* 206: 21, 26, 27.

expression in the Great Leap Forward era, they remained on the ideological scene after the forced retreat from the radical communization program and the reassertion of the power of urban-centered economic and political bureaucracies in the early 1960s. And they reemerged on the political scene with apocalyptic fury in the Cultural Revolution. However one wishes to interpret that most extraordinary upheaval, it was certainly (among other things) a direct attack on urban elites and an attempt to reverse the growing political and economic dominance of the industrializing cities over the countryside. It is perhaps overstating the case to describe the Cultural Revolution as "a movement of the countryside against the cities, and of the peasants against the workers," as Stuart Schram once suggested,[76] if only because peasants were not principal actors in the political drama. Nonetheless, the Cultural Revolution marked the resurgence of an ideology that spoke on the peasants' behalf and the pursuit of policies that tended to benefit the countryside rather than the cities and their "urban overlords." It resolved, at least for a time, one of the central policy issues involved in the political struggles of the preceding decade. The view, generally identified with Liu Shao-ch'i, that urban industrialization must precede the full socialist reorganization of the countryside gave way to the Maoist policy of committing a greater share of energy and resources to industrializing the countryside and providing the rural masses greater access to education and health services.

Perhaps the most significant expression of the utopian socialist strain in Maoism is the inversion of the Marxist-Leninist view of the relationship between town and countryside. Nothing could have been more repugnant to Mao than Marx's characterization of modern history as "the urbanization of the countryside," the Marxist assumption that industrialization demands urbanization, and the accompanying proposition that the complete dominance of town over countryside is the historical prerequisite for the achievement of communism. Just as Mao's revolutionary strategy was based on a faith in the revolutionary political potential of the peasantry, so his postrevolutionary strategy focused on the countryside as the point of departure for

76. Stuart Schram, *Mao Tse-tung* (New York: Simon and Schuster, 1966), p. 318.

radical socioeconomic change. It was a strategy designed to avoid what Marx regarded as the inevitable social consequences of industrialization and to eliminate the social inequalities and ideological impurities that the city was seen to foster even in a presumably socialist society. The Maoist aim was neither to "ruralize" the city nor to "urbanize" the countryside. It was, rather, to modernize the countryside. The cities were gradually to be absorbed into a modernized and communized rural milieu as society moved to the ultimate goal of abolishing the distinction between town and countryside.

Maoists, to be sure, adopted many of the measures Marx proposed as means to this end in the "transition" period following the socialist revolution: the "combination of agriculture with manufacturing industries," "a more equable distribution of the population over the country," and the "combination of education with industrial production."[77] But they flatly rejected his assumption that such measures could be pursued successfully only in advanced industrialized countries under the leadership of the cities and the urban proletariat. It was the Maoist insistence that such tasks must be undertaken in the here and now in a situation of economic scarcity, with the impetus coming from the countryside and a peasantry armed with the appropriate consciousness, morality, and leaders. It is not the utopian goal that distinguished Mao from Marx (and Lenin) and that gave Maoism its "utopian" character, but rather different conceptions of how and under what conditions the goal was to be pursued.

The inversion of the Marxist view of the relationship between town and countryside in modern revolutionary history is by no means a distinctively Chinese Marxist phenomenon. Along with similar intellectual affinities with utopian socialist thought, it is found in contemporary Marxist ideologies in other areas of the world—most notably in the Cuban version of Marxism-Leninism, in the neo-Marxist writings of Frantz Fanon, and in the "African socialism" of Julius Nyerere. For Castro, for example, "the city is a cemetery of revolutionaries and resources."[78] In Castroism, the urban areas are not only physi-

77. Marx and Engels, "Manifesto," p. 51.

78. Quoted in Regis Debray, *Revolution in the Revolution?* (New York: Grove Press, 1967), p. 69.

cally dangerous for revolutionaries but spiritually corrupting as well. As Debray, in his role as ideological spokesman for Castro put it, revolutionaries who remain in the cities will "lose sight of moral and political principle," and thus they are to "abandon the city and go to the mountains" because "the mountain proletarianizes the bourgeois and peasant elements" whereas "the city can bourgeoisify the proletarians."[79] And in the writings of Fanon, the peasantry is portrayed as the only revolutionary class since the foreign-built towns are populated by a privileged and conservative proletariat as well as a parasitic native bourgeoisie. For Fanon, the city and its sociopolitical life is "the world that the foreigner had built." Therefore, revolutionaries, who are to incarnate the elemental will of the peasantry, must live in the countryside both before and after political victory and "ought to avoid the capital as if it had the plague."[80]

The appearance in contemporary Marxist (or neo-Marxist) ideologies of ideas and conceptions similar to those characteristic of nineteenth-century European utopian socialist theories can be seen as a function of economic backwardness—as modern variants of a universal intellectual response (in new historical circumstances and ideological frameworks) to the effects of early industrialization or to the anticipation of them. In non-Western countries the hostility to the modern city has been particularly intense because the city not only manifests all the undesirable social consequences of early industrialism, but is also the symbol of foreign political, economic, and cultural dominance. The response, accordingly, is both a nationalist and a social one. It is this powerful combination of nationalist and socialist aspirations that has led many contemporary non-Western Marxists to endorse Marx's goal of abolishing the distinction between town and countryside while rejecting his analysis of the historical function of this division and his assumptions on the means by which it would be eliminated.

Such "utopian" departures from orthodox Marxism-Leninism have influenced profoundly both the revolutionary and postrevolutionary strategies of contemporary Marxists. In the making of revolution,

79. Ibid., pp. 70–77.

80. See Frantz Fanon, *The Wretched of the Earth* (New York: Grove Press, 1966), especially pp. 29–163.

perhaps the most important implication is the rejection of the urban bourgeoisie and proletariat as revolutionary classes in favor of the peasantry. And in the making of new social orders, what is involved is a special concern with the social price of modern economic progress, an explicit rejection of Western and Soviet models of development, an attempt to achieve industrialization without urbanization, and a search for means of economic growth that seem consistent with the ultimate achievement of socialist and communist goals. A good case can be made that non-Marxian "utopian heresies" have served well the needs of revolution where revolutions have been needed, and are better suited than orthodox Marxist and Leninist assumptions to the socioeconomic realities of economically backward lands. Certainly there is nothing in the modern Western historical experience to confirm Marx's prediction that socialism is the logical and necessary result of modern capitalism, and there is little in the Soviet historical experience to offer much hope that this particular "socialist" pattern of urban industrialization is likely to lead to any genuinely socialist future. It would be one of the supreme ironies of modern history (and of the history of Marxism in the modern world) if it should turn out that the peasant countries become the pioneers in the quest for Marxist socialist ends.

Yet before celebrating Maoist and other "new roads" to socialism, one might do well to keep in mind some of the dangers that Marx long ago warned against: the possibility of historical regression inherent in any attempt to bring about a socialist reorganization of society in the absence of highly developed productive forces; the particular forms of political elitism that tend to grow from historical situations characterized by a general weakness of social classes; and the tendency of countries with large peasant populations to foster Bonapartist personality cults—a phenomenon apparent in the appearance of charismatic leaders, such as Mao, Castro, and Nyerere, who emerge on the historical scene claiming special "spiritual bonds" to the masses.

Have we simply witnessed in Maoist China and elsewhere rather mundane and familiar processes where socialist ideologies and ostensibly socialist societies—as in the Soviet case but in new and strange forms—have been performing the historical work of capitalist economic development, ultimately producing more or less similar social results? Will it turn out, as Marx believed, that "the country that is more developed industrially only shows, to the less developed, the image of its own future?" Or is it rather the paradoxical case that old utopian ideas in new ideological gestalts and operating in unforeseen historical circumstances are projecting the image of a new future? Perhaps there is some light to be shed on these questions (and on the nature of Maoism) by comparing Mao with Lenin as well as with Marx, and by moving the inquiry from the perspective of Western European utopian socialist thought to another form of "utopian socialism"—nineteenth-century Russian Populist ideology.

3

Leninism and Maoism: Some Populist Perspectives on Marxism-Leninism in China

Isaac Deutscher once wrote that the Chinese Communist revolution presents the paradox of "the most archaic of nations avidly absorbing the most modern of revolutionary doctrines, the last word in revolution, and translating it into action. Lacking any native ancestry, Chinese Communism descends straight from Bolshevism. Mao stands on Lenin's shoulders."[1]

Deutscher's observation echoes a generally accepted view of the historical relationship between Maoism and Leninism. Most Western scholars of Chinese Communism take for granted that Marxism came to China in its Leninist form, and it remained in that form. And, for different reasons, Chinese Communist theoreticians claim that Mao Tse-tung is the true heir of Lenin. Indeed, the thought of Mao is celebrated as a new and higher stage in the development of a universally valid revolutionary theory still officially canonized as "Marxism-Leninism-Mao Tsetung Thought." In the Chinese Marxist pantheon, Mao stands on the shoulders of Lenin as firmly as Lenin presumably stands on the shoulders of Marx.

Yet while Mao may have had the last word (or at least the latest word) on revolution, it is by no means clear that the words he proclaimed were Leninist words. The whole question of the relationship between Leninism and Maoism is filled with ambiguities and

1. Isaac Deutscher, *Ironies of History* (London: Oxford University Press, 1966), pp. 89–90.

the historic tie between the two is a most tenuous one. How, after all, was it possible—during the Cultural Revolution—for "Leninist proletarian revolutionaries" to undertake to destroy the very organizational apparatus which Leninism teaches is the vanguard of proletarian revolution? If the Party is the incarnation of proletarian consciousness, as a Leninist must believe, then why is it that Maoists so often attributed true "proletarian consciousness" to individuals and groups completely outside of the Party structure? If Leninists have always regarded the "spontaneous" strivings and consciousness of the masses as not only inadequate but potentially dangerous for the revolutionary cause, why have Maoists so ardently prized the spontaneous revolutionary creativity of the masses? If Leninism teaches that the essential precondition for effective revolutionary action is the discipline and authority of the Party and its organizations, why was it that so much Maoist revolutionary action was so often directed against this organizational discipline? Indeed, how was it psychologically possible, much less politically and ideologically feasible, for Mao Tse-tung to issue the Cultural Revolutionary call for the masses to "rebel" against the Party organization that he himself was largely responsible for building and leading to revolutionary triumph?

Few answers to these questions are to be found in the writings of Chinese Marxist theoreticians. Maoists never abandoned their claim to be the inheritors of the Leninist tradition. Just as Lenin and his successors presented "Leninism" as the only true interpretation of Marxism, so Chinese Communists proclaim "Mao Tsetung Thought" as the only valid version of Marxism-Leninism. And in both cases the most significant departures, innovations, and revisions tend to be obscured by the use of orthodox ideological formulae and by psychological, intellectual, and political needs to reaffirm the tie to the inherited revolutionary tradition.

Thus, in attempting to understand the relationship between Maoism and the Marxist-Leninist tradition, it is not sufficient to examine exegetically Chinese Communists' writings on Marxism-Leninism and the role of the Party and compare them with the writings of earlier Leninists and Marxists. The literature itself does not always suggest the crucial questions, much less provide the answers. Indeed, some of the central problems involved in understanding the Maoist revolutionary mentality may not be apparent within a strictly

"Marxist-Leninist" framework; it may prove useful, therefore, to go outside the realm of formal ideology and approach Maoism in terms of broader intellectual and historical perspectives. One perspective that might prove suggestive is the thought of nineteenth-century Russian Populists. Rather than comparing Mao solely with his Marxist predecessors, it may be useful to explore the relationship between Maoism and Leninism by relating strands implicit in Maoist thought to certain general ideas and problems articulated in a "pre-Leninist" (and non-Marxist) "utopian" revolutionary movement.

In comparing Maoism with Russian Populism there is no intention of implying—for there is no evidence to suggest—that Mao or Maoists were influenced by Russian Populist ideas. Unlike Lenin, Mao (as far as one knows) did not read Herzen or Chernyshevsky, nor is there anything in the history of Maoism comparable to the lengthy anti-Populist polemics which occupied so much of Lenin's early revolutionary career. Rather, the concern is with the independent appearance of certain similar revolutionary modes of thought and a confrontation with certain common problems and dilemmas. Leninism was in part a response to ideas and problems expressed and raised by Populist revolutionaries and it is by identifying the distinctively Maoist response to similar ideas and problems in China that one may hope to measure something of the intellectual distance between Maoism and Leninism.

I. Russian Populism

Classical Russian Populism (ca. 1850–80) was, in large measure, the intellectual descendent of the early nineteenth-century tradition of Western European utopian socialist thought discussed in the previous chapter.[2] Nonetheless, it emerged under particular historical conditions (and in a historical time) that made it a distinct variant of

2. "Classical Russian Populism" generally refers to the movement (largely inspired by the writings of Herzen and Chernyshevsky) between about 1850 and 1880, the period prior to the degeneration of Populism into revolutionary terrorism and prior to the widespread influence of Marxism among the Russian intelligentsia. The discussion here will be confined to the intellectual rather than the political tendencies of the movement and will focus on those aspects of Populist ideology particularly relevant for contemporary comparative purposes.

the general ideological pattern. Like their Western predecessors, Russian Populist theorists were responding to the social disruptions of early capitalism and industrialism, but their response was conditioned by a consciousness of "backwardness," by a recognition that they were dealing with the specific problems of a largely agrarian country, where modern capitalism was in its infancy, in confrontation with the economically advanced capitalist countries of Western Europe. As Walicki has pointed out, "Russian Populism was not only a reaction to the development of capitalism *inside* Russia—it was also a reaction to capitalism *outside* Russia."[3] Moreover, whereas utopian socialism in the West preceded Marxism, Populism appeared when Marxism was already a well-formulated theory; thus not only were the Populists influenced significantly by Marxist ideas, but they developed their own ideas as an explicit alternative to the Marxist analysis of capitalism and its historical outcome.[4] One further general distinction might be noted: the utopian socialists (in their rejection of capitalism) spoke for what they perceived to be the interests of society in general, with a particular sympathy for the urban workers as the most exploited segment of society, whereas the Populists presented themselves as the spokesmen for "the people," defined essentially as the vast peasant masses, who were seen as the main victims of the capitalist encroachment. These features—the consciousness of "backwardness," the awareness of Marxism, and the special concern with the fate of the peasantry—gave Populist theory an ideological dimension not present in earlier utopian socialist ideologies and gives it a particular contemporary relevance.

3. A. Walicki, "Russia," in Ghita Ionescu and Ernest Gellner, eds., *Populism, Its Meaning and National Characteristics* (London: Weidenfeld and Nicolson, 1969), p. 91.

4. The first translation of *Capital* appeared in Russia, a fact that Marx viewed as "an irony of fate"; translation work was undertaken by Populists in 1868, only a year after the original German publication, and the Russian-language version was published in 1872, fifteen years before the first English translation. Russian Populists, many of whom were in semiexile in Western Europe in the 1850s and 1860s, were of course generally familiar with Marx's analysis of capitalism (and Marxist theory in general) well before the publication of *Capital*. For a perceptive analysis of the influence of *Capital* and other Marxist works on Russian Populist theorists, see A. Walicki, *The Controversy Over Capitalism* (Oxford: Clarendon Press, 1969), pp. 132–53.

Although Russian Populism was ideologically amorphous and its political manifestations diverse and complex, the Populists shared certain fundamental and identifiable beliefs and hopes. These beliefs have since died in Russia but similar ones remain very much alive in contemporary revolutionary movements in other areas of the world and have, therefore, more than a purely Russian historical significance.

Russian Populism was above all marked by a conception of "the people" as a more or less single entity with collectivistic social aspirations. The socialist reorganization of society, it was assumed, would be the quite natural result of the release of the inherent aspirations and revolutionary energies of the vast peasant masses.

This faith in the socialist potentialities of the "precapitalist" peasantry was closely associated with a fear of the intrusion of modern capitalist economic forces, which threatened to undermine these presumably innate socialist aspirations and destroy the traditional village *mir*, the idealized collective social organization that was to serve as the basis for the modern socialist reconstruction of society. Indeed, Populist ideology was shaped, in large measure, by a revulsion against the immediate social costs of modern capitalism and a fear of its ultimate historical consequences. The degradation and dehumanization wrought by nineteenth-century capitalist industrialism in the West were nowhere more vividly portrayed than in the writings of Marx and Engels, and this aspect of the Marxian critique became deeply etched on the Populist mentality. But whereas Marx assumed that the transformation of the masses into a dehumanized and alienated proletariat was the social price mankind must pay to achieve liberation, the Populists were neither willing to pay the price nor convinced that doing so would lead to the socialist outcome Marx predicted. It was not capitalism but rather precapitalist agrarian society that held socialist potentialities. That being the case, it was the duty of "enlightened men" to release the socialist instincts of the peasantry and build the new society on the basis of the collectivistic traditions of the *mir*—and to do so before these instincts and traditions were destroyed by capitalist forces of production.

Thus for the Populists, unlike the Marxists, capitalism was neither an inevitable nor a desirable stage of social development; it was not the harbinger of socialism but rather the specter of a possible future that might forever preclude its realization.

The Populists' determination to "bypass" capitalism expressed more than merely a desire to avoid the social evils of urban industrialism; it also reflected their conviction that capitalism led not to, but away from, socialism. Whereas the Western European countries were so corrupted by their economic "overmaturity" that they no longer had the energy and morality to realize their own socialist ideals, backward Russia, precisely because it was yet relatively unburdened by capitalism—and thus its "precapitalist" (and allegedly socialist) traditions were yet relatively uncorrupted—would be able to leap to the forefront of world civilization.[5] It was this consciousness of "backwardness"—a consciousness molded by agrarian Russia's coexistence with advanced industrialized nations and sharpened by the Marxist description of the tragic aspects of modern historical development—that shaped the specific Populist response to modern capitalism.

Reflected in these Populist notions was not only a desire to escape the social costs of capitalist industrialization—and a general contempt for Western bourgeois society—but also an impatience with history, an impatience that found expression in a faith in "precapitalist" Russia as the pioneer of socialist revolution. In this sense, the Populists can be seen as the ideological forerunners of the contemporary notion of "the advantages of backwardness." Tsarist Russia, they proclaimed, was closer to the achievement of socialism than the advanced industrialized states precisely because of the relative lack of capitalist development, precisely because of the moral and social virtues inherent in Russian "backwardness." Yet the Populists were by no means advocates of backwardness *per se*. They saw themselves as modern scientific men and advocated the appropriation of the latest fruits of Western European technology—but these borrowed fruits were to be utilized for the benefit of the people rather than as new instruments for their oppression.

5. These notions and views were first put forward by Alexander Herzen in the early 1850s, most notably in his highly influential letters to Jules Michelet entitled "The Russian People and Socialism" (1851). See his *From the Other Shore* (London: Weidenfeld and Nicolson, 1956), pp. 165–208.

Accompanying this "utopian" search for a means to bypass capitalism was a curious ambivalence in the Populist view of the role of historical traditions in the revolutionary process. The general theme was announced by Herzen shortly after the failure of the revolutions of 1848. His argument that Russia could achieve the socialist transformation that had eluded the Western countries was supported, on the one hand, by the view that Russia was relatively free from burdensome traditions. Whereas Europe was "exhausted" by the weight of its history, and its "energies" and "will-power" were insufficient to "sustain its own [socialist] ideas," backward Russia was unencumbered by the burden of tradition and thus able to bypass capitalism and proceed more or less immediately to socialism.[6] On the other hand, Herzen expressed the view that "the Russians were Socialists by tradition"[7] and appealed to the allegedly collectivistic traditions of the *mir* and *artel* which had survived in Russia but not in the West.[8] This ambivalent attitude toward tradition, i.e., that Russia's special socialist potential rested on the uniqueness of Russian historical traditions on the one hand, and on the other that Russia was uniquely unburdened by tradition, occurs throughout Populist thought.

Another central element of Populist ideology was the view that state and bureaucracy are inherently evil phenomena; the state was seen as an alien force which produces and perpetuates "unnatural" class divisions in society and precludes true human solidarity. Indeed, the Populists distrusted all forms of large-scale organization, whether political or economic. In their vision of a nonbureaucratic socialist future, they looked forward to a combination of "living and working" that was to be brought about by incorporating modern industry within the framework and in accordance with the principles of the traditional peasant commune.

Closely related to this profoundly antibureaucratic orientation was a general hostility to intellectual and occupational specialization, and

6. These ideas are expressed with particular clarity in Herzen's "The Russian People and Socialism."

7. Quoted in Franco Venturi, *Roots of Revolution* (New York: Grosset & Dunlap, 1966), p. 34.

8. Herzen, "The Russian People and Socialism," p. 189.

thus a certain enmity to formal higher education. Although they themselves were intellectuals and, for the most part, products of institutions of higher education, the Populists shared Rousseau's belief in "the goodness of simple men" and his distrust of intellectuals and specialists. At the heart of the Populist impulse was the intelligentsia's deep sense of isolation from society and the need "to merge" with the masses of the people.

Brief mention should be made of several other characteristic features of Russian Populism: the powerful antiurban bias which pictured the modern city as a foreign creation identified with the corrupting and dehumanizing influences of Western capitalism; and the all-pervasive mood of heroic self-sacrifice, an impulse which received its most noble expression in the ill-fated "go to the people" movement of the 1870s, when young Populist intellectuals did in fact leave the cities in an attempt to "merge" with the peasant masses. However, for the present discussion, particular attention should be given to two theoretical problems of special contemporary relevance which the Populists encountered: first, the problem of identifying the source and bearers of true socialist consciousness; secondly, the dilemma of reconciling revolutionary means with revolutionary goals.

Populist ideology was characterized by a profoundly voluntarist faith in the power of human consciousness to determine social reality. For the Populists, unlike the Marxists, the decisive factor in the making of history and revolution was not the inexorable movement of the material forces of production but rather the choices and actions of men; although socialism was ethically desirable and humanly possible, it was not historically predetermined. What was ultimately decisive, as Herzen declared, was "men who combine faith, will, conviction and energy."[9] The creation of a new society presupposed the emergence of those deeply dedicated and morally pure "men of the new age" so passionately portrayed in the writings of Chernyshevsky.

These "new men" were an elite of young intellectuals who were capable of imposing their socialist consciousness on historical reality and providing guidance for the masses. But the elitist implications

9. Quoted in Venturi, *Roots of Revolution*, p. 35.

of these notions were tempered by the basic, but perhaps conflicting, Populist faith that socialist consciousness resided ultimately in the people themselves, in the socialist traditions and ideals of the peasantry and the *mir*. The "new men" of the intelligentsia were to be only catalytic agents in a revolutionary process in which all would become "new men" in a new and just society.

Yet the Populists never succeeded in reconciling the conflict between their duty to enlighten and lead the masses and their desire to learn from and merge with them. These conflicting strands can be traced to Herzen, who called for men of consciousness and determination to "go to the people"; yet they were to go not with "ready-made works" but simply to reveal to the people "what is secretly stirring in their [the people's] spirits." Herzen emphasized the need for "men who combine faith, will, conviction and energy" who "do not necessarily spring" from the people. Yet he also insisted that these should be men "who will never divorce themselves" from the people but "who act within them and with them. . . . The man who feels himself to be so near the people that he has been virtually freed *by them* from the atmosphere of artificial civilization . . . will be able to speak to the people and must do so."[10]

The Populist world view thus rested on a central dilemma: a voluntaristic belief in the decisive revolutionary role of the consciousness of the intelligentsia was accompanied by a basic faith that the truly creative forces of revolution reside in the people themselves. On the one hand, the transformation of society was attributed to the knowledge and action of "men of culture"; on the other, it was held that the prime duty of the intellectual was to learn from the wisdom of the masses. This Populist dilemma was to be inherited by Lenin and, within a Marxist ideological framework, to be decisively "resolved" in a highly elitist fashion. It was also a dilemma that was to confront Mao Tse-tung and one not to be so easily resolved.

The problem of reconciling political methods with social goals, the problem of ensuring that the political means employed are consistent with the ends towards which those means are directed, is a dilemma confronting all who would engage in political activity; and the man-

10. Quoted in Venturi, ibid. (emphasis added).

ner in which the problem is treated—or ignored—is a matter that often has enormous practical historical consequences. Perhaps in no other revolutionary movement was this dilemma faced so explicitly and debated so seriously than among nineteenth-century Russian Populist intellectuals. The reasons why the dilemma assumed particular prominence in the Populist movement lie both in the nature of Tsarist Russian state and society and in the contradictory strands present in Populist ideology itself. The enormous gap in Russian society between the intelligentsia and the people, the political apathy of the peasantry and the general failure of the revolutionary intelligentsia to obtain mass support, the harsh police repression which made mass organizational activities virtually impossible, and the continuing erosion of the collectivistic traditions of the *mir*—such were some of the factors which fostered elitist and conspiratorial tendencies in the Populist movement. In the 1860s, and especially after the failure of the "go to the people" movement of 1874, many turned to terrorism, to Jacobin and even Blanquist notions and methods of revolution. Although political elitism was not inconsistent with one major strand in Populist thought—the belief in the decisive revolutionary role of enlightened intellectuals—it did not rest easily with the Populist faith in the spontaneous revolutionary energies and innate socialist aspirations of the people, the deep commitment to complete equality and popular democracy, and the acute distrust of anything imposed on the people from above. As the revolutionary movement turned to increasingly elitist and conspiratorial forms and formulae, the Populists were obsessed by the fear that the liberating and egalitarian ends of the revolution might be perverted by the means employed to attain them. It was this fear that lay behind their agonizing self-appraisals of the despotic and authoritarian implications possibly present in the conceptions and methods of revolution which developed in their own ranks. And it was this fear that led to their critique of the Marxist notion of the dictatorship of the proletariat in general and especially the application of that rather ambiguous Marxist formula to a country where the proletariat constituted only a tiny minority of the people. If the people could not or would not rise to build the new socialist order of freedom and equality, might not a revolution—or a revolutionary coup d'état—presided over by an elite of revolutionary intellectuals create new forms of inequality and despotism? This was the question Populists asked themselves and asked of the Marxists. It was a question which was to plague the history of the Marxist and Communist movement in Russia, but one which Russian Marxists were notably reluctant to confront.

The Populist impulse was expressed in very diverse political forms in late nineteenth-century Russia, but here it might be sufficient to note that an explicit recognition and a profound concern with the problem of the implications of revolutionary methods for the achievement of ultimate socialist goals is one of the more noteworthy features of Russian Populist thought. "The dilemma of means and ends," as Isaiah Berlin has remarked, "is the deepest and most agonizing problem that torments the revolutionary movements of our own day in all continents of the world, not least in Asia and Africa. That this debate took so clear and articulate a form within the Populist movement makes its development exceptionally relevant to our own predicament."[11] It was also, as shall be suggested, peculiarly relevant to Mao Tse-tung's predicament.

II. Leninism

Although Leninism is usually defined in terms of several crucial revisions and innovations in Marxist theory and strategy, it is also useful to understand Leninism in terms of its relationship to the Russian Populist tradition. Lenin was influenced significantly by certain Populist notions, especially in formulating his concept of the party; yet as a Marxist theorist he rejected virtually all the principal beliefs of the Populist world view. Lenin did not perceive "the people" as a collective entity, but rather saw Russian society as divided by irreconcilable class antagonisms. Although he had more to say about the possible revolutionary role of peasants than most of his Marxist predecessors, he did not attribute to the peasantry any inherent socialist tendencies. In the bourgeois-democratic phase of a revolution that might (under certain historical conditions) turn socialist, the peasantry could play a meaningful political role, but it would be no more than an auxiliary to the urban proletariat—or, more precisely, to the party that embodied "proletarian consciousness." In

11. Ibid., Introduction, p. xviii.

contrast to the Populists, Lenin's revolutionary hopes centered on the proletariat rather than on the peasantry.

Moreover, Lenin fully accepted Marxist theoretical views which directly contradicted fundamental Populist assumptions. Social class divisions and struggles, and the state power which rested upon them, were for Lenin entirely natural and inevitable historical phenomena and not alien forces introduced from without. Equally natural and inevitable were the Marxist-defined stages of sociohistorical development through which all societies must pass on their way to a socialist future. Lenin saw the forces of modern capitalist production in Russia as creating, rather than undermining, the historical preconditions for socialist revolution.

Furthermore, Lenin found few virtues in Russia's backwardness and rejected all the romantic notions and messianic beliefs which the Populists had derived from Russia's "special" historical situation; for Lenin backwardness posed special revolutionary problems but offered no special revolutionary advantages. Lenin hoped and worked for revolution in Russia on the basis of a realistic assessment of practical political situations and by seizing on immediate opportunities for revolutionary action which presented themselves, not because of any messianic faith in Russia's unique historical mission. Insofar as he believed that a revolution in Russia might occur before revolution in the advanced industrialized states, he generally conceived of it as the spark which would ignite the long-delayed—but ultimately necessary—proletarian revolution in the West.

The profound differences between the Leninist and Populist revolutionary world views can be more sharply defined by examining Lenin's confrontation with the two central dilemmas which had plagued the Populist movement: the problem of the relationship between the intelligentsia and the masses, and the problem of reconciling revolutionary means with revolutionary ends. In the first case, one notes certain Populist influences in Lenin's approach to the problem, but an ultimate solution that is profoundly non-Populist. In the second case, one is struck by Lenin's tendency to ignore the existence of the problem.

The problem of bridging the gap between the intelligentsia and the masses centers on the question of who are the bearers of true socialist consciousness and how that consciousness is to be fashioned into a historically dynamic revolutionary force. To most pre-Leninist Marxists this problem was of less concern than to the Populists, but the source and the role of the "proletarian consciousness," regarded by Marx as essential for the realization of socialism, is a fundamental question faced by all revolutionary Marxists. Although the problem of consciousness is a much more complex matter in original Marxist theory than is generally assumed, Marx tended to see true socialist consciousness as an attribute of the proletariat itself. Or, more precisely, he believed that the workers would develop socialist consciousness in the course of the practical revolutionary activities which their social and economic conditions would force them to undertake. "Orthodox" Marxists who followed Marx, with their unshakable faith in the workings of objective laws of economic development, tended to shift the focus from conscious man as the maker of history to man as the object through which the forces of "history" did their work. Consequently, the achievement of socialism came to be seen as the inevitable result of necessary and natural laws of historical evolution. As Kautsky typically put it, "the history of mankind is determined, not by ideas, but by an economic development which progresses irresistibly, obedient to certain underlying laws and not to anyone's wishes or whims."[12] The belief that the "march of history" guaranteed the arrival of socialism was the orthodox Marxist message which Lenin inherited from his Marxist mentor, Plekhanov. It was a message that Lenin was soon to reject, and the manner in which he did so was to have grave implications both for Marxist theory and for the entire Populist dilemma of the relationship between the intelligentsia and the masses.

With Lenin, the problem of consciousness became the most crucial theoretical and practical question of revolutionary politics. Even though Lenin accepted the general Marxist description of a historical movement toward a socialist utopia, he never acquired a firm Marxist confidence in the determining forces of history, nor did he ever really share Marx's faith in the revolutionary "self-activity" of the proletariat. His general distrust of the "spontaneity" of the masses precluded the latter, whereas his revolutionary activistic temperament precluded the former. Moreover, in a land where the material and

12. Karl Kautsky, *Class Struggle* (Chicago: Kerr, 1910), p. 119.

social prerequisites for socialism were still largely absent, Marxism implied that the revolutionary would have to passively observe a perhaps prolonged period of historical maturation. Neither by temperament nor intellectual orientation was Lenin any more willing than the Populists to wait in the political wings while the forces of capitalist production did their historical work. Just as Mao Tse-tung later was to learn from Soviet experience that the combination of state ownership of the means of production and industrialization does not automatically produce socialist and communist societies, so Lenin had learned from Western European historical experience that the existence of advanced industrialized economies and large working-class movements does not by itself produce socialist revolutions.

In the Leninist view, the natural history of the working-class movement inevitably culminated in the dominance of "revisionism" and "economism," both of which implied an eventual accommodation with the existing capitalist order. Forestalling such a nonrevolutionary outcome required active revolutionary intervention from without, which in turn presupposed that the sources of true "proletarian consciousness" be identified and brought into full historical play.

How then was "proletarian consciousness" to be fashioned into an instrument to guide the revolutionary movement? In dealing with this crucial problem, Lenin was profoundly influenced by Russian Populist ideas, especially the writings of Chernyshevsky. Like many of the Populists, Chernyshevsky derived from Hegelian philosophy the notion that consciousness was not merely a reflection of nature or history, but rather a phenomenon external to them. Furthermore, he seized on that strand in the Populist world view which attributed the essentially dynamic historic role to the will and initiative of the revolutionary intellectual.[13] However much obscured later by Marxist formulae, these fundamentally voluntarist (and largely Populist-inspired) assumptions remained essential features of Lenin's outlook, and became the intellectual foundation for the Leninist concept of the party.

13. For a highly perceptive discussion of the influence of Chernyshevsky on Lenin, see Leopold Haimson, *The Russian Marxists and the Origins of Bolshevism* (Cambridge, Mass.: Harvard University Press, 1955), especially pp. 97–103.

The attribution of so decisive a revolutionary role to the consciousness of the intelligentsia implied, of course, a much less important place for the masses, and this was made explicit in Lenin's distinction between the "consciousness" of the intelligentsia and the "spontaneity" of the masses, with the former category being superior to the latter. Whereas the spontaneous movement of the workers (which arose inevitably from objective socioeconomic conditions) was a necessary prerequisite for socialist revolutionary activity, it was an insufficient condition for revolution. True socialist consciousness would have to be imposed upon the amorphous movement of the masses by its carriers, the Marxist intelligentsia.[14]

The practical conclusion that Lenin drew from these beliefs is well known: only a highly centralized party apparatus, organized by a dedicated intellectual elite of professional revolutionaries, could ensure the development of socialist consciousness among the workers and discipline their spontaneous strivings into meaningful political action.

It should be noted that it is not Leninist organizational principles as such which give the party its central place in Marxist-Leninist theory (for the Leninist-type of party organization can exist quite apart from any particular ideology or social group), but rather its underlying intellectual assumption—the belief in the decisive revolutionary role of the consciousness of the Marxist intellectual elite. It is because the party is assumed to embody "proletarian consciousness" that it achieves its universally valid and sacrosanct character in the Marxist-Leninist world view.

Particularly noteworthy is the paradox that the Populist ideas so important in the formulation of the Leninist concept of the party were molded by Lenin into an ideology and a form of political organization profoundly antithetical to the Populist outlook. Whereas the Populist emphasis on the consciousness of the revolutionary intellectual was combined with (and modified by) the more basic Populist faith that the true revolutionary consciousness and creativity resided in the people themselves, Lenin seized upon the first strand and

14. These views, of course, are most clearly presented by Lenin in his treatise of 1902, *What Is to Be Done?*

totally rejected the second. For the Populists, the question of the relationship between the intelligentsia and the masses constituted an agonizing and unresolved dilemma, and the question of where consciousness resided remained problematic. With Lenin, the questions were settled with characteristic certainty and decisiveness. Nor was Lenin deeply troubled by the need to bridge the gulf between the intelligentsia and the people. What was a cause of profound concern to the Populists, Lenin converted into a Marxist revolutionary virtue. By drawing so sharp a distinction between the "consciousness" of the intelligentsia and the "spontaneity" of the masses, Leninist theory formalized the gulf between intellectuals and masses, and the Leninist practice of party organization served to institutionalize it. Nothing could have been more alien to the original Populist faith in the people than the highly elitist revolutionary formulae and strategies that Lenin based in part on borrowed Populist ideas.

Without questioning the sincerity of Lenin's commitment to the ultimate goal of an egalitarian socialist society which would, among other things, eventually abolish the distinction between "intellectuals" and "masses," Leninist political strategy raises the gravest questions as to whether the revolutionary means employed are compatible with the revolutionary ends sought. The dilemma of means and ends is nowhere more apparent than in the Leninist concept of the party. While the more dangerous implications of Leninist organizational principles were not to become evident until long after 1917, the problem was clearly recognized long before by another revolutionary Marxist. In 1904 Rosa Luxemburg wrote a critique of the "ultra-centralism" she perceived in the type of organization Lenin was advocating, a scheme which demanded "blind subordination" to "the party center, which alone thinks, guides and decides for all" and, more importantly, one which implied "the rigorous separation of the organized nucleus of revolutionaries" from the mass working-class movement.[15] She prophetically observed that there was "no greater danger to the Russian party than Lenin's plan of

15. Rosa Luxemburg, "Organizational Question of Social Democracy," in *Rosa Luxemburg Speaks* (New York: Pathfinder Press, 1970), p. 118.

organization. Nothing will more surely enslave a young labor movement to an intellectual elite hungry for power than this bureaucratic strait jacket. . . . What is today only a phantom haunting Lenin's imagination may become reality tomorrow."[16]

This "bureaucratic strait-jacket" was in fact to become political reality after the October Revolution. Lenin's political policies after 1917 derived more from the authoritarian principles of his concept of party than from the libertarian and antibureaucratic strains of the Marxist tradition he so eloquently evoked on the eve of the revolution. Again, no one analyzed the situation more perceptively and prophetically than Luxemburg, despite her own deep sympathy for the Bolshevik cause. Popular control and the initiative of the masses are indispensable for the life of the revolution, she wrote from her German prison cell in 1918, and "no one knows this better, describes it more penetratingly, repeats it more stubbornly than Lenin. *But he is completely mistaken in the means he employs*." (Emphasis added.) With general repression, the bureaucracy would remain the only active element in political life and the result would be not a dictatorship of the proletariat but a bourgeois, Jacobin "dictatorship of a handful of politicians." And such conditions, she predicted, "must inevitably cause a brutalization of public life."[17]

There were, of course, many factors which contributed to the growth of a massive bureaucratic dictatorship and institutionalized social inequality after 1917. And not the least important of these was the failure of the anticipated revolutions in the advanced industrialized states of the West and the consequent isolation of Bolshevik power in conditions of extreme social and economic backwardness. But the seeds of bureaucratic degeneration were also present in the elitist Leninist conception of revolution and political organization, and the failure of Leninist theory seriously to confront the dilemma of reconciling revolutionary means with revolutionary goals. As Barrington Moore has pointed out: "Lenin and his followers set out to achieve for humanity the goals of freedom and equality by means of an organization that denied these same principles. It was anticipated

16. Ibid., pp. 126–27.

17. Luxemburg, "The Russian Revolution," ibid., p. 391.

that the denial would be temporary and that the fruits of victory would bring the goals desired. Instead, discipline, authority and inequality had to be intensified after victory."[18]

The inconsistencies between Leninist political practice and Marxist goals were only exacerbated by Lenin's postrevolutionary economic policies, which emphasized employing capitalist forms of economic organization, labor discipline, and incentives to carry out a crash program of modern industrial development in the most economically efficient manner. At question here is not the efficacy of Leninist (and Stalinist) methods of achieving rapid industrial growth, but rather whether the means employed were consistent with the ultimate social goals that were sought. Lenin's celebrated remark that socialism could be defined as "electrification plus Soviets" proved to be an early formulation of what became and remains a prime Soviet ideological orthodoxy: the view that the combination of industrial development with state ownership of production guarantees the achievement of socialism and communism. As matters have turned out, it has only guaranteed the achievement of an industrialized society. In the process, economic development, which was originally seen as the means to a socialist end, became the end in itself. As Barrington Moore once observed: "While the [Leninist] ideology of ends has been much modified or discarded, the ideology of means has had lasting importance."[19] They remain of lasting and ultimate importance to the present day.

Leninism, in contrast to Populism, is a doctrine characterized by an almost total unconcern with the dilemma of means and ends. Lenin's preoccupation with the methods and immediate tactics of revolution was accompanied by his failure, in both theory and practice, to take into account the implications of these methods for the anticipated socialist future. The history of postrevolutionary Russia more than bears out the old Populist fear that a revolution presided over by an intellectual elite would succeed only in replacing old forms of despotism and inequality with new forms.

18. Barrington Moore, *Soviet Politics—The Dilemma of Power* (Cambridge, Mass.: Harvard University Press, 1959), pp. 81–82.

19. Ibid., p. 60.

III. Maoism

In comparing the modern Russian and Chinese intelligentsias, Benjamin Schwartz has remarked that "something like a populist strain emerges quite early in China, although it is speedily overwhelmed by the influence of the Russian Revolution." Schwartz further observed that after 1919 Marxism-Leninism cut short "the emergence of a full-blown Populism," and what survived in China was "the elitist rather than the anarchist brand of Populism."[20]

Yet it would seem to be the case that the influence of Marxism-Leninism never completely overwhelmed the Populist strain in China and that, in fact, a powerful Populist impulse was to become an integral component of the Maoist version of Marxism. Moreover, the form of Populism that did survive was, if not anarchistic, nevertheless profoundly nonelitist. It might also be suggesed that one of the more prominent features of the Maoist mentality was an unresolved tension between Leninist-type elitism and the more pristine Populist-type belief that the "people" themselves (and the peasantry in particular) possess a latent "general will" and an innate "socialist consciousness." In considering Maoism in light of Russian historical perspectives, one cannot fail to be impressed by striking affinities between many aspects of Maoist thought and the beliefs and dilemmas identified with classical Russian Populism; and the affinities seem to be most striking precisely in those areas where Lenin differed most sharply with the Populists.

Although Chinese Communist historians are inclined to periodize Chinese revolutionary history in terms of the history of the Russian revolutionary movement and have thus categorized the T'ung-meng-hui period (circa 1905–19) as the "Populist era" of the revolutionary movement,[21] this early Populist impulse was comparatively weak

20. Benjamin Schwartz, "The Intelligentsia in Communist China: A Tentative Comparison," *Daedalus* 89.3 (Summer 1960): 615.

21. See, for example, T'an Pi-an, "O-kuo min-ts'ui-chu-i tui t'ung-meng-hui ti ying-hsiang" [The Influence of Russian Populism on the T'ung-meng-hui], *Li-shih yen-chiu* [Historical research] 1 (1959): 35–44; and Jeng Meng-yüan, "Hsin-hai ko-ming ch'ien Chung-kuo shu-k'an shang tui Ma-k'o-ssu-chu-i ti chieh-shao" [The Introduction of Marxism in Chinese publications before the 1911 revolution], *Hsin chien-she* [New construction] 3 (1953): 9.

and appeared largely under the aegis of imported anarchist doctrines during the first two decades of the century. A much more significant Populist strain emerged in the May Fourth period—and, paradoxically, especially among young intellectuals attracted to Marxism. A strong Populist impulse is apparent in the ideas and actions of such student activist groups as the Mass Education Speech Corps in 1918, the Marxist-oriented students in Shanghai and elsewhere who went to the countryside to work with the peasants in 1920 and advocated "destroying the very concept 'intelligentsia,' " and in the activities of P'eng P'ai and members of the Socialist Youth Corps who went to the villages to organize the peasantry in the early 1920s.[22] Ideologically, Populism received its clearest expression in the writings of Li Ta-chao, China's first important convert to Marxism and a founder of the Chinese Communist Party. It is striking that Li's first political act after declaring himself a Marxist in 1918 was a passionate call to his student followers to leave "the corrupting life" of the cities and universities and "go to the villages," to "take up hoes and plows and become companions of the toiling peasants" while educating the peasant masses in the principles of socialism amidst "the wholly human life" of the countryside.[23]

Whereas in Russia the Populist phase of the revolutionary movement preceded the Marxist phase, in China a genuine Populist impulse appeared and grew more or less simultaneously with the introduction and spread of Marxist ideas. Whereas in Russia Populism tended gradually to be replaced by Marxism and Populist ideas and the Populist movement were ultimately suppressed by Leninism, in China a powerful Populist impulse survived to modify significantly the Leninist character of the Chinese Communist revolution.

22. Useful information on these student movements is provided in Ting Shou-ho, Yin Hsü-i, and Chang Po-ch'ao, *Shih-yüeh ko-ming tui Chung-kuo ko-ming ti ying-hsiang* [The Influence of the October Revolution on the Chinese Revolution] (Peking: Jen-min ch'u-pan she, 1957), especially pp. 137–42. On P'eng P'ai's agrarian revolutionary activities, see Robert Marks, "Peasant Society and Peasant Uprisings in South China: Social Change in Haifeng County, 1630–1930" (Ph.D. diss., The University of Wisconsin, 1978); and Roy Hofheinz, Jr., *The Broken Wave: The Chinese Communist Peasant Movement, 1922–1928* (Cambridge, Mass.: Harvard University Press, 1977).

23. On Li's Populist views, see Maurice Meisner, *Li Ta-chao and the Origins of Chinese Marxism* (Cambridge, Mass.: Harvard University Press, 1967).

The Populist-type beliefs which molded Li Ta-chao's adaptation of Marxism to the Chinese environment appear somewhat less explicitly, but no less powerfully, in the thought and actions of Mao Tse-tung. They are apparent from the very beginning of Mao's mature intellectual life and are not simply the latter-day product of what became a rural-based revolutionary movement. In his early political writings, published some months prior to his formal conversion to Marxism in late 1919, Mao perceived the Chinese people as a single and united political entity with enormous revolutionary potentialities. "Our Chinese people," he proclaimed, "possess great *intrinsic* energy" (emphasis added), and he called for a "great union of the popular masses," a momentous political action "which will not brook a moment's delay." Although the Chinese people had been oppressed and impotent for "thousands of years," this historic backwardness seemed to Mao to augur great political advantages for the present and future, for "that which has accumulated for a long time will surely burst forth quickly."[24] Here one detects a characteristically Populist faith in the inherent potentialities of the people, not a typically Leninist distrust of the spontaneity of the masses.

The Populist tendency is of course even more pronounced in the famous "Hunan Report" of 1927, when Mao presumably was firmly committed to Marxism-Leninism. Here Mao not only looked to the peasantry as the popular basis of the revolution, but attributed to the peasants themselves those elements of revolutionary creativity and standards of political judgment that Marxist-Leninists reserve for the party. For Mao, it was not the party that was to judge the revolutionary capacities of the peasantry, but the peasants who were to judge the revolutionary sufficiency of the party: "All revolutionary parties and all revolutionary comrades will stand before them to be tested, and to be accepted or rejected as they decide."[25] The Report emphasized throughout the revolutionary works that the peasants were ac-

24. From extracts from Mao's articles in the *Hsiang-chiang p'ing-lun* of July and August 1919, translated by Stuart Schram in *The Political Thought of Mao Tse-tung* (New York: Praeger, 1969), p. 163.

25. Mao Tse-tung, "Report of an Investigation into the Peasant Movement in Hunan," in Mao Tse-tung, *The Selected Works of Mao Tse-tung* (London: Lawrence and Wishart, 1954), vol. 1, p. 22.

complishing on their own initiative and was hostile to all external impingements and organizational restraints. In 1927 the spontaneous peasant movement seemed to Mao an elemental revolutionary force so great that it would sweep away everything before it, including those "revolutionary intellectuals" who proved unwilling or unable to become one with the masses. Then, as later, Mao expressed profound distrust for the "knowledge" brought by urban intellectuals and admiration for the innate "wisdom" of the peasantry.

In the mid-1920s, Mao found in the spontaneous revolutionary activities of the peasantry a concrete manifestation of the "great popular union of the masses" which he foresaw at the beginning of his revolutionary career in 1919. As Benjamin Schwartz once observed, Mao's "Hunan Report" of 1927 "might just as well have been written by a Russian *narodnik* as by a Marxist-Leninist. Nowhere here do we find those strictures on the independent revolutionary role of the peasantry which run through all Marxist-Leninist literature."[26] The Populist impulses so apparent in 1927 were never to be completely submerged by Marxist-Leninist influences, even though Mao's later officially published writings were to be presented in a more orthodox Marxist-Leninist vocabulary.

In the most general sense, the Populist strain in Maoism manifested itself in a strong tendency to view "the people" as an organic whole and to celebrate their spontaneous revolutionary actions and collective potentialities. Although Maoism was a doctrine that demanded class analysis and seemingly unending "class struggle," it also conceived of the Chinese people, or at least the overwhelming majority, as a potentially unified "proletarian" entity. As Mao so often proclaimed, 95 percent of the Chinese were basically revolutionary (or at least potentially so), and those who were not were to be excluded from membership in "the people," for they represented and reflected alien influences; they were, in effect, the "internal foreigners" who appear in so sinister a fashion in typically Populist world views.

Although Maoist doctrine emphasized the need for organization and discipline, those who by purely Leninist criteria presumably

26. Benjamin I. Schwartz, *Chinese Communism and the Rise of Mao* (Cambridge, Mass.: Harvard University Press, 1952), p. 76.

possessed the consciousness necessary to organize and lead the masses were urged repeatedly to "merge with the masses," to "learn from the masses," and indeed to "become students of the masses." When Maoists proclaimed that "the subjective activity of the popular masses" can overcome all objective material barriers, this may have reflected (in extreme form) Lenin's voluntarist emphasis on the role of subjective factors in history but not Lenin's insistence that these subjective factors are brought into being by an elite of revolutionary intellectuals and must be organized and disciplined by them. And when Mao, in commenting on the problem of overpopulation, insisted that "the more people there are the greater the ferment of ideas, the greater the enthusiasm and the energy,"[27] he echoed not simply an old anti-Malthusian Marxist bias but his own old Populist faith that true social creativity resided in the people themselves.

The much celebrated Maoist "faith in the masses" was, of course, essentially a faith in the peasant masses, the great majority of the Chinese people and the principal actors in the Chinese Communist revolution. Although Mao's successful revolutionary experiences in the countryside undoubtedly served to reinforce his rural orientation, he was of course drawn to the peasantry long before they proved their revolutionary worth. For half a century Maoist thought was characterized by a deep emotional attachment to the rural ideal of "the unity of living and working" and the rural traditions of "plain living" and "hard work." Though Mao never argued (as did the Russian Populists) that the peasantry was socialist by tradition (for there was after all no traditional Chinese equivalent to the Russian *mir* to celebrate), he did celebrate the revolutionary traditions of the Chinese peasantry and was romantically intrigued by the heroics of traditional peasant rebels. Even if there was no traditional Chinese peasant commune to save, there was a modern people's commune to create on the basis of what was perceived to be the "inherent socialist activism" of the modern Chinese peasantry. Or so Mao believed in 1958 and after. And that new commune was to realize the goal of combining agricultural and industrial production in an egalitarian and self-sufficient rural community (an old Russian Populist dream),

27. The comment was made during the utopian fervor of the early Great Leap Forward period. See *Hung-ch'i* [Red flag], 1 June 1958, p. 3.

a goal to be achieved long before there existed the Marxist-defined economic prerequisites for the abolition of differences between town and country. The "capitalist-bourgeois phase" of development was to be "bypassed" socially and economically as rapidly as it had been bypassed politically.

Yet however much the spontaneous revolutionary energies of peasants were praised, Mao never attributed "proletarian consciousness" to the peasantry as such. But if the peasantry was not the bearer of proletarian virtue, Mao always found many virtues among peasants. "I have spent much time in the rural areas with the peasants and was deeply moved by the many things they knew," Mao remarked in characteristically Populist tones on the eve of the Cultural Revolution. "Their knowledge was rich. I was no match for them."[28]

Mao's proclivity to look to the countryside and the rural masses for the sources of revolutionary creativity was quite naturally accompanied by a perception of the urban areas as sources of social and ideological impurities. This hostility to the cities was of course not unrelated to the objective conditions of modern Chinese Communist revolutionary history. While the rural basis of the Communist revolution led to a glorification of the peasantry as "the revolutionary people," Chinese cities, as Rhoads Murphey has observed, remained "the official and symbolic strongholds of the traditional Confucian order, of the Western imperialists . . . and of the Kuomintang. . . ."[29] Indeed, Mao's lack of interest in the urban proletariat during the revolutionary years was matched only by the almost total political apathy of the urban working class itself after 1927. The experience of a revolutionary situation in which the revolutionary forces of the countryside surrounded and eventually overwhelmed the nonrevolutionary cities undoubtedly served to confirm Mao's antiurban biases already present in the "Hunan Report," especially his contempt for the urban intelligentsia and his distrust of the revolutionary capacities of the urban proletariat.

These agrarian orientations remained dominant in the Maoist men-

28. *Joint Publications Research Service* 49826 (12 February 1970):30 (hereafter cited as *JPRS*).

29. Rhoads Murphey, "Man and Nature in China," *Modern Asian Studies* 1.4 (October 1967): 325–26.

tality in the postrevolutionary era. While Mao was consistently eloquent about the revolutionary virtues of the peasantry, he remained remarkably silent on the political role of China's rapidly growing urban working class. Indeed, urban people were sent to the countryside to become "proletarianized" and learn from the peasants the "proletarian virtues" of struggle, hard work and plain living. Maoist economic policies, at least since the Great Leap era, emphasized more the industrialization of the countryside than the industrial growth of the potentially "revisionist" cities. Moreover, the Chinese revolutionary experience was projected onto the global map so that in the uniquely Maoist conception of world revolution the "revolutionary countryside" of the backward lands of Asia, Africa, and Latin America were eventually to surround and overwhelm the economically advanced but reactionary "cities" of Europe and North America. And that most extraordinary of Maoist upheavals—the Great Proletarian Cultural Revolution—was directed primarily against newly emergent urban elites, the cultural and technological intelligentsias, and especially urban-based Party bureaucrats.

Whereas Mao's antiurbanism had nothing in common with either Marxism or Leninism, it shared certain similarities with a strain in the Western intellectual tradition, partly derived from Rousseau, which viewed the city as the embodiment of all social evils and moral corruptions, as a monolith threatening to crush the natural purity of the countryside. This idea found powerful expression in the writings of Russian Populists who regarded the modern city as an alien product of foreign capitalist forces which threatened to undermine the "socialist" institutions and traditions of the Russian countryside. Just as the Populists condemned the city as the source of bourgeois corruption, so Mao found in the cities the remnants of a corrupt old bourgeois culture and a breeding place for new bourgeois inequalities. And just as Russian Populists condemned the Western bourgeoisie and were generally contemptuous of the Western urban proletariat, so Mao combined a contempt for the modern social classes of the West with a fear that the new urban Chinese proletariat was all too susceptible to bourgeois corruption. In both cases, ultimate revolutionary hopes rested on a faith in the relative purity of the countryside and the inherent socialism (or potential socialist transformation) of the peasantry.

Perhaps the area in which the affinities between Maoism and Russian Populism are most profound lies in a particular perception of "the advantages of backwardness." What is involved here is not simply the ability of backward nations to borrow the technologies of advanced countries but rather a faith in the intrinsic virtues of backwardness. The Populist argument that the survival of traditional collectivistic forms of social life offered a unique opportunity for Russia to bypass capitalism was accompanied by a more general and pervasive belief that backwardness as such offered special moral and social advantages for a revolutionary future. Herzen saw revolutionary potential in a young Russia that was "full of vigour," but not in the Western countries that were infected by "crude egoism" and "the unclean worship of material gain."[30] Prospects for the West seemed no brighter to Chernyshevsky; history, he proclaimed, was like "an old grandmother who loves most her youngest grandchildren."[31] And other revolutionary Populists, in a manifesto of 1861 "To the Young Generation," announced that "we are a belated nation and precisely in this consists our salvation."[32]

Populist hopes for a socialist future were thus founded not only on the *mir* and on Russia's ability to speed her economic development by appropriating modern Western technology while avoiding Western social mistakes (itself an argument developed at great length in Populist writings), but also on a highly romantic and emotional celebration of the purity of backwardness itself. In the Populist world view, backwardness was both the cause of barbarity in Russian life and the source of potentially revolutionary virtues. And these were the virtues of youth (whether young nations or young people), freedom from traditions, freedom from the "overmature" history under which the West staggered, and freedom from the social and moral decadence that had stifled the revolutionary spirit in the more economically advanced countries. These prominent themes in Russian Populist writings are remarkably similar to a powerful strain in Maoist

30. Herzen, "The Russian People and Socialism," pp. 166–67.

31. As quoted by Walicki, "Russia," p. 84. For a somewhat different translation see A. Gerschenkron, *Economic Backwardness in Historical Perspective* (Cambridge, Mass.: Belknap Press of Harvard University, 1962), p. 173.

32. Quoted in Walicki, *The Controversy over Capitalism*, p. 117.

thought. In his early writings, Mao deplored China's backwardness but saw in that very condition of backwardness a reservoir of youthful energy and revolutionary creativity.[33] The culmination of this belief came in 1958 when Mao attributed to the Chinese people the special revolutionary virtues of being "poor and blank." The "blankest" of all were, of course, the youth; and it is therefore the young who were the most virtuous and the most revolutionary. From the worship of youth that characterized modern China's first cultural revolution of 1915–19 Mao derived, during the formative stages of his intellectual development, that special faith in the young which reached its political climax in the creation of the Red Guards during the Great Proletarian Cultural Revolution half a century later. Not only revolutionary energy but also intellectual creativity were seen to reside in youth. "Since ancient times," Mao remarked in a speech of 1958, "those who create new ideas and new academic schools of thought have always been young people without much learning."[34] As was the case with the Russian Populists, Mao believed in the special revolutionary capacities and creative energies of young people as well as young nations, for both were relatively "backward" and therefore relatively uncorrupted.

Closely associated with this romanticization of backwardness was an ambivalent attitude towards historical traditions. Along with the condemnation of the remnants of the feudal past one finds a celebration of revolutionary peasant traditions and praise for "the fine old culture of the people which has a more or less democratic and revolutionary character."[35] Yet more significantly, and more like the Populists, Mao also suggested that China was relatively unencumbered by the weight of historical traditions. Just as the Populists argued that Russia was a country without historical traditions (or at least Western historical traditions) and therefore potentially more revolutionary than other countries, so Mao found in China's "blankness" the conditions for her special revolutionary creativity. Just as

33. This idea is implicit in Mao's 1919 writings in *Hsiang-chiang p'ing-lun* referred to above (note 24).

34. *JPRS* 49826: 48.

35. Mao Tse-tung, *On New Democracy* (Peking: Foreign Languages Press, 1968), p. 62.

Herzen proclaimed that "we possess nothing" in proclaiming his faith in Russia's socialist future,[36] so Mao proclaimed China "a clean sheet of paper" and therein saw the promise of its future socialist greatness.

Several other aspects of the Maoist mentality which bear stronger similarities to the Populist world view than to Marxism-Leninism might briefly be noted: Mao's general distrust of centralization; his stress on local self-sufficiency and self-reliance; his extreme antipathy to occupational specialization (and to all things which threaten to divide "the people"); his deep and longstanding hostility to intellectuals;[37] and the romantic mood of heroic revolutionary self-sacrifice which pervaded his "thoughts" and which was so characteristic of so much of his life. Perhaps particularly noteworthy was Mao's striking lack of faith in the objective forces of history and his sense of indeterminateness about the future. It is, after all, rather extraordinary for the Marxist leader of a presumably socialist state to declare publicly (as he first did in 1957 and even more dramatically and explicitly in the Cultural Revolution) that the struggle between capitalism and socialism was yet to be decided;[38] and it is more extraordinary still to suggest in an interview with a foreign journalist (as Mao did in his conversation with Edgar Snow in 1965) the possibility of the future bourgeois corruption of the revolution he led.[39] There is something more here than an extreme version of Leninist voluntarism or an echo of Lenin's own impatience with the objective forces of history. It was, after all, the Populists, against whom Lenin fought so long, who argued that socialism was in no sense historically inevitable but rather entirely dependent on the wills, energies, and consciousness of men.

Rather than extending the list of affinities between Maoism and Populism, attention should be focused on Mao's confrontation with

36. Herzen, "The Russian People and Socialism," p. 199.

37. Mao, of course, was inclined to celebrate his own alleged status as a non-intellectual: "Being an unpolished man, I am not too cultured" were the words with which he prefaced a speech in 1959.

38. Mao Tse-tung, *On the Correct Handling of Contradictions among the People* (Peking: Foreign Languages Press, 1957), p. 50.

39. *New Republic*, 27 February 1965, pp. 17–23.

the two major dilemmas posed by Populist ideology and their implications for Mao's place in the Marxist-Leninist tradition; first, the problem of the relationship between the "consciousness" of the revolutionary intelligentsia and the "spontaneity" of the masses; and, second, the dilemma of reconciling revolutionary means with revolutionary ends.

As a master of political organization and revolutionary strategy, Mao may well have been a "natural Leninist," as Stuart Schram once suggested.[40] But intellectually, Mao was something other than a pure disciple of Lenin, for he never really succeeded in resolving the problem of the relationship between "consciousness" and "spontaneity" in a purely Leninist fashion. His conception of the Party (and its leaders) as the incarnation of "socialist consciousness" was modified and diluted by the conflicting belief that the masses of the people themselves (and the peasant masses in particular) were the sources of true knowledge and genuine socialist strivings.

To be sure, Mao always believed that the "great socialist activism" that the masses presumably embodied must be brought forth by the proper leaders and directed through the proper organizational channels; and he was, of course, the principal builder and leader of a party based on Leninist principles of organization, a party that was to supply leadership and direction for the spontaneous revolutionary strivings of the masses. But Mao's confidence in the Party and its organizations was never as absolute as was Lenin's, and Mao always expressed a faith in the spontaneity and wisdom of the masses that Lenin neither possessed nor expressed. Mao's appreciation of the practical revolutionary efficacy of Leninist principles of organization was combined with a Populist trust in the elemental revolutionary creativity of the masses and an essentially Populist impulse that all somehow must "merge" into the masses. His Leninist emphasis on the role of organization and discipline over the years was accompanied by constant exhortations to revolutionary intellectuals and Party cadres to "become one with the masses" (1939),[41] to "go to

40. Stuart Schram, *The Political Thought of Mao Tse-tung* (New York: Praeger, 1969), p. 33.

41. Mao Tse-tung, "The Orientation of the Youth Movement," in Mao Tse-tung, *The Selected Works of Mao Tse-tung* (London: Lawrence and Wishart, 1954), vol. 3, p. 20.

the countryside . . . put on coarse clothes . . . and learn what the peasants demand" (1945).[42] Whereas Mao the Leninist insisted that the Communists are to lead the people and are the vanguard of the revolution, Mao the Populist declared that "the masses are the real heroes while we ourselves are often ridiculously childish."[43] He stressed the need for Marxist intellectuals and Party cadres to bring socialist consciousness to the masses, yet warned that "many who have studied Marxist books have turned against the revolution, while illiterate laborers have often successfully mastered Marxism."[44] He emphasized (at least until the Cultural Revolution) the indispensable leadership role of the Party, but he also argued passionately that true revolutionary knowledge ultimately comes from the people themselves and that Party leaders and cadres must therefore "learn from the masses" and "acquire the good qualities of workers and peasants."[45] He insisted that it was necessary for Marxist intellectuals and cadres to be the pupils of the masses as well as their teachers, and that, indeed, it was necessary to learn from the people before it was possible to teach them.[46]

This pupil-teacher dichotomy, which in many forms appears so prominently in Maoist writings, is (within a new ideological framework and in the context of different historical circumstances) essentially the unresolved Populist dilemma of the role of the revolutionary intellectual: the dilemma of whether the prime duty of the intellectual (or would-be revolutionary leader) is to teach and lead the masses or to learn from and merge with them. Whereas Lenin had no doubts about where the true sources of "proletarian consciousness" resided, Mao never precisely defined the relationship between the organized consciousness of the Party and the spontaneous consciousness of the

42. Mao Tse-tung, "On Coalition Government," in Mao Tse-tung, *The Selected Works of Mao Tse-tung* (London: Lawrence and Wishart, 1956), vol. 4, p. 296.

43. Mao Tse-tung, "Preface and Postscript to 'Rural Survey,' " ibid., p. 8.

44. Mao Tse-tung, "Oppose Bookism," in John E. Rue, *Mao Tse-tung in Opposition* (Stanford, Calif.: Stanford University Press, 1966), p. 307.

45. Mao Tse-tung, "Draw in Large Numbers of Intellectuals" (December 1939), in Mao, *Selected Works*, vol. 3, pp. 70–71.

46. "It is my wish," Mao wrote in 1941, "that, together with comrades of the whole Party, I should continue to be a pupil of the masses and learn from them." *Selected Works*, vol. 4, p. 10.

masses. For Lenin, in this crucial realm, there was but one cardinal principle: faith in, and obedience to, the Party and its leaders. For Mao, there were two cardinal principles: "We must have faith in the masses and we must have faith in the Party. . . . If we doubt these principles, we shall accomplish nothing."[47]

This dual Maoist faith in the masses as well as in the Party was at least in part responsible for one of the most characteristic features of Chinese Communist politics during the Maoist period—the recurrent process, both before and after 1949, of encouraging spontaneous mass revolutionary activity and then imposing Leninist-type organizational restraint on that activity. In the late Maoist era, this phenomenon received dramatic expression in the Great Leap Forward campaign and the Great Proletarian Cultural Revolution. In launching the Great Leap, Mao looked not so much to the Party as he did to what he celebrated as "the boundless creative power" of the masses and their "potentially inexhaustible enthusiasm for socialism."[48] In the Cultural Revolution, he first bypassed the Party altogether and then called upon the masses to rebel against it and much of its leadership—until the chaos wrought by the upheaval caused him to reluctantly conclude that the authority of the Party was a political necessity. Neither the Great Leap nor the Cultural Revolution can be adequately understood without taking into account Mao's very non-Leninist "faith in the masses."

The tension in Mao's thought between conflicting Leninist and Populist tendencies had a great deal to do with the ambiguous Maoist attitude towards the Party and the curious situation during the Cultural Revolution of a nation, presumably guided by "Marxism-Leninism," where "proletarian consciousness" was attributed neither to the Party nor the proletariat. It is much too simple to dispose of this problem

47. Mao Tse-tung, "The Question of Agricultural Co-operation" (31 July 1955). For an earlier translation, using slightly different wording, see Robert R. Bowie and John K. Fairbank, eds., *Communist China 1955–1959, Policy Documents with Analysis* (Cambridge, Mass.: Harvard University Press, 1962), p. 96.

48. Introductory notes to volume 2 of the Chinese edition of *Socialist Upsurge in China's Countryside*. For the Peking rendition of these passages in the 1960s, see *Quotations from Chairman Mao*, pp. 118–21. In the 1957 English-language edition in one volume, the latter phrase is translated: "The people are filled with an immense enthusiasm for socialism": *Socialist Upsurge* (Peking, 1957), p. 44.

by concluding that Mao believed "proletarian consciousness" resided in his own person and thought.[49] Mao, no doubt, was as convinced of his own political and ideological infallibility as was Lenin. But the problem which confronted Lenin and Mao alike was not simply the question of what constitutes "correct" consciousness but rather how that consciousness might be fashioned to realize revolutionary socialist goals. There are many ambiguities in Leninism, but Lenin was quite explicit on who are the true bearers of proletarian consciousness and also on how that consciousness is to be organized, institutionalized, and activated. Here Maoist theory and practice was something less than clear and unambiguous. Mao adopted Leninist principles of party organization, yet his actions and speeches strongly suggest that he never fully accepted the intellectual assumptions upon which those organizational principles rested. His powerful Populist faith in the spontaneous revolutionary creativity and consciousness of the masses militated against a purely Leninist resolution. For Mao the problem of "consciousness" remained a Populist-type dilemma.

If Mao's non-Leninist attitude toward "proletarian consciousness" perhaps created unresolvable political and ideological dilemmas, he also raised and confronted a more general dilemma, often unrecognized by typical Leninists: the problem of reconciling revolutionary means with revolutionary ends. The concern was not the conventional (and usually oversimplified) ethical dilemma of whether "the ends justify the means," for there is little to suggest that Maoists have had any special ethical concern on the matter of revolutionary methods, but an unusual practical political and social anxiety that the socialist and communist goals of the revolution might all too easily be undermined by the means employed to attain them.

During the early years of the People's Republic the need to estab-

49. Proceeding from different lines of inquiry this is suggested by both Benjamin Schwartz in "The Reign of Virtue: Some Broad Perspectives on Leader and Party in the Cultural Revolution," *The China Quarterly* 35 (July–September 1968): 1–17, and by Stuart Schram in "The Party in Chinese Communist Ideology," *The China Quarterly* 38 (April–June, 1969): 1–26. Both of these articles appear in John W. Lewis, ed., *Party Leadership and Revolutionary Power in China* (London: Cambridge University Press, 1970).

lish and administer an effective state apparatus and to undertake the staggering task of modern economic development led to the creation of a new political elite of bureaucratic administrators (drawn largely from the Party and still within the Party) and an economic elite of industrial managers, scientists, and technicians. Whereas traditional Chinese patterns of bureaucratic behavior may have intensified this process of bureaucratization, it was facilitated specifically by the fact that the Communist revolution had destroyed old elites. As Weber demonstrated at considerable length, "every process of social leveling creates a favourable situation for the development of bureaucracy,"[50] and this was no less true in post-1949 China than it has been elsewhere.

Given Mao's extreme Populist hostility to all forms of bureaucracy—a phenomenon he condemned throughout his revolutionary career as the greatest of social evils[51]—it is not difficult to imagine how intolerable this potential bureaucratic institutionalization of the revolution must have seemed to him. Equally unbearable was the accompanying emergence of social patterns and value orientations which threatened to increase the economic and cultural gulf between the intelligentsia and the masses, especially the peasantry, and at the same time increase the separation between the cities and the countryside—the very gaps both Marxism and Populism demanded be closed. What Mao feared in the mid-1950s was not simply that economic growth was proceeding too slowly but that it was proceeding in a fashion that threatened to preclude the communist goals of the revolution.

What became distinctively Maoist in Chinese Communist thought and action may appear less irrational than it is usually pictured if it is seen in the perspective of the Maoist confrontation with the dilemma of means and ends, as a conscious attempt to pursue economic and social development in a way consistent (at least in the Maoist view) with the achievement of Marxist goals. In the realm of theory, the most significant attempt to reconcile means and ends was the explicit

50. Max Weber, *The Theory of Social and Economic Organization* (New York: The Free Press, 1964), p. 340.

51. "This great evil, bureaucracy, must be thrown into the cesspool," Mao typically demanded in 1933. *Selected Works*, vol. 1, p. 135.

recognition (which implicitly rejected both Leninist and Stalinist strategies of postrevolutionary development) that the existence of presumably "socialist relations of production" combined with economic development do not by themselves assure the realization of a socialist society, much less the transition from socialism to communism; rather, they were to be accompanied by "continuous" processes of the transformation of social relations and popular consciousness. This was formulated in various ways, but most notably in the doctrine of "uninterrupted" or "permanent revolution."[52] The most important Maoist innovations in social and economic policy were consistent with this doctrine and generally reflected the concern with the dilemma of reconciling the means and ends of revolution. The original aim of the people's communes, it should be recalled, was not only to release the productive energies of the masses, but also to combine industry with agriculture, reduce the gap between the cities and the countryside, and prevent the separation of the intelligentsia from the masses. The policies requiring intellectuals and Party cadres to engage in productive labor in rural areas, the *hsia-fang* ("sending down") movement, the various work-study schemes for combining education with productive activities, and the constant exhortations that the masses must make themselves masters of science and technology—all these were intended by Maoists (if not necessarily by other Communist leaders) to forestall the differentiation of a bureaucratic-professional vocational ethic from the communist political ethic and to prevent the stratification of new urban elites separated from the peasant masses.

The means which Maoists employed to achieve the ultimate communist ends envisioned were unprecedented in the history of Marxism-Leninism. They reflected a distrust of "revolution from above" in favor of spontaneous mass action from below, and exhibited powerful egalitarian and antibureaucratic impulses more characteristic of Russian Populism than Russian Leninism. And there was nothing Leninist, much less Stalinist, in the Maoist willingness to sacrifice the pace of economic development to preserve what were seen to be

52. For a definition and brief discussion of the concept, see Schram, *The Political Thought of Mao Tse-tung*, pp. 98–101. A fuller analysis is provided by Schram in *La 'Révolution permanente' en Chine* (Paris: Mouton, 1963).

essential social and ideological preconditions for socialism—and even to abandon the Party itself as the indispensable means to Marxist ends.

It would be unfair to Lenin (even if not to Leninism) to suggest that he was wholly oblivious to the social consequences of his political actions. On his deathbed he was haunted by the old Populist fear that the revolution he made had accomplished little more than the substitution of new for old forms of autocratic rule; a "bourgeois, tsarist mechanism" with "only a Soviet veneer" was Lenin's last bitter comment on the Bolshevik regime.[53] But in spite of these doubts, and even his sense of moral guilt, he was unwilling to recognize the profound inconsistency between the revolutionary means he devised and the revolutionary ends he sought. In his last assessments of the reasons for the bureaucratic corruption of the revolution, he did not refer to the implications of his scheme of party organization, but concentrated on Russia's isolation and economic backwardness, and especially on Russian cultural backwardness; it was above all the lack of *kulturnost* which had allowed old Tsarist bureaucratic traditions to overwhelm the Bolsheviks.

Whether Mao was consciously aware of the bureaucratic implications of Leninist organizational principles is problematic. Even if he had arrived at such a conclusion, it would have been impossible for him to acknowledge it without renouncing the entire Marxist-Leninist heritage to which he laid claim and within which he claimed to have made creative innovations. But Mao did adopt new means and methods which rejected the institutionalized, bureaucratic pattern of postrevolutionary development that so logically flows from Leninism, and he was sufficiently non-Leninist to question the revolutionary legitimacy of the Chinese Communist Party itself. Mao's particular concern with the problem of reconciling means and ends probably derived more from a sense of historical indeterminacy than from any profound moral crisis. While Lenin's Marxian faith in "history" was shaky, Mao's was virtually nonexistent. He was no more confident in the historical inevitability of socialism than were

53. For a poignant discussion of Lenin's views on the Soviet regime at the end of his life, see Isaac Deutscher, "The Moral Dilemmas of Lenin," in Isaac Deutscher, *Ironies of History* (London: Oxford University Press, 1966), pp. 167–173.

the Populists. In the Maoist view, postrevolutionary China could as easily revert to capitalism as proceed to communism; the historical outcome depended entirely on the consciousness, the wills and the activities of men. Mao, as did the Populists, believed that men are free to choose their ends and from this it follows that they must choose means which are consistent with the ends they seek. Whether the means Mao chose were leading China to the Marxist goals he envisioned is quite another matter. But whatever the future may bring, Mao was unique among Communist leaders, both past and present, in his willingness to confront the dilemma of the means and ends of socialism.

IV. Conclusion

Although there are certain remarkable similarities between Maoism and classical Russian Populism, Maoism is scarcely the twentieth-century resurrection of the nineteenth-century Russian creed. Mao was the conscious heir of Marx and Lenin and the author of what has been proclaimed to be a new and higher stage in the development of Marxist-Leninist theory. For all his Marxist-Leninist unorthodoxies, Mao's goals and categories of thought basically derived from the Marxist intellectual and political tradition with which he consciously identified. What Mao shared with Populism, on the other hand, was something unacknowledged and unperceived. Those aspects of the Maoist mentality which have been described as "Populist" in the preceding pages were viewed by Maoists as part of "Mao Tsetung Thought," a body of ideas celebrated as the most advanced expression of Marxist-Leninist theory.

The Maoist self-identification with the Marxist-Leninist tradition was of crucial importance in influencing thought and action; nevertheless the possibility is not precluded that Maoists may have been the unconscious bearers of beliefs and concepts common to (but not necessarily derived from) non-Marxian intellectual and political traditions. This chapter has suggested that much of what is distinctive in the Maoist version of Marxism-Leninism can be attributed to essentially Populist-type beliefs and impulses, and that this Populist component of Maoism has had profoundly important implications for what has too easily been assumed to be the purely "Leninist" character of Chinese Communist theory and practice.

The Populist strain in Maoism is an indigenous Chinese phenomenon which developed despite (not because of) the political and intellectual impact of the Bolshevik Revolution. Although the possible influence of traditional Chinese intellectual sources certainly is a matter that deserves investigation, an explanation for the emergence of this Populist strain is more likely to be found in factors present in the modern Chinese historical environment. Here it might be useful to note the conditions which have typically fostered Populist-type ideologies and movements: a traditional peasant-based society disintegrating under the forces of modern capitalism introduced from without and generally perceived as alien; the absence of a viable indigenous bourgeoisie; the emergence of an intelligentsia alienated from traditional values and existing society; and the desire of members of that intelligentsia to bridge the gulf that separates them from society by finding roots in the vast peasant masses and speaking on their behalf. In the broadest sense, Populism can be seen as a protest against modern capitalism and its human and social costs, particularly as those costs are borne by the peasantry.[54] Populism is not a peasant ideology, but a protest ideology of intellectuals speaking for what they perceive to be the interests of the rural masses. And perhaps especially pertinent to the Chinese situation, it has been noted that Populist tendencies typically spring "both from the tension between backward countries and more advanced ones, and from the tension between developed and backward parts of the same country."[55]

Viewed from these general perspectives, the Maoist combination of Marxism and Populism appears as a not illogical outcome of the

54. Although it is difficult to employ "Populism" as a general sociohistorical concept, the difficulties are no greater (and perhaps less misleading) than those involved in the use of such terms as "nationalism" and "modernization" as general concepts. Peter Worsley perhaps has made the most fruitful attempt to define and apply Populism as a general sociohistorical term. See *The Third World* (London: Weidenfeld & Nicolson, 1964), especially Chapter 4; and "The Concept of Populism" in Ionescu and Gellner, eds., *Populism*, pp. 212–50.

55. Angus Stewart, "The Social Roots," in Ionescu and Gellner, eds., *Populism*, p. 181.

history of Marxism in an economically backward and largely peasant land threatened by foreign capitalist political and economic forces. In Maoism, Marxist and Populist elements reinforced each other in opposition to the external capitalist order, both as that order had impinged on China in the past and as it threatened China in the present. Internally, the Populist component in Maoism reflected the tension between the backward (but relatively revolutionary) countryside and the relatively economically advanced (but nonrevolutionary) urban areas, and (both before and after 1949) expressed a revolutionary bias in favor of the former against the latter. Moreover, the Populist strain served to fashion Marxism into a revolutionary ideology that addressed itself to modern Chinese historical realities; in typically Populist fashion, Maoism was primarily concerned with the relationship between intellectuals and peasants, the two dynamic social groups in modern Chinese history, rather than with the traditional Marxist focus on the proletariat and the bourgeoisie, both relatively weak classes in modern Chinese society and ones only marginally involved in the Communist revolution.

What is unique in Chinese revolutionary history is not the emergence of a Populist strain, but its appearance within the Marxist movement rather than before it or in opposition to it. And it is this historical coincidence that has been responsible for much of what was unique about Marxism-Leninism in China. For however much Mao may have shared with Lenin, he did not fully share the most significant feature of Leninism—the intellectual assumptions on which the organization and role of the Leninist party are based.

A Populist-type hostility to capitalism is often accompanied by ambiguous attitudes toward modern life in general. Lenin described Russian Populist theory as "a Janus, looking with one face to the past and the other to the future."[56] For Lenin, the Narodniks were "progressive" in that they challenged the existing social order but "reactionary" insofar as they attempted to maintain traditional forms of production in opposition to modern capitalism. Many recent writ-

56. V. I. Lenin, "The Economic Content of Narodism," in V. I. Lenin, *Collected Works* (Moscow: Foreign Languages Publishing House, 1960), vol. 1, p. 503.

ers have also commented on the "Janus quality" of Populist ideologies, usually in terms of the Populist desire to preserve traditional cultural values and social forms in confronting "the modernization process."[57] Although in some cases this may involve a rejection of modern technology and industry in general, it is most typically manifested in an attempt to reach some sort of ideological synthesis between "traditionalism" and "modernity." In this realm, Maoism was not typically Populist. Explicitly antitraditional and deeply committed to modern economic development, Maoism presented not a "Janus face" but a single, basically progressive face. While Populist tendencies and dilemmas have contributed to a profound concern for the social costs and consequences of modern technology and industrialization, Maoism did not reject industrialization but rather the social forms it took in the Western capitalist world—and later the "bourgeois" Soviet world as well.

Yet there are disquieting similarities between some of the Populist aspects of Maoism and a recurring and purely reactionary syndrome of beliefs that Barrington Moore has labelled "Catonism." Where commercial relationships (and in modern times, specifically capitalist relationships) have begun to undermine a peasant economy, Moore has noted that "the conservative elements in society are likely to generate a rhetoric of extolling the peasant as the backbone of society." And the ideological rhetoric of this particular anticapitalist response involves a celebration of the "organic" life of the countryside; a deep hostility to the city and its "conspirators"; an emphasis on the need for moral regeneration, and the desirability of "comradeship" and "community"; antiintellectualism and the praise of the martial virtues; antiforeignism and a condemnation of "decadent" and "rootless" cosmopolitans; artistic notions which center around folk and provincial art; and opposition to "mere technical expertise" and to industrialism in general.[58]

Although it is easy enough to detect resemblances between "Catonism" and certain Populist features of Maoism, several crucial distinctions must be made. In modern times, Catonism has been part

57. See, for example, Stewart, "The Social Roots," pp. 186–91.

58. For a discussion of "Catonism," see Barrington Moore, *Social Origins of Dictatorship and Democracy* (Boston: Beacon Press, 1966), pp. 490–96.

of a reactionary ideological response to capitalism by the upper landed classes intent on preserving as much as possible of a traditional and oppressive agrarian social order; the celebration of the "rural virtues" is accompanied by a horror of social change. As Moore has pointed out, seemingly similar beliefs arise among the radical right and the radical left in the countryside when the traditional order is in a process of disintegration, but "the main distinction depends on the amount of realistic analysis of the causes of [peasant] suffering and on the images of a potential future. Catonism conceals the social causes and projects an image of continued submission. The radical tradition emphasizes the causes and projects an image of eventual liberation." The crucial differences center on the way these beliefs are combined and especially the ultimate purposes they are intended to serve.[59]

Maoism, at least during Mao's lifetime, remained firmly within the radical tradition. The Populist elements of Maoism were combined with Marxian social theory to promote revolutionary social change to realize a future egalitarian socialist society. Yet it is not inconceivable that very different social and political circumstances may develop in a post-Maoist China where these Populist elements (selectively interpreted) may become a dangerous and irrational "Maoist" ideological legacy easily turned to reactionary social ends.

In any general consideration of the history of Marxism-Leninism in China, one observes a paradox within a paradox. If it is paradoxical, as Deutscher suggested, that China, "the most archaic of nations," adopted Leninism, "the most modern of revolutionary doctrines," then it is more paradoxical still that within the Maoist version of "Marxism-Leninism" there emerged powerful "pre-Leninist" Populist-type ideas and beliefs which Lenin long ago consigned to the dustbin of revolutionary history. If Mao stood on Lenin's shoulders, he did so with an ideology bearing many of those "romantic" revolutionary notions and intellectual orientations which Lenin and Leninists time and again have condemned as "reactionary" and "utopian." Lenin indeed expressed great admiration for Herzen and Chernyshevsky and regarded them (although not most of their Populist successors) as progressive for their time; yet for Lenin

59. Ibid., pp. 494–95.

their time and the time for Populism had long since passed.[60] In strictly Marxist-Leninist terms, Populist tendencies constitute a "petty-bourgeois" revolutionary heresy. And not too surprisingly, it is precisely with this ideological sin that Mao was charged. As early as 1930, Ch'ü Ch'iu-pai, echoing Comintern complaints, accused Mao and his small band of revolutionaries of being "petty-bourgeois populists" who had turned their backs on the urban proletariat.[61] And the accusation has been revived by Soviet ideologists in more recent polemics.[62]

Yet, it is quite possible that a Leninist ideological heresy may have been something of a Marxist revolutionary virtue. Had it not been for the Populist orientations which drew Mao to the countryside in the first place, and also provided him with that very non-Leninist faith in the spontaneous revolutionary creativity of the peasant masses, it is most unlikely that there would have been a successful Communist revolution in China. And it is precisely the Populist aspects of the Maoist revolutionary mentality—particularly the hostility to bureaucratic elitism, the distrust of formal institutions and the special concern with the dilemma of means and ends—which have been crucial in keeping revolutionary hopes alive in postrevolutionary China. If Maoism did not create a genuinely socialist society in China, it did create a situation of permanent revolutionary ferment which left open the possibility of attaining (or, at least, pursuing) Marxian socialist goals. If Marx's injunction to change the world rather than simply interpret it is any standard by which to measure the credentials of a revolutionary Marxist, then Mao may perhaps eventually be judged a better Marxist than a Leninist. That indeed would be something of a paradox in view of all that Maoists and non-Maoists

60. "Once progressive, as the first to pose the problem of capitalism," Lenin wrote in 1897, "nowadays Narodism is a *reactionary* and *harmful* theory which misleads social thought and plays into the hands of stagnation and Asiatic backwardness." "The Heritage We Renounce," in Lenin, *Collected Works*, vol. 2, p. 516.

61. "Chung-kuo ko-ming ho nung-min yün-tung ti ts'e-lüeh" [The Chinese Revolution and the strategy of the peasant movement], *Pu-erh-sai-wei-k'e* [The Bolshevik] 3.4–5 (12 May 1930): 114, 141.

62. For example, the *Pravda* article "Scientific Socialism and Petty Bourgeois Ideology" (24 October 1966), in *Current Digest of the Soviet Press* 18.43:4–6.

have written about Mao's "Leninism." And it could be the strangest paradox of all if Mao's anti-Leninist (and non-Marxist) Populist notions were somehow to eventually facilitate the Chinese quest for the utopian social goals which Marxism prophesies.

Yet it cannot be assumed that the Populist strains in Maoism will long survive the passing of Mao. It remains to be seen whether the Populist strains in Chinese Marxism were peculiar to the thought of Mao Tse-tung or ones more deeply ingrained in the modern Chinese revolutionary consciousness.

4

Utopian Goals and Ascetic Values in Maoist Ideology

However much Mao Tse-tung may have championed the revolutionary virtues of backwardness, he did not believe that a socialist society could be built and maintained in conditions of perpetual economic scarcity. Having won power in a wretchedly impoverished land almost entirely lacking the Marxist-defined economic prerequisites for socialism, Mao, no less than other Chinese Communist leaders, saw the creation of those very prerequisites as the first and essential task confronting the new state. Maoism, perforce, thus became an ideology of development as well as a utopian prophecy, an ideology conveying the values of "modernization" as well as one promising a future communist utopia.

Conventional wisdom suggests that there is a contradiction here. Modern economic development, we are told, requires a rationality and stability that is incompatible with the social and political convulsions fostered by utopian ideologies and visions. But modern historical experience, both Western and Chinese, also suggests that the values conducive to economic modernization are closely bound up with utopian visions. What is the link between Maoist utopianism and the modernizing values the doctrine conveys?

The ethical values and norms which are to guide social behavior in the People's Republic are often imparted to the people through fables and stories. One might begin the inquiry with one of the most popular of such fables. The story is from traditional Chinese folklore, but it became a part of the Chinese Communist tradition when it was retold by Mao Tse-tung in his concluding speech to the Seventh National Congress of the Chinese Communist Party in June of 1945:

In ancient China there was a fable: "How Yu Kung Removed the Mountains." It is the story of an old man in North China in ancient times, by the name of Yu Kung of the North Mountain. His house faced south and its doorway was obstructed by two big mountains, Taihang and Wangwu. With great determination, he led his sons to dig up the mountains with pickaxes. Another old man, Chih Sho, witnessed their attempts and laughed, saying: "What fools you are to attempt this! To dig up two huge mountains is utterly beyond your capacity." Yu Kung replied: "When I die, there are my sons; when they die there will be their own sons, and so on to infinity. As to these two mountains, high as they are, they cannot become higher but, on the contrary, with every bit dug away, they will become lower and lower. Why can't we dig them away?" Mr. Yu Kung refuted Mr. Chih Sho's erroneous view and went on digging at the mountains day after day without interruption. God's heart was touched by such perseverance and he sent two celestial beings down to earth to carry away the mountains on their backs.[1]

There was a contemporary lesson to be drawn from the ancient fable: "We must work persistently, work ceaselessly, and we too may be able to touch God's heart. This God is no other than the masses of the people throughout China."[2]

In late 1966 Mao's speech of 1945 (retitled "The Foolish Old Man Who Removed the Mountains") was canonized as one of "the three constantly read articles," which, it was proclaimed, summed up the essence of Maoist wisdom.[3] In addition to the emphasis on the ethical value of hard work and the promise that diligence in the present will be rewarded in the future, the other two of the "three constantly

1. Mao Tse-tung, "How Yu Kung Removed the Mountains," in Mao Tse-tung, *The Selected Works of Mao Tse-tung*, vol. 4, (London: Lawrence and Wishart, 1956), pp. 316–17.

2. Ibid., p. 317.

3. The other of the "three constantly read articles" are "Serve the People," (a speech delivered in 1944) and "In Memory of Norman Bethune" (an essay written in 1939). On the "canonization" of the articles see "Maxims for Revolutionaries—The 'Three Constantly Read Articles,' " *Peking Review*, 6 January 1967, pp. 7–8.

read articles" praise the values of struggle, courage, and sacrifice, and especially the virtue of unselfishness: "We must all learn the spirit of absolute selflessness. . . . A man's ability may be great or small, but if he has this spirit, he is already noble-minded and pure, a man of moral integrity and above vulgar interests."[4]

The values expounded in the homilies of Mao are typical of those which in various ways and forms have been propagated and popularized in China since 1949. The sin of selfishness and the virtue of self-denial, the ethical value of hard work, frugality, self-discipline, diligence, and honesty—such are the moral maxims constantly imparted to the Chinese people, and especially to Chinese youth.

Whether conveyed through writings of Mao himself, or through the didactic hero tales in newspapers and popular magazines, the "Maoist" values which presumably orient social behavior in the People's Republic are not ones which should unduly upset the moral sensibilities of most Westerners, for they are values which Westerners generally take for granted, at least as implicit ideals even if they are not always reflected in actual social behavior. Diligence, frugality, self-discipline, honesty, the moral value of work, and unselfishness are the most common of the original bourgeois virtues, and ones deeply imbedded in modern Western thought and morality. These are of course essentially ascetic values, analogous to those which Max Weber attributed to the "Protestant ethic" of the rising capitalist class of Western Europe in the sixteenth and seventeenth centuries, values conducive (and some would say essential) to the economic and industrial transformation of the Western world in its modern capitalist form.

Ascetic values, however, are rarely ends in themselves, but rather are usually seen as means to serve higher interests and attain ultimate goals, as such goals may be defined in a comprehensive religious or political ideology. The active, ascetic life-orientation of the Calvinist saint, for example, was understood as an ethical obligation to serve the glory of God, for, according to Calvinist ideology, a transcendental and inscrutable God had decreed that it was the duty of all men (those condemned to eternal damnation as well as those granted

4. Mao Tse-tung, "In Memory of Norman Bethune," *Peking Review*, 17 February 1967, p. 5.

eternal salvation) to labor to establish the Kingdom of God on earth.[5] Similarly, the ascetic pattern of life demanded by Chinese Communist ideology is not an end in itself but is seen as a means by which people can transform themselves and transform nature to realize the "truly human life" which Marxist theory historically locates in the communist utopia of the future.

Thus the ascetic values of Maoism are not autonomous elements or final ends. They are part of a wider ideological structure, elements of a comprehensive world view which proclaims universal truths and ultimate goals and thus provides the context within which adherence to the prescribed values becomes meaningful. While it is undoubtedly true that it is social and cultural values, and the norms of behavior derived from them, which most directly govern social action, it is equally true that seemingly analogous values which exist within the framework of different ideological world views and conceptual structures may produce very different forms of social action and tend toward dissimilar historical results.

For the study of Chinese Communist ideology, it is a matter of special importance to understand the relationship between values and goals and to understand how the former are made "meaningful" in terms of the latter. This is demanded not only because of the strongly utopian, "goal-oriented" impulses so obviously present in the Maoist mentality but, more important, because the Chinese Marxist conceptual structure (both in its Maoist and post-Maoist forms) itself explicitly links the social consciousness and values of the present with the communist goals of the future. Indeed, one of the most characteristic and significant features of the Maoist version of Marxist theory—as distinguished from Soviet Marxism—is the recognition that economic development and the existence of "socialist relations of production" do not by themselves automatically guarantee the future realization of communist goals. Communism cannot be achieved, it constantly has been emphasized, unless Marxist goals are consciously pursued, embryonic forms of communist social or-

5. For an excellent analysis of the Calvinist world view, see Michael Walzer, *The Revolution of the Saints* (Cambridge, Mass.: Harvard University Press, 1965). Also, Max Weber, *The Protestant Ethic and the Spirit of Capitalism* (New York: Scribner's, 1958), pp. 98–128.

ganization implemented, and the proper social values popularized and internalized *in the process,* and for the purpose, of creating the material prerequisites for the future communist society.

This point can perhaps be demonstrated by briefly examining the Maoist treatment of the Marxist goal of abolishing the distinction between mental and manual labor, a goal widely popularized over the years and extensively discussed in Chinese Marxist theoretical literature. In brief, Maoist theorists have argued that the basic "antithesis" between mental and manual labor has been eliminated in Chinese society but that the differences remain, even though in "nonantagonistic" form. It is emphasized, however, that an ever-present danger exists that these differences may become "antagonistic" in the course of social and economic development. What is required to combat the danger are intensive ideological and political efforts and concrete social policies designed to promote the combination of physical and mental labor. As the matter was put by one theoretician in 1960: "Although a high level of social productivity is the material foundation for the elimination of the difference between mental and manual labor, this difference will not automatically disappear no matter how high the level of productivity. The only path to eliminate this difference lies in the revolutionary transformation of social relations."[6] Or, as more radically formulated, "mere reliance on changes in the relations of production" cannot abolish the difference between physical and mental labor, for the distinction "exists not only in the economic realm but also in the political and ideological realms."[7]

The development of the necessary material prerequisites for communism therefore must be accompanied by equally necessary and continuous processes of ideological transformation and revolutionary social and political action. This, in part, is what Maoists meant by the much-celebrated doctrine of *"pu-tuan ko-ming,"* the notion of "uninterrupted" or "permanent revolution." As often formulated in Maoist theoretical literature, it is a doctrine that recognizes that

6. *Kuang-ming jih-pao,* 26 September 1960.

7. See, for example, Yün Hsi-liang, "Physical Labor and Mental Labor in Socialist Society," *Ching-chi yen-chiu* [Economic research] 2 (1965), in *Selections from Chinese Mainland Magazines,* 507:9.

"the ideals of communism" can be achieved only in the future, but it also demands that revolutionary practice in the present must proceed in a "continuous" fashion so as "to pave the way for the realization of these ideals."[8] As characteristically put, there can be no "Great Chinese Wall" between the presumably socialist society of the present and the future communist utopia.

The essential virtue of the "theory of uninterrupted revolution" for Maoists lay less in a belief in its validity as a "scientific" description of objective laws of historical development than in the belief that if "the spirit of uninterrupted revolution" is "grasped by the revolutionary masses," it will guide their consciousness and motivate their actions—for, as was so often proclaimed, "it is the masses of the people who are the creators of history."[9] As applied to the question of eliminating the differences between mental and manual labor, the demand was for action in the here and now to eradicate the traditional Chinese disdain for manual labor and to implement concrete social policies designed to promote the combination of physical and mental work—measures such as those requiring intellectuals and administrative cadres to participate in physical labor on a more or less regular basis and others to popularize scientific and cultural knowledge among the masses through a variety of "spare-time" and "work-study" educational programs.[10]

There was much that was utopian but little that was teleological in the Maoist mentality. The faith in the "inevitability" of communism was not based on any firm confidence in the workings of "objective" historical laws but on a faith in the revolutionary activism of the masses and their determination to consciously puruse and implement communist goals *while* building the material prerequisites for com-

8. Hsü Li-chun, "Tsung shih-fou i-ching tao-le kung-chan chu-i' shuo-ch'i" [Is it correct to speak of "having already reached communism?"], *Hung-ch'i* [Red Flag] 12 (December 1958): 20–24.

9. Chao Feng-ch'i and Wu Shih-k'ang, "Pu-tuan-ko-ming-lun ho ko-ming fa-chan-chieh-tuan-lun ti t'ung-i" [The unity of the theory of uninterrupted revolution and the theory of revolutionary development by stages], *Hsin Chien-she* [New construction] 2 (February 1959): 27.

10. For an excellent analysis of the "work-study" programs, see Donald J. Munro, "Maxims and Realities in China's Educational Policy: the Half-Work, Half-Study Model," *Asian Survey* 12.4 (April 1967): 254–72.

munism. And that faith presupposed, in turn, that the masses were imbued with the proper consciousness and values, particularly the ascetic values of struggle and hard work that would foster activistic life orientations in the present to build the communist society of the future.

The Maoist propagation of ascetic values was closely associated with an attack on traditional Chinese values. The link between Maoist asceticism and antitraditionalism follows a Western pattern of intellectual and socioeconomic development. Just as the asceticism of Protestant sects such as Calvinism and Puritanism demanded a radical devaluation of all traditional and magical beliefs in order to allow true believers to carry out God's demands to rationally transform the world toward a more ethical status, so "Mao Tsetung Thought" demanded of its believers a radical break with traditional values and superstitions in order to enable them to achieve a modern socialist future.

In considering the social function of Maoist antitraditionalism in broader historical perspectives, it might be recalled that Western capitalism (and "the spirit of capitalism") was a profoundly antitraditional force which broke apart the old family system, promoted the ascendency of universal ethical values over particularistic kinship values, encouraged the liberation of the individual from traditional family obligations, and fostered the emergence of the modern nuclear family within the larger disciplinary system of the modern nation-state. The rise of modern capitalism was associated with the rise of modern skepticism, rationalism, and science—and consequently was accompanied by a radical attack on traditional magical, superstitious, and mystical beliefs. Western capitalism, moreover, both brought and presupposed fundamentally new attitudes toward work; the notion that work was a burden to be carried on at a leisurely pace and for the purpose of subsistence was replaced by the view that work was an ethical duty and a moral obligation, a value orientation highly conducive to the new and disciplined work patterns modern capitalist forms of production required.

Maoist antitraditionalism performed a similar modernizing role, albeit in different historical circumstances and by different means and methods. Just as the ideal of "Christian fellowship" of the Protestant sects broke apart the traditional Western family and its values, so the Maoist ideal of "serve the people" undermined the sacred values of the traditional Chinese family system. In both cases the social result has been the consolidation of the nuclear family within larger social and political structures, with individual family members free and able to engage in modern secular work and vocations. And much in the fashion that the modernization of the West presupposed the modern work ethic, Maoist ideology ethically praised "the dignity of labor," manifesting itself most forcefully in an attack on the sharp distinction between mental and manual work so deeply ingrained in the traditional Chinese value system.[11]

Ascetic and antitraditional values, it is widely agreed, were highly favorable (and perhaps necessary) for the modern economic development of the Western world, and it may safely be assumed that asceticism and antitraditionalism in their Maoist forms have similarly promoted the "modernization" of China. In the Maoist view, the assault on traditional values was seen as necessary to remove the psychological barriers to the building of the envisioned new society while ascetic values were regarded as necessary to instil the work ethic required to establish the material prerequisites for the communist future. And both asceticism and antitraditionalism were ethically sanctioned by the utopian social goals prophesied in Marxist theory.

The nature of the relationship between utopian goals and social values in Maoist ideology perhaps can be illustrated by examining the "red and expert" formula which appeared so prominently in Chinese

11. Modern Chinese antitraditionalism has of course taken a far more extreme form than antitraditionalism in the West, partly because of the peculiarly conservative character of the old Confucian heritage and partly (and correspondingly) because of the radical iconoclastic impulses that marked the thought of the modern Chinese intelligentsia. But perhaps the more important factor was timing. In the West the break with tradition was a relatively gradual process, spanning several centuries and accompanying the relatively gradual growth of modern forms of economic life. In China, modern economic and cultural change was telescoped into several decades, rather than centuries, and thus the break with the past was a far more traumatic experience and one that assumed a more radical character. For a different explanation of the origins of radical iconoclasm in modern China, see the sophisticated argument brilliantly pursued by Lin Yü-sheng in *The Crisis of Chinese Consciousness: Radical Antitraditionalism in the May Fourth Era* (Madison: University of Wisconsin Press, 1979).

Communist ideology after 1957. The "red and expert" notion combined Marxist utopianism with several other characteristic features of the Maoist mentality—the insistence that communist social patterns and values be created in the course of building the economic and technological foundations of communism (for, in the Maoist view, the material preconditions for communism in no sense automatically guarantee its realization), the conflicting Leninist and Populist impulses to both manipulate and "merge with" the masses, and the proclivity to fashion model personalities who typify universally valid—and universally attainable—social values and life orientations. The ideally portrayed "red and expert" exemplified not only the prescribed ascetic social values and norms of behavior of the present but also embodied the communist goals of the future.

The "red and expert" notion was initially an attempt to politicize the values of two new intellectual elites which had emerged as a consequence of economic and political developments of the early years of the People's Republic. One was an economic elite of industrial managers, technicians, and scientists; the other was a political elite of party cadres who were rapidly becoming bureaucratic administrators and functionaries in the new state apparatus. The two elites not only tended to become separated from each other on the basis of two different kinds of knowledge and value orientations, but both were separated and increasingly alienated from the masses of workers and peasants. The traditional gap between mental and manual work, as in the case of the Soviet Union, was in the process of becoming institutionalized in new sociohistorical circumstances. High levels of economic development and technological expertise were prerequisites for the attainment of communist goals; but the means employed to create these prerequisites were also creating social conditions and intellectual orientations which tended to vitiate these goals as meaningful guides to social action, and thus threatened to preclude their future realization.

Although the "red and expert" formula was first directed to the professional intelligentsia and to political-administrative cadres, it was soon transformed into a universal social ideal to be attained by workers and peasants as well. The great rallying cry heard during the Great Leap Forward period was that "the masses must make themselves masters of culture and science" in order to break the intelligentsia's "monopoly" of knowledge and meet the needs of "the mass technological revolution." As ideally conceived in Maoist theory anyone could become—and everyone was urged to become—"red and expert." Thus, the "red and expert" formula served (or at least was intended to serve) not only as a means to integrate the professional elite of "experts" and the political elite of "reds," but also to narrow the gap between both elites and the common people.

What emerges from the vast body of Maoist writings on the "red and expert" notion is the Chinese prototype of the future "all-round" communist man.[12] It is a prototype drawn both from the more utopian pronouncements of Karl Marx and the heroic strands in the Chinese Communist revolutionary tradition. The "red and expert" was conceived as the product of existing socialist society, the exemplifier of the ascetic life-orientation deemed necessary in the present, the carrier of a more advanced "communist consciousness," and thus the producer of the greater social goals proclaimed in the Marxist vision of the future. As characteristically described, the "red and expert" was the model for a new "generation of all-round men who combine a capacity for mental labor with a capacity for manual labor"; he was a politically conscious "jack of all trades" (*to-mien-shou,* literally, "many-sided hand") capable of engaging in "scientific and cultural undertakings" as well as in physical labor. He was an exemplar of "communist" social and moral values. He was typically antitraditionalist, for he knew (or was told) that those who make creative accomplishments are those who have freed themselves from "the fetters of tradition." He was "a fully developed red and expert laborer who can handle both civilian and military work," combining theory with practice, "brain work with brawn work," and thus capable of switching from one job to another as the needs of society dictated. He was, in short, the "new Communist man, red and expert," who would realize Mao Tse-tung's dream of a whole nation of "socialist-conscious, cultured laborers."

It is perhaps less important to ask if there were or are many—if any—such people in China than to ask what influences such widely propagated images of the ideal personality had in orienting social

12. The following description and quotations are drawn from a variety of articles in *Chung-kuo ch'ing-nien* [China youth], 1958–66.

values and social actions. In one sense, paradoxically, the less the "red and expert" ideal existed in Chinese social reality the more important it was. To the extent that the goals and values exemplified by the ideally portrayed "red and expert" were accepted (as they were presented) as morally and ethically good, there was instilled a sense of moral duty to practice these values and realize these goals. The more radical the contrast between ideal and real life-orientations, the greater was the tension generated to transform real life in accordance with ideal patterns. And tension, Maoist theory emphasized, was not only inevitable but potentially good—for tension promoted efforts and activities which, if guided by the proper consciousness, led people to transform themselves and transform society in accordance with the highest ideals of human life; that is to say, it promoted efforts to build socialism and communism. Therefore, tension and pain in the present would not only result in pleasure and happiness in the future but were themselves pleasurable and of ethical value.

Divested of their particular ideological jargon, Maoist ethical commentaries and biographical sketches of model "red and experts," popularized over the years, might easily be mistaken for Calvinist-inspired moral tracts rather than products of the "Marxist-Leninist" thoughts of Mao Tse-tung. The ideal young "red and expert" was not only inspired by a deep sense of mission and purpose ("to serve the people"), but also burdened with a self-imposed sense of guilt and sin; he was therefore to constantly employ "the weapon of self-criticism" to examine his consciousness "for the presence of bad thoughts" and continually struggle against "shortcomings and mistakes," for he was aware that if he "makes a mistake, thousands of people might suffer." Thus he was to carry out "a lifelong revolution in [his] own mind" for he was forever obligated to serve the party, society, the people and, needless to say, the "thoughts of Mao Tse-tung." Such burdens could be relieved, and such obligations fulfilled, not simply by "faith" but by the practical demonstration of one's faith in the self-disciplined and diligent pursuit of revolutionary goals and values. His disciplined activity was not for the purpose of securing happiness for himself or his family, but for the purpose of serving society, the nation and indeed all of mankind. He recognized that manual labor was the source of all social wealth and "the prime want of human life"; labor (and laborers) were "noble" and thus if not already a worker or peasant, he engaged regularly in manual labor and fostered a "fervent love for labor" and love for the laboring masses. He felt that work was not a burden but a joy that carried its own rewards. Indeed, if there was any dominant social value the "red and expert" activist personified, it was the ethical value of hard and disciplined work.

The ideal "red and expert" was, above, all, unselfish and the embodiment of the "communist spirit of altruism." He subordinated all personal pleasure to the duty of serving the party and the people, for the only true source of joy and happiness was struggle in behalf of, and together with, the masses; such struggle was "saintly and divine," and from it one derived strength and happiness. Moreover, the ideal "red and expert" lived "the frugal and simple style" of workers and peasants—for self-denial, economy, and thrift were virtues, whereas indolence, luxury, and waste were sinful. Not only was material waste sinful but waste of time even more so, for "time is something cunning; if one does not grasp it, it will slip away."[13] Thus what was ethically demanded was a highly activistic life orientation, disciplined and controlled by the internalization of the prescribed moral values and ascetic norms of behavior.

Yet it would be highly misleading to suggest that Maoists preached asceticism simply for its own sake and advocated struggle for the sake of struggle alone. To be sure, joy and happiness were to be derived from struggle and an ascetic life orientation but only because such struggle was the means to the realization of great ends—the transformation of the world in accordance with the communist vision of the future. As typically formulated in Maoist ethical treatises: ". . . one has the greatest pleasure and happiness when one wages a heroic struggle for a noble goal, a great ideal, and a political direction, particularly when one sees that such goals, ideals and political directions are finally realized after many sacrifices have been made by revolutionary martyrs. One's pleasure and happiness is the greatest when one devotes oneself to a definite cause by means of which to transform society and promote the wellbeing of mankind, especially when one sees that one's work is achieving brilliant successes. . . ."[14]

13. *Chung-kuo ch'ing-nien* 10 (1960):12.
14. *Chung-kuo ch'ing-nien* 11 (1960):11.

It was, in short, the expectation of the realization of a communist utopia that made revolutionary struggle meaningful, and provided the ultimate ethical sanction for the ascetic pattern of life such struggle demanded. Struggle might be inevitable and infinite—it might be inherent in the human condition—but it resulted in continuous social transformation and self-transformation toward a more ethical status; it was "arduous struggle for the great cause of communism." Ascetic struggle was of ethical value only because it was the means to ethically valued Marxist goals.

Yet the Maoist notion of the "new man of all-round ability" engaged in both mental and manual labor was not Karl Marx's "all-round communist man" pure and simple. What Maoists "added" to the original Marxian notion were the repressive values which corresponded to a historical stage Marx had assumed would have been long transcended with the advent of socialism. For the ascetic values which the model "red and expert" exemplified were essentially the early bourgeois values which both Marx and Weber identified with the initial phases of modern capitalist economic development. If Maoist ideologists chose to describe these values as "socialist" or "communist," this did not make them so, nor did it in any way mitigate their fundamentally repressive character; in original Marxian terms, these values could be described as a reflection of conditions of "alienated labor." That the "red and expert" prototype combined early bourgeois ascetic values with "post-bourgeois" Marxist goals is one of the curious paradoxes of modern Chinese history and one of the paradoxes of the history of Marxist theory in the modern world.

What Maoists added to the original Marxian notion of the "all-round" man is also what they subtracted. For what is most glaringly absent in the ideally portrayed "red and expert" is any real sense of individual human freedom, and this is no more apparent than in the failure of Maoist theory to deal seriously with the problem of human self-alienation—a problem which is so central in Marx's discussion of the future communist man who would achieve "self-consciousness" by realizing his own human potentialities. For the "red and expert," by contrast, "self-consciousness" was not self-realization but the internalization of prescribed values and norms of behavior. "Freedom" was essentially self-disciplined service in behalf of the party, and particularly its leader, not the free realization and free expression of the individual human personality.

Yet even though perceived in a highly nonlibertarian fashion and applied in a repressive social and political environment, utopian Marxist goals were key historical determinants in the Maoist era of the People's Republic. Much of that history will remain incomprehensible unless it is understood from the standpoint of historical actors whose social and political actions were guided and inspired by a Marxist vision of the future. And it is only in terms of that vision, and by the promise that it would be realized, that the enormous Maoist emphasis on the ascetic values of struggle and hard work were morally justified and ethically sanctioned.

An eminent social psychologist has said that "there is often much we can learn about the nature of a society and its dominant values by examining the dreams that it has produced."[15] Maoists dreamt Marxist dreams and attempted to impart the ethical and moral values they believed would transform their dreams into reality. Both their dreams and their values have had practical social and economic consequences, and a moral significance. And we should make some effort to understand both their dreams and their values (and the relationship between them) in terms that are historically and humanly comprehensible. Their ascetic values should not be dismissed as meaningless banalities because they seem familiar and banal to those who study them. Nor should their dreams be dismissed as "irrational" because they were utopian; to do so would be to ignore the historical truth that "man would not have attained the possible unless time and again he had reached out for the impossible."[16] Dreaming, to be sure, is not reality, but what people dream has a great deal to do with how they shape reality and make history.

15. Herbert C. Kelman, "From Dystopia to Utopia; an Analysis of Huxley's *Island*," in Richard Farson, ed., *Science and Human Affairs* (Palo Alto: Science & Behavior Books, 1965), p. 168.

16. Max Weber, "Politics as a Vocation," in Hans Gerth and C. Wright Mills, eds., *From Max Weber: Essays in Sociology* (New York: Oxford University Press, 1958), p. 128.

5

Images of the Paris Commune in Chinese Marxist Thought

On 21 May 1968, seven hundred thousand Chinese demonstrated in Peking in support of rebellious French students and striking French workers who had paralyzed the Fifth Republic of Charles de Gaulle. Over the next week, according to Chinese Communist reports, twenty million people marched through the streets of various Chinese cities ("in the spirit of proletarian internationalism," it was said) to express their solidarity with "the revolutionary struggles of the people of France."[1] Perhaps it was not without some sense of historical irony that the Peking correspondent of *Agence France Presse* noted that the most prominent slogan of the Chinese demonstrators was "long live the revolutionary heritage of the great Paris Commune."[2]

The Paris Commune of 1871, half-forgotten by Marxists in France, long has been celebrated by Marxists in China. In 1961 the ninetieth anniversary of the Commune was commemorated in China by academic symposia and public meetings, and by the publication of books and articles devoted to explaining the historical significance of the Commune and the theoretical significance Marx attributed to it. In March 1966, the ninety-fifth anniversary of the Paris uprising was marked by the opening (first in Peking and then in Shanghai) of

1. For a description of the demonstrations, see *Peking Review*, 31 May 1968, pp. 9–17.

2. *The New York Times*, 23 May 1968, p. 15.

an exhibit of historical documents of the Commune. And despite the Maoist aversion to specialization, Chinese newspapers reported on the work of "Chinese scholars specializing in the study of the Paris Commune."[3]

At the same time—and the time, significantly, was the eve of the Great Proletarian Cultural Revolution—Chinese Marxist theorists were writing lengthy treatises discussing the contemporary relevance of the Commune and the revolutionary lessons it had bequeathed. These lessons soon were to become important themes in the turbulent events of the following years.

That the Marxist interpretation of the Parisian revolutionary uprising of 1871 was deemed relevant for the revival of revolution in China almost a century later was a view officially put forth in the "Sixteen Points" of August 1966, the "charter" of the Cultural Revolution. Red Guard manifestoes of the time attributed to Mao Tse-tung a statement to the effect that the "Peking People's Commune" was the twentieth-century version of the Paris Commune, and they also proclaimed (among other things) that it was now the "true proletarian revolutionaries" of China who were the legitimate bearers of "the red banner of the Paris Commune."[4] In the ensuing months, ideas, images, and concepts derived from the Parisian events of 1871 (or, more precisely, from Marx's recreation of those events) played a prominent role in the Maoist call for the masses to rebel against existing organs of state and party and replace them with genuine forms of "proletarian dictatorship." Ch'en Po-ta and others close to Mao at the time frequently and explicitly suggested the Paris Commune as the revolutionary model to emulate. And an article in the August 1966 issue of *Red Flag,* the major Maoist theoretical journal, elaborating on one of the "Sixteen Points," proclaimed the universal validity of the Commune's electoral system and the need for its application in China. It was the Commune principle that the people had the right to elect, supervise, and recall officials that

3. "Exhibition on the Paris Commune Opens in Peking," *Survey of the China Mainland Press* 3671 (30 March 1966):39–40.

4. For a sampling of typical references to the Paris Commune in the literature of the period, see K. H. Fan, ed., *The Chinese Cultural Revolution: Selected Documents* (New York: Grove Press, 1968), especially pp. 161–96, 239–58.

would permit Chinese revolutionaries to realize the Marxist goal of transforming the state "from the ruler into the public servant of society."[5]

The use of the Paris Commune as a model for the reorganization of political power culminated in the abortive "Shanghai People's Commune" of February 1967, an attempt (however flawed it was from the beginning) by more radical Maoist leaders to establish a "proletarian dictatorship" in accordance with what they understood to be the revolutionary principles set forth by Marx in his analysis of the Parisian events of 1871. The demise of the Shanghai Commune, after a brief nineteen-day history, marked the beginning of the Maoist retreat from the more utopian aims of the Cultural Revolution and the beginning of a tortuous process of restructuring Chinese political life on the basis of "revolutionary committees," a process that eventually resulted in the reestablishment of the total political supremacy of the Chinese Communist Party. Although the Marxist description of the Paris Commune no longer served as a literal guide for political action after the early months of 1967, many of the concepts and much of the revolutionary imagery of the Commune remained a significant strand in the radical Maoist ideological tradition.

The special Chinese interest in the Commune, and its political use in the 1960s, is one of the more intriguing features of Maoist thought and action. Twentieth-century China and nineteenth-century France, after all, are separated by more than time and space; the Chinese Cultural Revolution and the Commune of Paris were products of vastly different processes of historical development and radically dissimilar social and political circumstances. Whatever else they may have been, the Red Guards were not the Parisian Communards reincarnate and the People's Liberation Army of Lin Piao was hardly the historical resurrection of the proletarian battalions of the popularized National Guard of Paris.

Why, then, did Chinese revolutionaries of the 1960s look back across so much history to the Paris of 1871? Why did Red Guards and "revolutionary rebels" of recent years adopt the names, the

5. Liu Hui-ming, "The General Election System of the Paris Commune," *Hung Ch'i* [Red flag], August 1966. Translated in *Selections from Chinese Mainland Magazines* 543 (21 August 1966):1–3.

slogans and the political forms of the workers of Paris of a century ago, or, at least, the slogans and forms that Marx attributed to them? Why did Chinese Marxist theorists insist that Mao Tse-tung inherited (and also "developed and enriched"), the experience of the Paris Commune? If China is a blank sheet of paper on which the newest revolutionary words can be written—as Mao Tse-tung proclaimed and Maoists so often repeated—why then was it necessary to look back to historical precedents, and ones so distant in historical time and space? And if the Cultural Revolution was a completely new, original, and unprecedented phenomenon in human history, then why did many of the actors in that contemporary drama attempt to model their actions, and to justify them, by reference to what happened at a very different historical time and place?

It is not difficult to offer cynical answers to these questions. A convenient one is suggested in an essay by Karl Marx. Commenting on Hegel's remark that all great historical events occur twice, Marx observed (with reference to Napoleon III) that Hegel forgot to add: "the first time as tragedy, the second as farce." If the Paris Commune of 1871 was a tragedy, was the Shanghai People's Commune merely a farce? Did Red Guards and "revolutionary rebels" who imitated the Parisian Communards make history or merely act out a historical parody? Was the Cultural Revolution really revolutionary or only a caricature of revolution?

For the spectator, it is tempting to view the Cultural Revolution as a gigantic farce; so much the easier, then, to dismiss the whole business as a case of mass hysteria. Not history, some might suggest, but a historical parody played out by madmen in Peking under the supervision and direction of the Marquis de Mao. A farce need not be taken seriously and thus there is no need to seriously inquire into the motivations of those who took part in so bizarre a play.

There are, of course, less cynical ways to view the Cultural Revolution and more serious approaches to the question of why revolutionaries who attempt to achieve a radical break with the present look back to precedents of the past. One such approach is suggested in another well-known passage from Marx:

> At the very time when men appear engaged in revolutionizing things and themselves, in bringing about what never was before, at such very epochs

of revolutionary crisis do they anxiously conjure up into their service the spirits of the past, assume their names, their battle cries, their costumes to enact a new historic scene in such time-honored disguise and with such borrowed language.[6]

There is a sense of historical parody implied here, but more importantly, a sense of the real drama involved in the way in which men make history, how they use the past—and at the same time how they are restrained by a need to retain forms and concepts inherited from the past—in their attempts to create a new future. Why then did contemporary Chinese revolutionaries use notions taken from a Marxist European past in attempting to bring about "what never was before" in China?

I. The Paris Commune in the Marxist Tradition

There is no need here to reproduce Marx's analysis of the Commune or trace its complex and controversial role in the Marxist intellectual and political tradition. Suffice it to note that for "orthodox" social-democratic Marxists, Marx's *The Civil War in France* has tended to be seen as something of an utopian aberration, an unfortunate regression to what was regarded as the outmoded Jacobin revolutionism of 1848. While appropriate lip service was paid to what became a canonical Marxian text, the entire notion of the "dictatorship of the proletariat"—and especially the utopian revolutionary definition Marx gave it in 1871—proved largely and logically irrelevant to the historically deterministic Marxist theory and reformist political practice of the late nineteenth-century Marxian social-democratic labor movement. For Kautsky, and orthodox Marxists in general, the Paris Commune was a heroic event of a revolutionary past, but one safely buried in the past; it was to be commemorated on appropriate occasions, to be sure, but no longer really relevant to contemporary political needs. As Martin Buber once observed: "What

6. Karl Marx, *The Eighteenth Brumaire of Louis Bonaparte* (Chicago: Kerr, 1919), pp. 9–10.

Marx praised the Paris Commune for, the Marxist movement neither wanted nor achieved."[7]

With Lenin one enters a much more complex realm of affairs, for what Lenin apparently wanted from Marx's interpretation of the Commune he obviously was unable (or perhaps unwilling) to achieve. Lenin, of course, in reviving the revolutionary and utopian strains of original Marxism, made frequent and glowing references to the Commune as the model for the dictatorship of the proletariat, reiterated the major themes of *The Civil War in France* in *State and Revolution,* and described the Russian Soviets as identical with the Commune "in their social and political character." Yet nowhere is the gap between Leninist theory and practice more glaring than between the classic Marxian revolutionary principles so passionately proclaimed in *State and Revolution* and the actual policies Lenin pursued during and after the Bolshevik seizure of power. It was by no means accidental that the increasingly repressive and bureaucratic character of the new Soviet state was accompanied by the virtual disappearance of references to the Paris Commune in Lenin's writings and speeches after mid-1918. And it is entirely consistent with familiar patterns of postrevolutionary institutionalization that the political model of the Commune, along with Marxian socialist goals in general, should have become ritualized in Stalinist and "post-Stalinist" Russia. Here it need only be observed that Lenin's *State and Revolution* (however little it had to do with actual Soviet political practice) became a canonical text in the evolving Marxist-Leninist orthodoxy and thus served to transmit to other lands Marx's model of the Commune and the utopian revolutionary imagery associated with it.

Since Marxist theory celebrates the Paris Commune as the first historical example of the dictatorship of the proletariat, it is rather paradoxical that this model should have assumed special prominence in the thought and writings of Marxists in China who led a revolution in which the proletariat was only marginally involved. And it is even more curious that it was not before, but almost a decade after, the victory of 1949 that the Marxist image of the Paris Commune became a significant factor in Chinese Communist politics.

7. Martin Buber, *Paths in Utopia* (Boston: Beacon Press, 1958), p. 98.

Although Marx's interpretation of the Commune was known to China's first converts to Marxism in the early 1920s, there is little in the general history of Chinese Marxist thought—and even less in the history of the Communist revolution that Mao led—which foreshadowed the very special importance Maoists eventually came to attribute to it. To be sure, *State and Revolution* was one of the most influential of Marxist-Leninist writings from the very beginning of the Communist movement in China and it was by way of Lenin's famous pamphlet that Chinese Marxists were introduced to Marx's description of the Commune. The model of the Paris Commune became part of the Chinese Communist ideological heritage and was duly celebrated in standard Marxist-Leninist fashion over the years, but prior to recent years there was nothing distinctive about Chinese Marxist comments and commentaries on the subject. In the *Selected Works of Mao Tse-tung,* there appear only a few passing (and rather insignificant) references to the Paris Commune.

Given the nature of the revolutionary situation in China, there is, of course, no particular reason why Mao should have been drawn to the writings of Marx and Lenin on the Commune. For the Maoist strategy of mobilizing revolutionary peasant armies in the countryside to surround and eventually overwhelm the nonrevolutionary cities, nothing could have been less relevant than the classic model of urban proletarian revolution presented in *The Civil War in France.* The revolutionary self-activity of the urban proletariat which Marx so passionately praised in his description of the Paris Commune was totally incongruous with Mao's ardent faith in the revolutionary creativity of the rural masses and his longstanding distrust of the revolutionary capacities of the Chinese proletariat—and incongruous with his powerful antiurban biases in general. Moreover, in twentieth-century China (unlike nineteenth-century France and Tsarist Russia), there was no powerful, centralized bureaucratic state to destroy; rather the revolutionary task in China, as Mao perceived and practiced it for two decades, was to build new military and political organizational nuclei in an historical situation characterized by incredible political disintegration and fragmentation—and to do so in a process of "protracted revolutionary warfare." Thus the central theme of Marx's interpretation of the Paris Commune—the need to "smash" the existing centralized bureaucratic-military state apparatus and replace it with an entirely new form of political organization (the proletarian dictatorship) which would return to society as a whole the powers usurped by the state—was simply largely irrelevant to Chinese historical conditions prior to 1949.

Nor did Marxist-Leninist writings on the Paris Commune provide even ideological support for the Chinese Communist revolution or the post-1949 People's Republic. Whereas the Marxian significance of the Commune was that it was the model for the dictatorship of the proletariat, in Maoist theory (prior to the late 1950s) proletarian dictatorship was explicitly rejected as an unsuitable revolutionary formula for a country characterized by "semifeudal" and "semicolonial" conditions—and, in fact, was proclaimed to be unnecessary for the eventual achievement of socialism and communism. According to the Maoist modification of the Leninist notion of a "two-stage" revolutionary process for precapitalist lands, the Chinese revolution was to result in the establishment of "a new-democratic state," a "joint dictatorship" based on an alliance of the four "democratic classes" of workers, peasants, petty bourgeoisie, and national bourgeoisie. While this alliance of classes was to be led by the "proletariat," i.e. the Chinese Communist Party, Chinese historical conditions dictated, according to Mao, "a particular form of state and political power," a system of "new democracy" that was to be "different in principle from a socialist state under proletarian dictatorship" and one "distinguished from the Russian system."[8]

These views about a distinctively Chinese form of state, suggested in Mao's writings between 1939–1945, were reaffirmed and formally summarized in 1949. With the revolutionary victory of that year, Mao proclaimed not a dictatorship of the proletariat but rather a "people's democratic dictatorship," a term which became duly enshrined in the Constitution of 1954. What is noteworthy about Mao's well-known essay on that topic, and generally characteristic of Maoist theoretical writings until 1956, is the view that a socialist society could be built in China without the need for state power to take the orthodox Marxist form of the dictatorship of the proletariat. While

8. Mao Tse-tung, *On Coalition Government* (Peking: Foreign Languages Press, 1955), pp. 55–56. See also Mao Tse-tung, *On New Democracy* (Peking: Foreign Languages Press, 1954), passim.

Mao, in 1949, promised the classical Marxist vision of a classless society, in which "parties and the state machinery" would "lose their function, cease to be necessary [and] therefore gradually wither away and end their historical mission," this Chinese road to socialism and communism was to be travelled through the vehicle of a "people's dictatorship," not a proletarian dictatorship.[9] Nevertheless the road to socialism and communism was to be a long one, Mao implied, and the immediate needs of the time were political order and economic development.[10] In the increasingly institutionalized social and political conditions which resulted from the pursuit of these two tasks in the 1950s, the revolutionary utopian themes of Marx's interpretation of the Commune struck no particularly responsive chords. Although the anniversary of the Commune was one of eight official holidays decreed in the Constitution of the People's Republic, this ritualistic observance was no more than merely *historically* significant (to borrow Joseph Levenson's suggestive phrase),[11] no more than part of the general historical and ideological legacy handed down from one generation of Marxists to the next.

What made the Marxian concept of the Commune (and the revolutionary imagery it conveyed) *really* historically significant and a truly dynamic factor in Chinese Communist thought and politics was the unique Maoist attempt to forestall the bureaucratic degeneration of the revolution. The specifically "Maoist" policies pursued over the last two decades of the Maoist era reflected a distrust of working through formal state and party institutions and a growing faith that the more or less spontaneous activities of the masses (and especially the peasantry) could effect the radical social transformations Marxists envision. The tendency to bypass official bureaucratic channels by direct appeals to the masses (and to celebrate their inherent revolutionary creativity and socialist strivings) was apparent in the accelerated drive for agricultural collectivization in 1955–56 and especially

9. Mao Tse-tung, "On the People's Democratic Dictatorship," in Mao Tse-tung, *The Selected Works of Mao Tse-tung* (Peking: Foreign Languages Press, 1961), vol. 4, p. 411.

10. Ibid., pp. 412ff.

11. On the utility of the distinction between the "merely *historically* significant" and the "historically really *significant*," see the fascinating discussion in Joseph Levenson, *Confucian China and Its Modern Fate* (Berkeley: University of California Press, 1965), vol. 3, especially pp. 85–125.

in the communization program of the Great Leap Forward period. Behind this tendency lay a Maoist perception that existing state and party organs were no longer effective instruments for achieving Marxian socialist ends—and a Maoist fear that the works of the revolution were threatened by an increasingly routinized political apparatus which stood above society and by new bureaucratic elites separated from the masses and potentially hostile to Marxist goals and Maoist values.

It was by no means entirely coincidental that the growing Maoist suspicion of existing state and party organizations was accompanied (in the realm of theory) by an increasing Maoist emphasis on the notion of the dictatorship of the proletariat. Whereas it had been standard Chinese Marxist doctrine that peculiar Chinese historical conditions permitted the attainment of socialism and communism through a "people's dictatorship" (which, as noted, was explicitly distinguished from the concept of the "dictatorship of the proletariat"), in 1956 and after it became standard Maoist doctrine that the "dictatorship of the proletariat" was essential to the achievement of Marxist ends—a view that was to become a central ideological theme of the Cultural Revolution. The distinctively Maoist treatise of 1956 "On the Historical Experience of the Dictatorship of the Proletariat" proclaimed both its universal validity and its particular Chinese historical necessity.[12] Since original Marxist theory identifies the Paris Commune as the model for the dictatorship of the proletariat, it is hardly surprising to observe a growing Chinese interest in classic Marxist writings on the lessons of the 1871 Parisian uprising. Nonetheless, the question of what constitutes "proletarian dictatorship," and the particular form that it would or should take in China, remained (and indeed remains) highly ambiguous.

II. The Paris Commune and Chinese People's Communes

In view of the increasing Maoist emphasis on the concept of the dictatorship of the proletariat in the late 1950s, it is of some interest

12. *On the Historical Experience of the Dictatorship of the Proletariat* (Peking, 1959). The document appeared originally on 5 April 1956 as an editorial in the *People's Daily*.

to note certain political implications of the Great Leap Forward campaign. In examining the theoretical literature on the communization movement in 1958, it is difficult to escape the impression that Maoists originally conceived the rural people's communes as organs of "proletarian dictatorship," albeit *sans* urban proletariat. The communes were to be not only more or less self-sufficient socioeconomic units (combining industry with agriculture and education with productive activities—two of the classically defined functions of the "transition" period), but they also were seen as organs of revolutionary political power. The Maoist theoretician Kuan Feng, for example, interpreted the commune's appropriation of the administrative function of the *hsiang* as making the commune not only a new form of social and economic organization but, more importantly, a political unit "performing the functions of state power" and "the most desirable organizational form" for the period of the transition from socialism to communism.[13] At the same time, editorials in *Red Flag* and *People's Daily* stressed that the communes were not mere productive organizations but rather ones which "combined economic, cultural, political and military affairs,"[14] and merged "workers, peasants, merchants, students and militiamen into a single entity."[15] Special emphasis was placed on the political role of the commune, the "merging" of the basic economic organization of society with the basic "organs of state power,"[16] and on the crucial role of the commune in carrying out the "transition from socialism to communism," a process during which the internal functions of the state (now theoretically assigned to the commune) would gradually disappear.[17] Indeed, in the Maoist vision of 1958, the people's commune was to be the agency to perform all the social and political

13. Kuan Feng, "A Brief Discussion on the Great Historical Significance of People's Communes," *Che-hsüeh yen-chiu* [Philosophic research] 5 (1958). The *hsiang* is the basic and lowest unit in the state administrative structure, generally encompassing several villages and a local market town.

14. *Jen-min jih-pao* [People's daily] editorial, 3 September 1958.

15. Wu Chih-pu, "From Agricultural Producer Cooperatives to People's Communes," *Hung Ch'i* [Red flag] 8 (August 1958). For a translation see *Selections from Chinese Mainland Magazines,* 147:1–10.

16. Ibid., p. 5.

17. Kuan Feng, "A Brief Discussion."

tasks which Marxists traditionally have identified with the "transition period" of the dictatorship of the proletariat—everything from the abolition of the distinctions between town and countryside, between mental and manual labor, between industry and agriculture, and between workers and peasants to the very "withering away" of the state itself. The commune was to be "the organizer of living" as well as the organizer of production; it was conceived as the means to realize ultimate communist ends as well as the embryonic social unit of the future communist utopia.[18]

Quite apart from other similarities, there is a rather striking affinity between this Maoist scheme for the decentralization of political power in the people's communes and Marx's "federalist" inclinations in his analysis of the Paris Commune. The Commune, Marx had observed, was not to be a centralized, Jacobin-type dictatorship over all of France, but rather was to serve as a model for more or less autonomous communal units in the rural provinces as well as for the secondary industrial centers; the old centralized form of government would "have to give way to the self-government of the producers" in the local areas. "In a rough sketch of national organization which the Commune had no time to develop," Marx wrote with apparent approval, "it is clearly stated that the Commune was to be the political form of even the smallest country hamlet" and "the rural communes of each district were to administer their common affairs by an assembly of delegates in the central town."[19] Moreover, the decentralization of administrative functions into the hands of the actual producers was not relegated to a distant communist future but was seen as an integral part of the revolutionary process itself, a process in which the Commune (and the communes) would function as political organs for revolutionary social change while at the same time shedding their purely political character. Although Lenin later insisted that Marx showed no "deviation" from centralism in this conception of the dictatorship of the proletariat, it is interesting to note

18. See Wu Ch'uan-ch'i, "Communism Seen Through People's Communes," *Jen-min jih-pao* [People's daily] 1 October 1958 in *Survey of the China Mainland Press,* 1887:9–13, for a typical example.

19. Karl Marx, "The Civil War in France." From the 1902 translation reprinted in Karl Marx and Friedrich Engels, *The Paris Commune* (New York: Labor News Co., 1965), pp. 75–77.

that Engels (who was certainly more given to centralist proclivities than Marx) praised the Commune's plans for a "free federation" of local communes as opposed to "those agencies of oppression in a centralized government."[20] And in his well-known critique of the 1891 Erfurt program, Engels criticized German centralist tendencies by pointing to earlier French revolutionary precedents where "every French department [and] every parish" possessed "complete self-administration."[21]

The extent to which the Maoist conception of the decentralization of political power in the people's communes was influenced by earlier Marxian writings on the Paris Commune is problematic. The similarity, however, did not go unnoticed at the time. A Chinese Marxist theoretician writing in September 1958, for example, observed that "the integration of the *hsiang* with the commune will make the commune not very different from the Paris Commune, integrating the economic organization with the organization of state power."[22] More important than the possible influence of Marxist precedents is that the political function which Maoists originally assigned to the communes posed a fundamental challenge to existing party and state bureaucracies. Had the people's communes actually developed in the manner Maoists first envisioned, centralized political power in China would have been gravely undermined—much in the way in which Marx attributed to the Paris Commune the potentiality of restoring to the producers those social powers which had been usurped by the state. As matters turned out, the economic and organizational chaos of 1959–60 (which Mao later attributed in part to the resistance of a conservative bureaucracy) gravely undermined Maoist plans for the people's communes—and the latter emerged only in modified and disfigured form.

The problem for Maoists became acute—and acutely political—with the forced retreat from the radical socioeconomic policies of the

20. In his Introduction to the 1891 German edition of Marx, "The Civil War in France," p. 17.

21. Karl Marx and Friedrich Engels, *Werke* (Berlin: Dietz, 1963), vol. 22, p. 236.

22. Wu Chih-pu, "On People's Communes," *Chung-kuo ch'ing-nien pao* [China youth journal], 16 September 1958 in *Selections from Chinese Mainland Magazines*, 524:5.

Great Leap Forward period, and the reassertion of the power of regular state and party bureaucracies in the early 1960s. While Mao remained the master of ideology, others paying little more than lip service to Maoist ideas and slogans were the masters of political and economic organization—and of science and technology. While Maoists were proclaiming the theory of "permanent revolution," Chinese society was dominated by the seeming permanence of bureaucracy. At no time in the history of the People's Republic was the gap between theory and practice so great and so glaring.

III. The Paris Commune and the Cultural Revolution

That most extraordinary historical phenomenon known as the Great Proletarian Cultural Revolution, which burst forth in the spring of 1966, was (among many other things) a dramatic attempt to close the gap between radical Maoist social theory and conservative bureaucratic social and political practice. One of the most striking features of the Cultural Revolution was the remarkable charge that not only the state but also the party (in large measure) had fallen into the hands of "counterrevolutionary revisionists" and authorities "taking the capitalist road," who, it was alleged, had betrayed the "dictatorship of the proletariat," established organs of "bourgeois dictatorship," and were preparing the way for the restoration of capitalism.

No less remarkable were the proposed remedies. Presumably degenerate state and party bureaucracies were not to be reformed from within—or rectified by other bureaucracies from without—but rather were to be overthrown by mass revolutionary action from below. To the masses came Maoist directives that "to rebel is justified" and injunctions to "struggle to seize power." And as the Cultural Revolution turned increasingly political, one of the most celebrated slogans of the time, drawn from the lessons of the Paris Commune, was "the Marxist principle of smashing the old state machinery."

Thus, in the early phases of the Cultural Revolution, existing state and party organs were condemned as conservative and potentially counterrevolutionary structures opposed to the general interests of society—and the presumably revolutionary masses were encouraged to "seize," "overthrow," and "smash" them and in their place establish true forms of "proletarian dictatorship." It was in this political and ideological context that the example of the Paris Commune was removed from the museum of Marxian historical exhibits and declared relevant to the making of history in the present. In the chaotic political struggles of the Cultural Revolution, the "Paris Commune" was invoked as the model for the restructuring of political power, and the revolutionary battle cries that Marx and Lenin attributed to the Communards were heard throughout the land. A celebrated Marxist interpretation of a long-past European historical event came (for a time) to be celebrated as a guide for contemporary Chinese political action.

To return, then, to a question which was posed earlier: why did the example of the nineteenth-century Paris Commune assume such prominence in the twentieth-century Chinese Cultural Revolution? One answer, of course, is that immediate Maoist political purposes were served. If the Chinese Communist state and party had fallen into "bourgeois" hands and were becoming parasitic bureaucratic structures, as was alleged, then revolutionary Marxism demanded the destruction of these oppressive forms of political power. The Commune provided a historical example and a source of revolutionary inspiration for the masses to rally to the Maoist call for a rebellion to return political power to true "proletarian" revolutionaries. And it provided Maoists with the theoretical support of the classic Marxist model of proletarian revolution.

Yet the Chinese revival of the original Marxist view of the Paris Commune was not simply a matter of immediate political utility and ideological convenience. No less significant than the role of the Commune model in the politics of the Cultural Revolution were notions and ideas in Marxist writings on the Commune which Maoists found intellectually attractive as well as politically useful. Indeed, it was precisely because there were striking affinities between basic tendencies in Maoist thought and themes which Marx announced in interpreting the events of 1871 that the Marxian model of the Commune acquired a particular Maoist political utility—and it is this broader realm of intellectual affinity which makes the matter more than one of purely transient interest.

Without undertaking a detailed analysis of Chinese Marxist writings on the Paris Commune, several of the more prominent themes should briefly be noted. First and foremost, Maoists drew from the original Marxian interpretation of the Commune powerful support for their profoundly antibureaucratic impulses and their general hostility to formal state organizations and institutions. What is especially noteworthy is that Maoist writings not only stressed the standard Marxist-Leninist formula that the old state machinery must be destroyed and not simply taken over (although that particular "lesson" of the Commune invariably appeared) but also placed special emphasis on the general Marxist notion that a true "proletarian dictatorship" must be "a basic negation" of state power.[23] A recognition of the need to "smash" what Marx referred to as "the ubiquitous organs of standing army, police [and] bureaucracy" was accompanied by a general concern with the question of the nature and organization of political power in the postrevolutionary era and a deep anxiety that a new parasitic bureaucracy could all too easily once again rise to stand above society. The crucial question posed in Chinese Marxist literature on the Commune—and especially during the time of the Cultural Revolution—was, as it typically was put, the question of "how to prevent state organs under the dictatorship of the proletariat from degenerating into the opposite of what they were intended to be," to forestall the threat of the state "changing from the servant to the master of society,"[24] a phrase borrowed from Engels' Introduction to the 1891 German edition of *The Civil War in France*.

The measures which many Maoists proposed to deal with this problem were precisely those antibureaucratic safeguards which the Communards introduced and which Marx had hailed with such great enthusiasm. In order to restore political power to society, the producers were to be organized in working (and not parliamentary) bodies which combined executive and legislative functions and which were to carry out the revolutionary tasks of socialist transformation. Such administrative functions as were socially necessary were to be performed not by appointed officials but by those selected from and by

23. Liu, "The General Election System," p. 1. On the role of the Paris Commune in the ideology and politics of the Cultural Revolution, see John Bryan Starr, "Revolution in Retrospect: The Paris Commune Through Chinese Eyes," *The China Quarterly* 49 (January–March 1972):106–25.

24. Chen Chih-ssu, "Great Revelations of the Paris Commune," *Hung Ch'i* [Red flag], 24 March 1966, in *JPRS* 35137 (21 April 1966):14–17.

the masses, persons who were to be directly responsible to (and constantly supervised by) the people, and who were subject to immediate popular dismissal and replacement. And those performing public service were to do so at ordinary workers' wages and were not to be granted special privileges or status. Such were some of the more practical political "lessons" which Maoists derived from Marx's description of the Paris Commune. The importance of these measures were emphasized time and again in Chinese writings on the Commune, for they accorded with the longstanding Maoist hostility to bureaucracy and with the idealized egalitarian political practices Maoists celebrated as part of their own revolutionary heritage.

The powerful antibureaucratic and egalitarian impulses which characterize Marx's description of the Commune—and which received special attention in Maoist commentaries on the subject—were closely related to another Marxian theme which Maoists prized: a faith in the spontaneous revolutionary creativity of the masses. The nonbureaucratic picture of proletarian dictatorship that Marx drew rested on the creative and heroic qualities of the Parisian workers which he so eloquently praised in *The Civil War in France*. Nowhere does he discuss the role of parties or even say much about leaders. The entire emphasis is on the initiatives undertaken by the workers themselves—for in the Commune, Marx above all found historical confirmation of his original confidence in "the revolutionary self-activity" of the proletariat. It is this confidence in the revolutionary potential of the masses that Maoists found so appealing in quoting from (or paraphrasing) Marx's account, even though it was the revolutionary spontaneity of the people in general (rather than that of the urban proletariat in particular) that was celebrated. And thus when Chinese writers characterized the Paris Commune as "a crystallization of the creativity of the masses" and argued that it was "the activism and initiative of the masses which was the source of the strength of the Commune,"[25] they both reflected and reinforced Mao Tse-tung's own longstanding (and non-Leninist) faith in "the inherent socialist activism of the masses."

Several other aspects of Marx's analysis of the Paris Commune, often neglected in Western Marxist writings, occupy a prominent

25. Ibid., pp. 12, 14.

place in Chinese Marxist interpretations. Of particular interest is the manner in which Marx blends nationalist and internationalist themes. Although the Commune, as the product of a genuine proletarian revolution, was necessarily basically internationalist in character and purpose, the Communards nonetheless were the true defenders of the French nation against foreign invaders. The workers' government was "emphatically internationalist," Marx wrote, yet at the same time, the Commune was "the true representative of all the healthy elements of French society and therefore the truly national Government" in resistance to the Prussian army.[26] By contrast, bourgeois counterrevolutionaries were seen as being driven by their class interests into becoming national traitors; in the conflict between national duty and class interest, Marx declared, "the Government of National Defense did not hesitate one moment to turn into a Government of National Defection."[27] Adolphe Thiers, the epitome of bourgeois class corruption, was portrayed as the leader of bourgeois national capitulation to the foreign enemy—the instigator of a civil war carried on "by the special permission of Bismarck," the solicitor of "the immediate occupation of Paris by Prussian troops," and the leader of "a slaveholders' rebellion protected by foreign invasion."[28] Whereas the history of the Commune proved that the bourgeoisie—by recognizing Prussia as "the supreme arbiter in internal French politics"—was no longer capable of disguising class rule "in national uniform,"[29] the Parisian workers proved to be the defenders of French national integrity as well as the harbingers of international proletarian revolution. From Marx's comments on the Paris Commune, it is easy enough to derive the notion (as Chinese Marxist writers have) that there is nothing inconsistent between a national war against foreign aggression and the international character and mission of the proletariat. The picture of bourgeois class rule taking on a reactionary and spurious "international" character, while proletarian revolutionaries become genuinely "national" in pursuing genuinely internationalist aims, was highly attractive to Maoists—for it provided a Marxist sanction to reconcile their strongly Chinese

26. Marx, "The Civil War in France," p. 84.
27. Ibid., pp. 47–48.
28. Ibid., pp. 51–59, 69.
29. Ibid., pp. 95, 104.

nationalist impulses with their internationalist claims and aspirations.[30]

Another theme of special contemporary Chinese relevance is the antitraditionalist strain in Marx's analysis of the Commune. For Marx the Communards attempted not only a revolutionary break with the old socioeconomic and political order but also a radical break with the conservative traditions, habits and values of the past in general. In the French situation the focus was on the destruction of the repressive "spiritual force" and "parson-power" of the Church; this was to be accompanied, Marx observed, by the freeing of science and education in general from "the fetters which class prejudice and governmental force had imposed" upon them.[31] In the original Marxian conception of proletarian revolution, it was presupposed that the emergent new society would radically devalue all of the traditions, beliefs and values associated with the doomed old society. This antitraditionalist impulse which Marx attributed to the Commune frequently has been noted in Chinese Marxist writings, for it was very much in accord with the Maoist belief that material social and economic change must be accompanied by a "spiritual transformation" which will bring forth "new men" freed from the burden of old habits and ideas. It was thus particularly relevant to the era of the Cultural Revolution when the call for "proletarian revolution" was accompanied by a fiercely iconoclastic assault on all traditional values and beliefs.

Chinese Marxists have emphasized many other themes in Marx's description of the Commune. The acts of revolutionary heroism and the ascetic values of devotion and self-sacrifice for which Marx so ardently praised the Communards were no less fulsomely reproduced and celebrated in Maoist accounts. Many of the grandly heroic char-

30. It is interesting to observe that it is this "nationalist" aspect of proletarian revolution which was emphasized in perhaps the earliest Chinese commentary on the Paris Commune—by Li Ta-chao (the first Chinese convert to Marxism) in 1923. "The people of Paris," he stressed, "rose up to resist a traitorous government." "I-pa-ch'i-i nien ti Pa-li 'K'ang-miao-ssu' " [The Paris "Commune" of 1871] in Li Ta-chao, *Li Ta-chao Hsüan-chi* [Selected writings of Li Ta-chao] (Peking: Jen-min ch'u-pan she, 1959), pp. 447–56. The general theme reappears in much of recent Chinese Marxist literature on the Commune.

31. Marx, "Civil War in France," pp. 74–75.

acteristics of the Commune which Marx extolled were precisely what Maoists prized in their own revolutionary history and what they celebrated as the spirit of "revolutionary romanticism." Marx's description of simple workers efficiently performing the tasks of displaced bourgeois officials and experts nourished the general Maoist distaste for occupational specialization and fortified the Maoist faith in the "self-reliant" masses capable of mastering all specialized technological knowledge as well as basic administrative functions. Particular attention was given to Marx's comments about the necessity of proletarian revolutionary violence to counter inevitable bourgeois violence (thus reaffirming the well-known Maoist maxim that the masses must recognize "the importance of taking weapons in their own hands") and, as the suppression of the Commune proved, the need for constant revolutionary vigilance and even ruthlessness in the face of the "savagery" and "barbarism" of the forces of counterrevolution (thus offering Marxist historical testimony to the Cultural Revolution slogans that "the revolution must be carried through to the end" and that "the enemy must be given no breathing spell"). Marx's general picture of the Commune (and therefore of the "dictatorship of the proletariat") as a community of armed workers also was reproduced to support Maoist notions that proletarian revolution necessarily involves the militarization of the masses, the Maoist emphasis on the importance of the people's militia, and the Maoist distrust of a professionalized standing army.

IV. Maoism and Marxism

There is of course much (and much that is crucial) which separates Maoism from classical Marxist theory. Marx's faith, after all, rested with the actual proletariat as the agent of universal human liberation, and the dictatorship of the proletariat was the agency by which that class would carry out its appointed historical mission. For Maoists, "proletarian dictatorship" was not exercised by the proletariat as such but rather by those deemed to possess "proletarian consciousness." While the cluster of beliefs and values which constitute this "consciousness" has been defined and redefined in Maoist ideology, its particular social carrier is not so easy to identify. "Proletarian consciousness" was neither an attribute of a specific social class (as

Marx believed), nor, for that matter, did it reside in a specific institution (the Communist party, as Lenin insisted). Although the claim was made that Mao developed and enriched the experience of the Paris Commune, the social and political content of the Maoist version of the "dictatorship of the proletariat" remained vague and unfulfilled.

While one may ponder the ambiguous implications of the Maoist use of the term "dictatorship of the proletariat," there can be little doubt that Maoists looked to the rural people's communes as the main institutional basis for revolutionary social and economic transformation. Here one observes another obvious departure from classical Marxism. Whereas Marx assumed that the proletarian revolutionary process necessarily would bring "the rural producers under the intellectual lead of the central towns," as he put it in his report on the Paris Commune, Mao's revolutionary hopes rested primarily on a faith in the creative energies of the peasantry. In Maoist eyes, it was the communes of the countryside upon which the survival and continuation of the revolution depended.

On the most fundamental issue raised in Marx's analysis of the Commune—the relationship between state and society—the Maoist view remained rather equivocal. Even though the Maoist orientation was profoundly antibureaucratic and exhibited a good deal of hostility to centralized state power, Chinese Marxist theorists were reluctant to fully accept the original Marxist proposition that all political power is a form of alienated social power, just as they failed to confront the problem of human self-alienation in general. There has been, to be sure, a greater concern with the question of the relation between state and society than generally has been the case with Marxists in power, and Maoists explicitly have rejected the Stalinist (and typically conservative) notion of an organic, nonantagonistic relationship between state and people. Yet there remained an unresolved tension between Leninist and Stalinist conceptions of the leading role of a strong state in promoting postrevolutionary social and economic development, on the one hand, and a general Populist-type distrust of the state on the other. The latter tendency was often reinforced by quotations from Marx on the alien nature of state power, but the discussions of this matter are much too brief (and usually much too superficial) to determine whether the question ever was one of genuinely serious theoretical concern.

Despite these and other obvious differences, many aspects of the original Marxian conception of proletarian revolution struck responsive chords in the Maoist mentality. The utopian strains in Marx's description of the Paris Commune were revived and popularized because they were intellectually and politically conducive to promoting that "uninterrupted" process of radical social transformation seen as essential for the survival of the revolution. In China the revolution was to continue; its thrust was to change the world in accordance with the Maoist vision of ultimate Marxist social goals, and not to fall victim to what Maoists called the "typical pragmatic fallacy" of "adaptation to reality." The concepts and images derived from the model of the Paris Commune served for a time as a stimulus for change and as a barrier against tendencies to institutionalize existing social and political reality.

It is indeed more than dubious that the principles of the Marxian model of the Commune have had (or will have) any lasting influence on the political life of the People's Republic; yet the Maoist celebration of the Paris Commune is a matter of more than passing intellectual and historical significance. The appeal to the classic Marxist model of the dictatorship of the proletariat was not only one way Maoists attempted to reassert their political and ideological authority, it was also a way to reaffirm Mao's claim to be the true heir of Marx. For when Chinese Marxists invoked the revolutionary tradition of the Paris Commune, as that tradition was created by Marx, they looked across Russia to the "workingmen's Paris" that Marx proclaimed would be "forever celebrated as the glorious harbinger of a new society." And in looking across Russia to Paris, they implicitly rejected much of the Russian Revolution, or at least (and less implicitly) condemned the contemporary results of that revolution. It is rare to find a Chinese commentary on the Paris Commune that fails to point to the Soviet Union as a "negative example" in the history of postrevolutionary society. And thus the assertion that only Maoists are capable of exercising "proletarian dictatorship" in accordance with the principles of the Commune served to support the larger claim that Mao had raised Marxism to a "higher stage" by resolving the theoretical and practical revolutionary problems which the Russians proved incapable of solving. Unlike "Soviet revisionists," Maoist revolutionaries, it was said, had both the will and theoretical understanding to prevent "the restoration of capitalism," to build and maintain genuine forms of "proletarian dictatorship," and thereby to prepare the way for the transition to socialism and communism.

Much more was involved in these grandiose claims than the desire to score political points in anti-Soviet polemical battles. Also very much reflected in them was a universal human need to feel part of a living historical tradition that establishes some coherent relationship between past, present and a conception of a socialist future that is to be. Having rejected both traditional Chinese and modern Soviet precedents, Maoists attempted to fill the void by searching for roots in original Marxist sources, by tying Mao to Marx in an uncorrupted and universally valid tradition of Marxist revolutionary history. Chinese claims that they inherited and enriched the Marxian concept of the Commune reflected this search for a link to a viable and useful past—and this is one reason why Maoists felt the need to "conjure up into their service the spirits of the past" and use "borrowed language" to enact new revolutionary dramas.

Thus the Maoist search for roots in the Marxist tradition had an important psychological dimension as well as a political and ideological significance. For, as E. H. Carr has suggested, those who believe that they are going somewhere in history must believe that they have come from somewhere as well.[32] Maoists wished to believe that they came from the revolutionary Marxist tradition, for that is a tradition which not only sanctions, but also demands, radical departures from the present in order to create a radically new future.

32. Edward Hallett Carr, *What Is History?* (New York: Vintage Books, 1967), p. 176.

6

The Cult of Mao Tse-tung

In April 1956 the leaders of the Chinese Communist Party made their first official response to Nikita Khrushchev's "secret" speech denouncing Stalin and his "cult of personality," delivered almost two months before at the closing session of the Twentieth Soviet Party Congress. The Chinese commentary, which appeared in the form of a lengthy editorial in the *People's Daily*, offered a rather orthodox Marxist explanation of the phenomenon of "personality cults," attributing it to the survivals of agrarian backwardness:

> The cult of the individual is a foul carry-over from the long history of mankind. The cult of the individual is rooted not only in the exploiting classes but also in the small producers. As is well known, patriarchism is a product of a small-producer economy.[1]

Although Russia's small-producer economy had been abolished a quarter of a century earlier, the Chinese editorial explained that "certain rotten, poisonous ideological survivals of the old society may still remain in people's minds for a very long time." The cult of the individual was a reflection of this persisting "force of habit of millions," and Stalin had unfortunately succumbed to the influences

1. "On the Historical Experience of the Dictatorship of the Proletariat," in Robert R. Bowie and John K. Fairbank, eds., *Communist China 1955–1959: Policy Documents* (Cambridge, Mass.: Harvard University Press, 1962), p. 147.

of a "backward ideology," thereby "bringing losses to the cause and hampering the initiative and creativeness of the masses of the people."[2]

The commentary failed to mention that China's far more massive and deeply ingrained small-producer economy was only just then in the process of being abolished in the course of the agricultural collectivization campaign of 1955–56. If the Stalin cult was attributable to the "ideological survivals" of Russia's agrarian backwardness, then Chinese soil clearly provided far more fertile ground for the growth of such a cult. But it was nonetheless suggested that the Chinese Communist Party, unlike the Russian, had established the necessary political safeguards against the "cult of the individual": a tradition of "relying on the wisdom of the masses"; prudence and modesty among leaders; the proper practice of Leninist principles of "democratic centralism"; and especially methods of leadership based on the hallowed principles of "the mass line." The Chinese Communist Party, it was claimed, "has incessantly fought against elevation of oneself and against individualistic heroism."[3]

Yet if the Chinese Communist Party was opposed to "the cult of the individual," this was not necessarily the case with its Chairman and many of his more ardent supporters. Just two years after the Chinese response to Khrushchev's famous speech, with the launching of the Great Leap Forward campaign in 1958, Mao Tse-tung was to do precisely what Khrushchev had condemned Stalin for doing, although not necessarily for the same reasons and purposes—he was to "place himself above the party,"[4] appearing on the historical scene as supreme leader and utopian prophet, largely bypassing formal political institutions and speaking directly to and for the masses. And half a decade later, during the Great Proletarian Cultural Revolution, the cult of Mao was to manifest itself in forms far more extreme than Stalin's "personality cult" ever had assumed.

2. Ibid.

3. Ibid., p. 148.

4. The phrase is taken from Khrushchev's February 1956 speech and was the Soviet leader's main explanation for the evils of the Stalin era.

I. The History of the Mao Cult

Although the cult of Mao Tse-tung (and the more bizarre rituals it generated) was not to emerge full-blown until the Cultural Revolution of the late 1960s, its origins are to be found in China's rural hinterlands three decades earlier, during a more heroic and legendary time in the history of the Chinese Communist movement. When Edgar Snow made his way to the tiny Communist base area in the mountains of northern Shensi province in 1936 to interview Mao Tse-tung—at a time when Mao was best known to the outside world (and to most of the Chinese world) for the $250,000 bounty Chiang K'ai-shek had offered for his head—Snow discovered that the 43-year old Mao was already known in the Red areas as a man who led "a charmed life."[5] That perception undoubtedly owed much to the heroic ordeal of the Long March, concluded only a year before. For those few who survived that incredible six-thousand mile trek through the wilderness, and for the many more who were inspired by the story of their miraculous survival, there emerged a faith in Mao as the prophet who would lead his devoted followers to the promised land. The Long March was not only the time when Mao achieved political supremacy in the Chinese Communist Party; it was also an experience that lent a sacred character to the revolutionary mission he now led—and led to a belief that Mao was the invincible One who was destined to successfully complete that mission. Indeed, the stories and legends which emerged from the Long March often read like Biblical tales of Moses and the Exodus. And the traditions and beliefs born in the early days of the Yenan era retained their sacred character three decades later, when, during the Cultural Revolution of 1966, youthful Red Guards embarked on their own exhausting "long marches" as testimony to their faith in Mao and in the power of his "thought."

Yet it was among the peasants living in and around the early Communist base areas, perhaps more than among the veterans of the Long March, that the emerging cult of Mao found its deepest and most significant roots. The Red Army, formally commanded by Chu Teh, was popularly known as the "Mao-Chu army," but in some of

5. Edgar Snow, *Red Star Over China* (New York: Random House, 1938), p. 67.

the more remote areas of the Chinese countryside "Mao-Chu" was thought to be a single personage who would free the peasants from their oppressors and restore justice in the world. As Party history was rewritten to magnify the revolutionary accomplishments of Mao, and diminish the role of other leaders, the Mao-Chu myth soon became the Mao myth, the savior who promised deliverance from suffering.[6]

Suggestions of the peasant sources of the Mao cult are to be found in the early observations of that first and most perceptive of students of the Chairman, Edgar Snow. In writing his first "subjective impressions" of Mao in 1937, Snow dismissed the notion that there could be any one "savior" of China, but went on to prophetically observe:

> Yet undeniably you feel a certain force of destiny in him. It is nothing quick or flashy, but a kind of solid elemental vitality. You feel that whatever extraordinary there is in this man grows out of the uncanny degree to which he synthesizes and expresses the urgent demands of millions of Chinese, and especially the peasantry—those impoverished, underfed, exploited, illiterate, but kind, generous, courageous and just now rather rebellious human beings who are the vast majority of the Chinese people. If these demands and the movement which is pressing them forward are the dynamics which can regenerate China, then in this deeply historical sense Mao Tse-tung may possibly become a very great man.[7]

"As yet, at least," Snow noted, there was "no ritual of hero-worship built up around him," but "the role of his personality in the movement was clearly immense."[8] And, no less prophetically, Snow commented: "Yet I doubt very much he would ever command great respect from the intellectual elite of China, perhaps not entirely because he has an extraordinary mind, but because he has the personal habits of a peasant. The Chinese disciples of Pareto might think him uncouth."[9]

6. As the history of the Party was rewritten, the title "Father of the Red Army," originally conferred on Chu Teh, was transferred to Mao.

7. Snow, *Red Star Over China*, pp. 66–67.

8. Ibid., p. 69.

9. Ibid., p. 73.

The popular cult that had begun to grow around Mao Tse-tung during the early days of the Yenan era was soon reinforced by official decrees. The rectification campaign of 1942–44 established Mao's writings as the orthodox ideology of the Chinese Communist Party. Party historians began to rewrite the history of the revolution to place Mao at the center of political events since the May Fourth era. The Seventh Party Congress in 1945 not only solidified Mao's political supremacy but also canonized "The Thought of Mao Tse-tung" as the sole guide for the Party's policies and actions. Indeed, the congress was largely a celebration of Mao's leadership. All speakers at the congress lavished praise on Mao and his thought, but, ironically, no one more ardently than Liu Shao-ch'i, who proclaimed Mao "the greatest revolutionary and statesman in Chinese history" and China's "greatest theoretician and scientist," and told the assembled delegates that the main task of the Party was to study the thought of Mao Tse-tung.[10] Several years later, in 1949, Liu declared that Mao's thought marked a new and higher stage in the development of a universally valid body of Marxist-Leninist theory, and proclaimed that "the road of Mao Tse-tung" was the revolutionary path to be followed by the peoples of all colonial and semicolonial countries.[11] Liu Shao-ch'i played no small part in fashioning the cult that was to bring about his own political downfall less than two decades later.

The Communist victory of 1949, the confirmation of Mao's prophecy of the triumph of the revolutionary countryside over the conservative cities, naturally served to enhance the Chairman's already enormous personal prestige and power—and to reinforce popular

10. Liu Shao-ch'i, *Collected Works of Liu Shao-ch'i* (Hong Kong: Union Research Institute, 1968), pp. 30–31.

11. Ibid., p. 179. In praising the accomplishments and the thought of Mao, Liu Shao-ch'i also took the lead in rewriting—and distorting—the history of the Revolution in the process. At the Seventh Party Congress in 1945, for example, he proclaimed that "following the road of Mao Tse-tung, our Party and the Chinese people launched the great pre-1927 revolutionary movement, of which Comrade Mao Tse-tung was the organizer. During the Agrarian Revolution (1927–37), the great Red Army was created with Comrade Mao Tse-tung as its founder and leader. In the War of Resistance to Japanese Aggression, the great liberated areas and the people's armed forces were created—the Eighth Route Army and the New Fourth Army, of which Comrade Mao Tse-tung was again the founder and the leader." (Ibid., p. 14).

perceptions that he was indeed a "savior" and "the star of salvation." Yet however great his personal power, during the early years of the People's Republic Mao did not use that power to impose his will on the new postrevolutionary Party-State, perhaps because the will of the leader and the policies of the Party largely coincided. To be sure, Mao suffered from no lack of popular and official adulation during the time; few official writings and speeches failed to pay due homage to the wisdom of the Chairman and the greatness of his thought.[12] But this already developing cult of Mao was not employed to break the bureaucratic rules which governed the functioning of the new state. The leader of the revolution, and the institutions that the revolution had produced, seemed to be in harmony.

That seemingly harmonious relationship was shattered in the summer of 1955 when Mao defied the majority of Party leaders by launching, very much on his own initiative, the accelerated drive for agricultural collectivization. His 31 July speech "On the Question of Agricultural Cooperation" was delivered not to the central committee of the Party, where Mao found himself in a minority on agrarian policy at the time, but rather to an informal gathering of provincial Party secretaries who happened to be in Peking for a session of the National People's Congress. Relying on his personal prestige, Mao bypassed and overruled the Party leadership and appealed to local rural Party cadres and, through them, to the rural masses. It was not until three months later that the Party central committee convened to formally ratify the collectivization campaign, which now was already well underway. The demonstration that a massive social movement involving hundreds of millions of peasants could be initiated by the words of the leader of the Party, and did not require the word of the Party as an institution, was one factor contributing to a new political climate conducive to the further growth of the Mao cult. The lesson was not lost on other Party leaders. As the veteran revolutionary Ch'en Yi caustically remarked at the time,

12. Typically, Ch'en Po-ta's 1951 treatise commemorating the thirtieth anniversary of the founding of the Chinese Communist Party concluded: "The theory of Mao Tse-tung is a development of Marxism-Leninism in the East. . . . for the entire world struggle as a whole, it is of universal significance." Ch'en Po-ta, *Mao Tse-tung on the Chinese Revolution* (Peking: Foreign Languages Press, 1953), p. 86.

Mao's speech on collectivization "settled the debate [on agrarian policy] of the past three years."[13]

No less significant for the blossoming of the cult was the manner in which Mao perceived the relationship between the Chinese Communist Party and the peasant masses in his July 1955 speech. It was a perception that harkened back to the "Hunan Report" of 1927, the document which had announced the appearance of "Maoism" on the political-ideological scene, and it was accompanied by a revival of much of the populist imagery and spirit of the revolutionary years. In 1927 Mao had found the true sources of revolutionary creativity residing not in the Party but rather in the spontaneous movement of the peasantry. It was not the Party that was to judge the revolutionary capacities of the peasantry but rather it was the actions of the peasants themselves that was to be the criterion to judge the revolutionary sufficiency of the Party. "All revolutionary parties and revolutionary comrades will stand before them [the peasants] to be tested, and to be accepted or rejected as they [the peasants] decide," Mao had declared in 1927.[14] In 1955 he once again contrasted a revolutionary peasantry with a party described as insufficiently revolutionary. While hailing the majority of peasants as striving for radical social change, Mao complained that many Party officials were "tottering along like a woman with bound feet." "As things stand today, the mass movement is in advance of the leadership," he declared, and Party leaders who argued that the collectivization movement was proceeding too rapidly and had "gone beyond the understanding of the masses" merely revealed their own lack of faith in the masses.[15] Implicit in these pronouncements was the claim that Mao himself, not the Party as such, best represented and expressed the desires and interests of the peasantry. It was a claim that served, consciously or not at the time, the purposes of cult-building.

13. As quoted in James P. Harrison, *The Long March to Power* (New York: Praeger, 1972), p. 470.

14. Mao Tse-tung, "Report of an Investigation into the Peasant Movement in Hunan," in Mao Tse-tung, *Selected Works of Mao Tse-tung* (London: Lawrence and Wishart, 1954), vol. I, p. 22.

15. Mao Tse-tung, "The Question of Agricultural Cooperation" (31 July 1955), in Bowie and Fairbank, eds., *Communist China 1955–1959: Policy Documents*, pp. 94 and 101.

Other Party leaders—and, not entirely coincidentally, many who were later to be among the political victims of the Mao cult—soon found the opportunity to blunt the growing personal dominance of Mao over affairs of state. Seizing upon Khrushchev's condemnation of Stalin's personality cult, Liu Shao-ch'i and Teng Hsiao-p'ing championed the principle of "collective leadership" at the Eighth Congress of the Chinese Communist Party held in September 1956—and they underscored the point by having the assembled delegates delete from the Party constitution the phrase that the Party was "guided by the Thought of Mao Tse-tung." And Teng, the eminently Leninist Secretary-General of the Party, declared: "Love for the leader is essentially an expression of love for the interests of the Party, the class, and the people, and not the deification of an individual."[16]

The tension between the Party and its Chairman intensified during the Hundred Flowers campaign when Mao, determined to break down bureaucratic resistance to the radically new socioeconomic policies he now was advocating, began again to question the revolutionary credentials of the Party. And by doing so, he fostered the political processes which were to make him more than simply the Chairman of the Party. Indeed, the crucial ideological rationale for the leadership cult, which was soon to blossom, was set forth by Mao himself in the most celebrated theoretical treatise of the time—the speech "On the Correct Handling of Contradictions Among the People." Delivered at a non-Party forum in February 1957, Mao enumerated many contradictions in Chinese society, but among them he emphasized the contradiction between "the leadership and the led," between the Party and "the people." In pursuing the matter, Mao suggested that responsibility for the contradiction rested more with the leaders of the Party than with the people they led, and further suggested that on certain issues Party leaders might be wrong and the people might be right. And if the Party was thus not ideologically infallible, as its Chairman now implied, it was therefore per-

16. Teng Hsiao-p'ing, "Report on the Revision of the Constitution of the Communist Party of China," delivered at the Eighth National Congress of the CCP, 16 September 1956. *Eighth National Congress of the Communist Party of China*, (Peking: Foreign Languages Press, 1956), vol. I (Documents), p. 200.

missible and indeed desirable for "the people" to criticize the Party from without—and for Party members to learn from criticisms and views which came from outside their ranks.[17]

The argument had profound implications for the relationship between the leader and the institution over which he presided. For if the people were now free to criticize a party which may have gone ideologically and politically astray, then who was ultimately to speak for "the people" if not Mao himself? Mao, after all, was not merely the Chairman of the Communist Party and Chairman of the People's Republic, but also, and more importantly, he was the acknowledged and celebrated leader of the people's revolution—and thereby possessed special bonds to the masses no one else could claim. If "the people" were to speak, then clearly it was Mao who was their preeminent spokesman. Mao was thus freed from the Leninist discipline of the Party and free to criticize the institution from without in his unique and transcendent role as the representative of the will and wisdom of "the people."

That was precisely the role Mao assumed in launching the Great Leap Forward campaign in 1958. During the rural communization movement, which aroused chiliastic expectations of the more or less immediate advent of a communist utopia, Mao appeared on the new historical stage in the guise of a utopian prophet who promised to lead those who followed his teachings and instructions to a classless and stateless society. Through direct and visionary appeals to the masses, Mao ignored and bypassed regular bureaucratic channels and established state and Party procedures—and, for a time, forged a direct bond between himself and the peasant masses, a bond between his own utopian visions and popular aspirations for social change and economic abundance. The chiliastic character of the early phase of the mass movement in the countryside was accompanied by an unprecedented glorification of both the person and thought of Mao Tse-tung.

Mao himself did not object to his deification and the semisacred aura that had come to surround the position of supreme leadership he had assumed. Indeed, he personally promoted the process. At the

17. Mao Tse-tung, *On the Correct Handling of Contradictions Among the People* (Peking: Foreign Languages Press, 1957), pp. 9 and 49–58.

beginning of the Great Leap, he provided a quasi-ideological rationale for personality cults by distinguishing between good and bad varieties. He observed in a secret speech delivered in March 1958:

> There are two kinds of the cult of the individual. One is correct, such as that of Marx, Engels, Lenin, and the correct side of Stalin. These we ought to revere and continue to revere forever. It would not do not to revere them. As they held truth in their hands, why should we not revere them? . . . Then there is the incorrect kind of cult of the individual in which there is no analysis, simply blind obedience. This is not right. Opposition to the cult of the individual may also have one of two aims: one is opposition to an incorrect cult, and the other is opposition to reverence for others and a desire for reverence for oneself. The question at issue is not whether or not there should be a cult of the individual, but rather whether or not the individual concerned represents the truth. If he does, then he should be revered.[18]

It is safe to assume that Mao believed he possessed the "truth," and thus deserved reverence.

Nor did Mao seem to have reservations about even the most blatantly petty forms of cult-building. He prefaced his remarks on "correct" and "incorrect" forms of personality cults, for example, by suggesting that he stood as high, if not higher, than Stalin in the Marxist pantheon and should be portrayed as such, complaining that "when Chinese artists [in the early 1950s] painted pictures of me together with Stalin, they always made me a little shorter, thus blindly knuckling under to the moral pressure exerted by the Soviet Union at that time."[19]

Reverence for Mao Tse-tung declined as the Great Leap campaign faltered, and the bond between Mao and the masses was undermined as the movement disintegrated into organizational chaos and economic crisis. Confronted with what was becoming an increasingly desperate struggle for sheer physical and national survival, utopian hopes faded, the hungry masses turned politically apathetic, and

18. Mao Tse-tung, "Talks at the Chengtu Conference" (10 March 1958), Stuart R. Schram, ed., *Mao Tse-tung Unrehearsed: Talks and Letters 1956–71* (Middlesex: Penguin Books, 1974), pp. 99–100.

19. Ibid., p. 99.

regular Party and state bureaucracies reestablished their authority. During the "bitter years" of 1960–62, Mao yielded the center of the political stage to those who wielded power in his name but ignored his policies and paid only ideological lip service to his "thoughts." It was a time when the Chairman was treated as "a dead ancestor," as he later complained. And it was a situation which created both a political and psychological need to refashion and revive the cult.

The process of cult-building which took place in the years immediately preceding the Cultural Revolution was markedly different in character than the previous manifestations of the phenomenon. Hitherto, the cult of Mao had been identified with the heroism of the revolutionary years and the radicalism of mass movements launched in the postrevolutionary era. It had grown in at least a partly spontaneous manner during the course of a distinctively Maoist revolutionary history that spanned the period from the heroics of the Long March to the utopianism of the Great Leap Forward campaign. In the early 1960s, by contrast, the rebuilding of the cult was undertaken at a time when a conservative Party and routinized state apparatus ruled a politically quiescent population. The cult of Mao was now a patently manufactured product, deliberately contrived for immediate political ends. And, incongruously, the task of fabricating it fell largely to the People's Liberation Army, the most bureaucratic and hierarchical agency of the state apparatus, but the one which provided Mao with his main political base at the time and the only institution he regarded as still uncorrupted by "revisionist" ideology. It was the Political Department of the Army that published the first edition of *Quotations from Chairman Mao* in May of 1964, and then proceeded to print almost a billion copies of "the little red book" over the following three years, along with 150 million copies of *The Selected Works of Mao Tse-tung*. It was the head of the Army, the then eminently Maoist Lin Piao, who orchestrated the 1964–65 campaign to study Mao's works, to the virtual exclusion of all other writings, and who made the most extravagant claims for the power of Mao's thought. "Comrade Mao Tse-tung is the greatest Marxist-Leninist of our era," Lin proclaimed, and his genius had raised the doctrine to "a higher and completely new stage." Masses and cadres alike were enjoined to "study Chairman Mao's writings, follow his teachings, act according to his instructions and be his good fighters," for once grasped by the people Mao's thought was "an inexhaustible source of strength" and nothing less than "a spiritual atomic bomb of infinite power."[20] The heroic figures popularized as models for emulation during the years immediately preceding the Cultural Revolution, moreover, were mostly PLA soldiers who invariably attributed their miraculous deeds to the inspiration derived from the "thought of Mao Tse-tung."

Although control over the Party apparatus remained largely in the hands of those Mao soon was to condemn as "capitalist roaders," by 1965 the Mao cult had become all-pervasive. When Edgar Snow visited the People's Republic in January of that year, he was shocked by the "immoderate glorification" of the Chairman:

> Giant portraits of him now hung in the streets, busts were in every chamber, his books and photographs were everywhere on display to the exclusion of others. In the four-hour revolutionary pageant of dance and song, *The East is Red,* Mao was the only hero. As a climax of that performance—presented with a cast of 2,000 . . . I saw a portrait copied from a photograph taken by myself in 1936, blown up to about thirty feet high. It gave me a mixed feeling of pride of craftsmenship and uneasy recollection of similar extravaganzas of worship of Joseph Stalin seen during the wartime years in Russia. . . . The one-man cult was not yet universal, but the trend was unmistakable.[21]

In a January 1965 interview with Snow, Mao candidly acknowledged the existence of the cult, and indeed acknowledged that he regarded personality cults as political assets, suggesting that Nikita Khrushchev's fall from power (which had occurred three months earlier) might well be attributed to the fact that Khrushchev "had no cult of personality at all."[22]

If the cult of Mao fashioned in the early 1960s was a contrived phenomenon, the events of the latter half of that decade dramatically demonstrated that its seemingly artificial character in no way dimin-

20. Lin Piao, *Quotations from Chairman Mao Tse-tung,* 2nd ed. (Peking: Foreign Languages Press, 1966), Foreword.

21. Edgar Snow, *The Long Revolution* (New York: Random House, 1972), pp. 68–69.

22. Ibid., p. 205.

ished its political potency. Personality cults, if they are to be historically significant, demand cult-worshippers—and the launching of the Cultural Revolution soon revealed that China was a land seething with discontented people longing to worship both the person and "thought" of Mao, and eager to vow loyalty to the now deified Chairman. When Mao issued the Cultural Revolutionary call for the masses to "dare to rebel" against the established authority of the Party and its organizations, tens of millions mobilized (or were mobilized) to do battle in what was described, in the typically chiliastic utopian terms of the time, as a "life and death" struggle to determine whether the revolution would survive to realize its socialist mission or degenerate into a "bourgeois restoration," and succumb to "ghosts, monsters, and demons," the deathly forces of counterrevolution. And in the course of the titanic and chaotic conflicts which ensued, Mao loomed larger than ever before as utopian prophet and supreme leader, directly linked to the "revolutionary masses" through his "thoughts" and his "vision," issuing "instructions" and "directives," which millions of faithful followers translated into new (and often bizarre) forms of revolutionary action.

The earliest and most ardent cult-worshippers of the Cultural Revolution were the youth of China, who viewed Mao as the sole repository of the purity of a romanticized revolutionary past and the prophet who promised to cleanse the corruptions of the present and create a radically new and better future. Those "courageous and daring pathbreakers," as Mao christened the Red Guards, travelled over the land in an iconoclastic crusade against the "four olds," carrying copies of "the little red book" (to which they often attributed semimagical properties), and issued manifestoes proclaiming that "supernatural powers" were to be derived from "Mao Tse-tung's great invincible thought." Political legitimacy was conferred on their sometimes dubious exploits on 18 August 1966, in one of the more chiliastic moments of the Cultural Revolution. Hundreds of thousands of Red Guards gathered in the square beneath the Gate of Heavenly Peace ecstatically awaiting the presence of Mao, who finally appeared at sunrise atop the gate in godlike fashion and donned a red armband to become "Supreme Commander" of the Red Guards.

The prominence of young people in the early phases of the Cultural Revolution conveyed the themes of revolutionary revivalism and rebirth which the cult of Mao symbolized and promoted. Had the movement which proceeded under the aegis of the cult remained a youth crusade, perhaps it might have proved little more than a somewhat exotic episode for sociological investigation. But the movement spread rapidly to encompass other social groups, and soon it became apparent that Mao-worshippers were to be found throughout Chinese society. By the latter months of 1966, the urban proletariat, China's most modern social class and a presumably secular one, responded to the Maoist call to rebel against the Communist Party and its organizations. The multitude of working-class organizations which appeared so massively and rapidly on the new Cultural Revolutionary political stage expressed a diversity of social grievances and economic interests, but all proclaimed total loyalty to Mao, professed faith in his teachings, and performed the rituals of his cult. And although the peasantry was only marginally involved in the battles of the Cultural Revolution, the Mao cult spread throughout the countryside as well. Villages constructed communal "rooms of loyalty" dedicated to Mao's thought, individual peasant households often had their own "tablets of loyalty" where family members gathered in mornings and evenings to pay reverence to the Chairman, and it became customary to recite sayings from "the little red book" before meals. The cult was so all-pervasive that even Mao's most formidable foes were forced to march (if they were to do any political marching at all) under Mao's banners and slogans. As Edgar Snow suggested: "In one sense the whole struggle (of the Cultural Revolution) was over control of the cult and by whom and above all 'for whom' the cult was to be utilized."[23] The question of "for whom" the cult was used will be addressed shortly.

One of the most striking features of the cult in its Cultural Revolution manifestations was its infusion with traditional religious symbolism. Just as Chinese emperors of old were "Sons of Heaven" whose virtue linked the social order with the cosmic order, so "Heaven" became the symbol of Mao and he was identified with the forces of the cosmos. In an uneasy fusion of traditional Chinese and modern revolutionary symbolism, the "Mao-sun" was hailed as "the reddest of all suns" whose radiance dwelt in the hearts of all true

23. Ibid., p. 66.

revolutionaries. Drawing on the imagery of Taoist mysticism, the "thoughts of Mao" were said to be a "magic weapon" that would vanquish his foes, while the foes themselves were condemned in demonic Buddhist terminology as hellish "monsters," "demons," "cow-ghosts," and "snake-gods." Exhibition halls commemorating Mao's revolutionary deeds were built across the land, their halls facing east to the source of light, their floors laid in traditional-style mosaics decorated with sunflowers. The official press referred to these halls as "sacred shrines," and peasants who paid reverence to Mao before their "tablets of loyalty" did so much in the same fashion as they traditionally venerated ancestral tablets.

The strongly traditional and strangely religious forms the Mao cult assumed during the Cultural Revolution were of course wholly incongruous with the purposes of the movement it was intended to serve. The Cultural Revolution had begun with a fiercely iconoclastic assault against the traditions of the Chinese past (as well as against Western bourgeois traditions) and was undertaken on the assumption that the destruction of old values was the precondition for the modern revolutionary transformation of the consciousness of the people, which, in turn, was the essential prerequisite for political action to safeguard China's transition to socialism. The traditional forms and symbols surrounding the cult were invoked by the leaders of the Cultural Revolution to bury tradition and convey a modern revolutionary content. Yet it may have been the case that the traditional forms and archaic rituals themselves had a greater impact on popular consciousness—and on the character of Chinese political life—than the new revolutionary values which Mao and Maoists hoped to impart.

There is of course nothing uniquely Chinese about the spectacle of revolutionary iconoclasts promoting the worship of traditional-type icons. As Karl Marx once observed: "At the very time when men appeared engaged in revolutionizing things and themselves, in bringing about what never was before, at such epochs of revolutionary crisis do they anxiously conjure up into their service the spirits of the past . . . to enact a new historic scene in such time-honored disguise and with such borrowed language."[24]

24. Karl Marx, *The Eighteenth Brumaire of Louis Bonaparte* (Chicago: Kerr, 1919), pp. 9–10.

As the fervors of the Cultural Revolution waned in 1968, and as Mao Tse-tung increasingly moderated the radical thrust of the mass movement he had called into being, the cult of the Chairman, ironically, grew ever more extravagant. Mao's writings were printed and distributed in ever greater numbers, to the exclusion of virtually all other writings. His portraits, statues, and plaster busts grew both in size and volume. But whereas in the early days of the Cultural Revolution the cult had been identified with a genuine and largely spontaneous mass revolutionary movement, it now manifested itself more in the performance of the established rituals of an orthodox church. In Peking, in the summer of 1968, observers noted "a grimness reflected in the faces of a people who still marched behind crimson banners and portraits of the Chairman, but who did so out of habit."[25] And it was reported that "PLA teams fostered group therapy sessions all over Peking, at which members of opposing factions sat together and embroidered portraits of the Chairman."[26] Schoolchildren, rather than saying "good morning," began the day by chanting "May Chairman Mao live ten thousand years ten thousand times," which, it was boasted at the time, were the first words taught children attending schools for the deaf.[27] Increasingly massive numbers of people came on organized pilgrimages to pay homage at the "sacred shrines" built to commemorate the life of Mao Tse-tung. The test of loyalty to Mao came to be measured less by revolutionary acts inspired by his "thought" than by the ability to memorize his maxims and sayings, and by the size of his portraits carried in the streets and hung in homes. At the beginning of the Cultural Revolution, the Mao cult had stimulated the masses to take revolutionary and iconoclastic actions; at the end of the upheaval it simply produced icons for the masses to worship.

Perhaps the bizarre and alienating way in which the Cultural Revolution came to an end was inherent in its political origins. From the beginning of the movement, the cult of Mao, which demanded the subordination of the people to the all-embracing wisdom of one man,

25. David Milton and Nancy Dall Milton, *The Wind Will Not Subside: Years in Revolutionary China, 1964–1969* (New York: Pantheon, 1969), p. 330.

26. Ibid., p. 335.

27. Snow, *The Long Revolution*, pp. 106–7.

stood in striking incongruity with the announced principle of the Cultural Revolution that "the only method is for the masses to liberate themselves, and any method of doing things in their stead must not be used."[28] Yet it was under the legitimizing authority of the cult, by "offering one's loyal heart to Chairman Mao," that the masses rose in rebellion. Having proceeded under so alienated a form of political authority, under the auspices of a cult which attributed all political and moral wisdom to Mao alone, it was perhaps unnatural but not illogical that the politically apathetic and disillusioned masses who had physically and spiritually exhausted themselves in the battles of the Cultural Revolution, and who had fought those battles in the name of the Chairman, should now prostrate themselves before the manufactured icons of the cult of Mao.

In the end, the Cultural Revolution failed to yield viable political institutions to take the place of the Chinese Communist Party, and Mao was forced to reestablish the authority of the Party in its old Leninist and pre-Cultural Revolution form, although now with the Chairman as its real as well as titular head. The cult of Mao, or more precisely, its more extreme and irrational aspects, were discarded in direct proportion to the process of Party rebuilding in the early 1970s.

Stuart Schram has suggested that the decision to dismantle the cult was due, in part, to Mao's belated recognition that the blind worship of his "genius" and the rote learning of precepts drawn from his "thought" could not liberate the Chinese people and revolutionize their consciousness.[29] This is perhaps too charitable an interpretation. It would be closer to the truth of the matter to say that the cult was dismantled, and then only in part, only after it had served its Maoist political purposes. Indeed, Mao himself candidly acknowledged as much in his December 1970 talk with Edgar Snow. The cult, he then said, had been deliberately employed as a weapon against a Party bureaucracy over which he had lost control. Now that he had regained supremacy over the institution, and presumably

28. *Decision of the Central Committee of the Chinese Communist Party Concerning the Great Proletarian Cultural Revolution* (Peking: Foreign Languages Press, 1966), p. 4.

29. Stuart R. Schram, ed., *Authority, Participation and Cultural Change in China* (Cambridge, England: Cambridge University Press, 1973), p. 104.

cleansed it of its "revisionist" elements, the time had come for the cult to be "cooled down."[30] The more excessive forms of adulation of Mao were in fact "cooled" in the following years, although the cult remained (even if in attenuated form) and was intimately involved in the Byzantine political struggles and palace intrigues among the Chairman's would-be successors which marked Chinese political life during Mao's last years.

II. Social Origins and Functions of the Cult

How does one explain the emergence of so archaic a form of political authority as the cult of Mao Tse-tung, and one so incongruous with the teachings of Marxism on the form that political power is to assume in a socialist society? It is tempting to view the phenomenon through the prism of the well-known "totalitarian model" and offer a conventionally satisfying explanation. It is widely assumed that the Mao cult was forged much in the same mold as other twentieth-century personality cults and thus can be attributed to the drive for personal aggrandizement on the part of a totalitarian leader determined to remove all barriers to his absolute political supremacy. As Franz Michael typically has argued, the Mao cult was fabricated to create "the image of personal infallibility," similar in nature and function to the cults of Mussolini, Hitler, and Stalin.[31] Operating from more elaborate theoretical perspectives, Leonard Schapiro and John Lewis have argued that Mao sought to build a "*führerist* type" Communist party "in which his will was supreme." This effort engendered a continuous and increasingly bitter conflict between the leader of the Party and the Party as an institution, for the Party is "an autonomous and competing power base with independent strengths" which tends to undermine rather than reinforce the power of the leader. Just as in the case of Stalin, the supremacy of Mao and "the thought of Mao" required diminishing the role of the Party. Thus, Schapiro and Lewis conclude, "Mao's assault on the Party in

30. Snow, *The Long Revolution*, pp. 18–19.

31. Franz Michael, "Ideology and the Cult of Mao," in Frank N. Trager and William Henderson, eds., *Communist China, 1949–1969* (New York: New York University Press, 1970), p. 27.

his old age bears many striking resemblances to the all-out attack launched by Stalin on the Communist Party in 1936. . . . Just as was Stalin, Mao is intent on bypassing the Party as the supreme, monopolistic instrument of power; as once did Stalin, Mao is seeking to break the institution so that it cannot thwart the will of the leader. . . . both Stalin and Mao, as they become personal dictators, so they seek to circumscribe any independent role of the Party which might present any kind of challenge to their own personal, unlimited and arbitrary authority."[32]

Needless to say, the conflict between the person of Mao Tse-tung and the institution of the Chinese Communist Party has been one of the overriding themes in the history of the People's Republic, with which the Mao cult has been closely intertwined. From the collectivization campaign of 1955 to the wholesale attack on the Party and its organizations in the Cultural Revolution, the supremacy of Mao (and the flourishing of his cult) can be more or less directly correlated with undermining the authority and power of the Leninist party. Moreover, there are of course striking similarities between the cults of Stalin and Mao. Apart from the more obvious and outward forms of official adulation and popular idolatry, many of the political and ideological elements that went into the building of the Stalin cult were used to fashion the Mao cult. Just as Stalin's first effort in cult-building was to establish his dominance in the realm of Marxist philosophy,[33] so Mao's Yenan writings on philosophy and literature came to be treated as holy writ to establish the Chairman's credentials as a creative Marxist theoretician.[34] Just as the Stalin cult required the rewriting of party history to portray Stalin as "Bolshe-

32. Leonard Schapiro and John Wilson Lewis, "The Roles of the Monolithic Party under the Totalitarian Leader," in John Wilson Lewis, ed., *Party Leadership and Revolutionary Power in China* (Cambridge, England: Cambridge University Press, 1970), pp. 114–15.

33. On the relationship between the Stalin cult and Stalinist philosophic dogmas in the early 1930s, see Robert C. Tucker, "The Rise of Stalin's Personality Cult," *American Historical Review* 84. 2 (April 1979):349–52.

34. By the mid-1940s, Mao's talks on art and literature at the Yenan Forum of 1942 and his philosophical essays "On Practice" and "On Contradiction" (both written in 1937) had become virtually unchallenged Chinese Marxist dogma and pervaded all aspects of Chinese Communist intellectual and cultural life.

vism's second Lenin,"[35] so the history of the Chinese Communist Party was rewritten and embellished to magnify Mao's revolutionary role to the neglect or denigration of others—a feat more easily accomplished in China than in Russia since Mao could claim to be the Lenin as well as the Stalin of the Chinese revolution.[36] And just as the Stalin cult came to be associated with the ubiquitous phrase "classical works of Marx, Engels, Lenin, and Stalin," so Mao's writings were elevated to a new and higher stage of presumably universally valid revolutionary theory and canonized as "Marxism-Leninism-Mao Tsetung Thought." In both cases, the political supremacy of the leader demanded, and was reinforced by, a celebration of his ideological creativity and infallibility.

Yet however similar in forms and methods, the cults of Mao and Stalin differed radically in their origins and especially in their sociopolitical functions. The cult of Mao grew and was constructed around the acknowledged leader of a popular revolution, and one who enjoyed enormous prestige among the masses both before and after the revolutionary victory. Stalin, by contrast, was a shadowy figure among Bolshevik leaders, never acquiring a popular prestige remotely comparable to that enjoyed by Lenin and Trotsky, or even a host of lesser figures. Stalin achieved political dominance by working within party circles and manipulating its organizational apparatus behind closed doors. Such popular prestige as he acquired was manufactured under Lenin's shadow (and, indeed, in Lenin's name) through the agency of the officially constructed cult.

More importantly, the Mao cult was identified with a massive popular movement during the revolutionary years and retained that identity in the postrevolutionary era through the mobilization of the masses for radical social change. The Stalin cult, by contrast, was a wholly postrevolutionary phenomenon utilized by the leader of a centralized state to convey bureaucratic orders to the masses from

35. See Tucker, "The Rise of Stalin's Personality Cult," pp. 352–65.

36. One way the leaders of the post-Mao era have pursued to diminish Mao's stature, without directly criticizing the late Chairman, has been to encourage historical writings which emphasize the importance of early Party leaders long neglected in official Maoist historiography (such as Li Ta-chao, P'eng P'ai, and Tsai Ho-sen) and which laud the revolutionary contributions of Mao's opponents within the Party over the years, especially P'eng Te-huai and Liu Shao-ch'i.

above. Whereas the Stalin cult was historically associated with (and served to reinforce) the bureaucratic institutionalization of the new Soviet order, the cult of Mao was wholly antithetical to bureaucratic routinization and the institutionalization of the postrevolutionary state. Moreover, the Stalin cult was employed to carry out a crash program of urban industrialization (based, in large measure, on the exploitation of the countryside), whereas the Mao cult came to prominence (in 1955 and after) as an instrument Maoists utilized to break away from the Soviet model of development and forge a new agrarian road to socialism. Furthermore, the Stalin cult was compatible with stability and the revival of old Russian traditions, but the Mao cult (in content if not in form) was profoundly antitraditional, and hardly conducive to either social or political stability.

These differences suggest that the cult of Mao Tse-tung cannot be adequately understood simply as an instrument fabricated by a leader to break down institutional resistance to his political supremacy, although it undoubtedly had and served that purpose. Nor can it be simply explained in terms of a need for personal gratification, although it may safely be assumed that Mao, no less than Stalin, derived no small measure of satisfaction from popular and official adulation. How, then, might it be understood?

In reviewing the history of the Mao cult, it is striking how consistently the phenomenon was identified with the Chinese peasantry and with social movements which purported to express the interests and aspirations of peasants. The cult was born in the rural revolutionary environment of the early Yenan era and the earliest and most ardent cult-worshippers were impoverished peasants who believed that Mao was their "savior" and "star of salvation," who would establish (or perhaps reestablish) justice in the world. Although Mao held little appeal for intellectuals and was largely unknown among the politically inactive urban working class, he was extraordinary (as Edgar Snow wrote in 1937) because of "the uncanny degree to which he synthesizes and expresses the urgent demands . . . [of] the peasantry. . . ."[37] It was on the basis of peasant support that the Communists triumphed and Mao was elevated atop the Gate of Heavenly Peace. And it was before that ancient gate that peasants

37. Snow, *Red Star Over China*, pp. 66–67.

continued to worship their leader in traditional fashion. "During the early years of the revolution there was a strange thing," a high Chinese Communist official once related. "When peasants came to the October anniversary and went past the reviewing stand, many did the *k'ou-t'ou* before Chairman Mao. We had to keep guards posted there to prevent them from prostrating themselves. It takes time to make people understand that Chairman Mao is not an emperor or a god. . . ."[38]

If peasants worshipped Mao as a deity, Mao celebrated the revolutionary creativity of the peasantry and what he rediscovered (during the rural collectivization movement of 1955–56) to be their "inexhaustible enthusiasm for socialism."[39] Indeed, it was with the launching of the agricultural collectivization campaign that the cult was politically activated in a movement whose purpose, Mao stated at the time, was to allow impoverished peasants "to throw off poverty, improve their standard of living and withstand natural calamities."[40] And from that time on, the cult was employed in increasingly explicit fashion to serve peasant interests, at least as Mao perceived them, in a continuing conflict between the cities and the countryside over the allocation of scarce resources. "The peasants' burden of taxation is too heavy while the price of agricultural products is very low, and that of industrial goods very high," Mao complained in 1956,[41] and the complaint reflected deep resentments over the exploitation of the rural areas for the benefit of the industrializing cities. The Soviet-modeled First Five Year Plan, which was turning the peasants who made the revolution into the victims of the revolution, was soon abandoned in favor of a distinctively Maoist economic strategy which emphasized the development of the countryside. It was a strategy which culminated in the ill-fated Great Leap Forward campaign, when the Mao cult reached unprecedented heights and

38. The story was related to Edgar Snow in 1965 by Kung P'eng, then vice-minister of foreign affairs. Snow, *The Long Revolution*, p. 69.

39. *Socialist Upsurge in China's Countryside* (Peking: Foreign Languages Press, 1957), pp. 44, 160.

40. Mao, "The Question of Agricultural Cooperation," p. 99.

41. Mao Tse-tung, "On the Ten Great Relationships" (25 April 1956), in Schram, ed., *Mao Unrehearsed*, p. 64.

was employed to prophesy a communist utopia to be realized through the organization of the peasantry into more or less self-sufficient communes combining industrial and agricultural production. In the Maoist Great Leap vision, it is significant to note, it was the rural people's communes composed of peasants, not the urban proletariat, which were assigned the tasks of carrying out what was then hailed as China's "transition from socialism to communism."

Although the prophecy of the Great Leap failed, the prophet and his cult remained—and remained identified with rural and peasant interests. In the early 1960s, as Mao's power over Party and state bureaucracies eroded, he relied increasingly on the People's Liberation Army, an army composed mostly of peasants, one that was heir to a heroic tradition of rural revolutionary warfare, and the institution which undertook the task of rebuilding and refashioning the cult of Mao. The Socialist Education Movement of 1962–65, although it proved abortive in its Maoist purpose, aimed at mobilizing poorer peasants to combat bureaucratic elitism and corruption in the countryside. And it was during these years that the antiurban strains in Mao's thought were expressed in increasingly strident tones, as he called for equity between town and countryside and lashed out at "urban overlords" who administered the educational and health care systems for the benefit of the urban areas and to the neglect of the peasantry. "Don't crowd into the cities," he advised in 1961. "Vigorously develop industry in the countryside and turn peasants into workers on the spot . . . rural living standards must not be lower than in the cities. They can be more or less the same or slightly higher than in the cities. Every commune must have its own economic center and its own institutions of higher learning to bring up its own intellectuals."[42] And in 1965 he caustically commented: "The Ministry of Public Health is not a Ministry of Public Health for the people, so why not change the name to the Ministry of Urban Health, the Ministry of Gentlemen's Health, or even to the Ministry of Urban Gentlemen's Health? . . . The methods of medical examination and treatment used by hospitals nowadays are not at all appro-

42. "Reading Notes on the Soviet Union's 'Political Economy,' " *Mao Tse-tung ssu-hsiang wan sui* [Long live the thought of Mao Tse-tung] (Taipei: n.p., 1969), pp. 389–99.

priate for the countryside, and the way doctors are trained is only for the benefit of the cities. And yet in China over five hundred million of our population are peasants."[43]

It was of course during the Cultural Revolution that the cult of Mao Tse-tung assumed its most extreme and bizarre forms and expressions. The events of that most extraordinary of movements unfolded mainly in the urban areas of China; its great battles were fought in the cities and the principal political actors were urban workers, students, and intellectuals. During the years when the cities were in turmoil, most of the countryside remained politically quiescent, save for more fervent and widespread performances of the rituals of the Mao cult. Yet in many respects, however indirectly, the Cultural Revolution assumed the form of a war of the countryside against the cities. If the peasants watched the struggles of the time from the political sidelines, they observed an upheaval (proceeding under Mao's mantle) which aimed to strike down urban bureaucrats and the intellectual and technological elites of the cities. They heard an ideology which celebrated the traditions of rural revolutionary struggle and extrolled the old peasant traditions of "plain living and hard work." And such social benefits as the cataclysm eventually yielded, although the benefits hardly justified the human and economic costs exacted, went to the countryside. For what emerged from the chaos of the Cultural Revolution and the spiritual ruin of the cities were new Maoist policies announcing the revival of the program for rural industrialization, the expansion of education in the rural areas, and a reformed health care system which emphasized the needs of the peasantry.[44] While the gap between town and countryside remained enormous, the inequities were mitigated by a significant reallocation of resources and emphasis from the cities to the rural areas. The social policies which followed from the Cultural Revolution were in accord with, even if they did not fulfill, the

43. Mao Tse-tung, "Directive on Public Health" (26 June 1965), in Schram, ed., *Mao Unrehearsed,* pp. 232–33.

44. For perceptive and balanced analyses of post-Cultural Revolution economic policies and educational reforms in the countryside, see Jon Sigurdson, "Rural Industry and the Internal Transfer of Technology," in Schram, ed., *Authority, Participation and Cultural Change in China,* pp. 199–232, and John Gardner and Wilt Idema, "China's Educational Revolution," ibid., pp. 257–89.

demands for equality between the urban and rural areas which Mao had championed in the years immediately preceding the cataclysm.

The cult of Mao survived the death of Mao in 1976, and it is hardly surprising that it has survived mostly in the countryside where it originated four decades earlier. Much of the peasantry, by all accounts, still venerate the dead peasant leader as something of a deity, just as the urban intelligentsia (in their own fashion) worship Chou En-lai.[45] As Mao's successors in Peking pursue "de-Maoification" in the cities, as they seek to replace the personal authority of Mao with the impersonal bureaucratic authority of an authoritarian state, they must ponder the political implications of the persistence of the cult of Mao among the great majority of the people over whom they rule.

The close association between peasantries and the "personality cults" of dictators is a modern historical phenomenon that has been frequently noted. Karl Marx, for one, noted it in the case of mid-nineteenth-century France under the rule of Napoleon III, when the French state appeared "to have made itself completely independent" of society. Yet state power, Marx argued, was "not suspended in midair," for "Bonaparte represents a class, and the most numerous class of French society at that, the small-holding peasants." It was, in part, the superstitious beliefs of peasants that was responsible for the ascendancy of Louis Bonaparte: "Historical tradition gave rise to the belief of the French peasants in the miracle that a man named Napoleon would bring all the glory back to them. And an individual turned up who gives himself out as the man because he bears the name of Napoleon. . . . After a vagabondage of twenty years and after a series of grotesque adventures, the legend finds fulfillment and the man becomes Emperor of the French. The fixed idea of the Nephew was realized because it coincided with the fixed idea of the most numerous class of the French people." But the social basis of the superstition—and the political phenomenon—was to be traced to

45. The veneration of Chou En-lai by present-day Chinese intellectuals perhaps confirms Edgar Snow's 1937 prediction that while Mao expressed the demands of the peasants it was doubtful that "he would ever command great respect from the intellectual elite of China. . . ." Snow, *Red Star Over China,* p. 73.

the isolated and largely self-sufficient character of rural society: "In so far as there is merely a local interconnection among these small-holding peasants, and the identity of their interests begets no community, no national bond and no political organization among them, they do not form a class. They are consequently incapable of enforcing their class interest in their own name, whether through a parliament or through a convention. They cannot represent themselves, they must be represented. Their representative must at the same time appear as their master, as an authority over them, as an unlimited governmental power that protects them against other classes and sends them rain and sunshine from above. The political influence of the small-holding peasants, therefore, finds its final expression in the executive power subordinating society to itself."[46]

Marx's explanation of the cult of Louis Bonaparte provided the theoretical perspectives for the Chinese Communist explanation of the cult of Stalin a century later. In the 1956 treatise "On the Historical Experience of the Dictatorship of the Proletariat," it might be recalled, the Stalin cult was attributed to "a small-producer economy," or, more precisely, to the survivals of a "backward ideology" which such an economy had produced.[47]

The notion that peasant life and traditions have a great deal to do with leadership cults is by no means an exclusively Marxist argument. The political scientist Robert C. Tucker, for example, explains the Stalin cult, in part, in the following manner: "For centuries the Russian people, overwhelmingly composed of peasants, had been monarchist in outlook. The Revolution had opened the door for many peasant sons to have careers in the new society. Industrialization and collectivization resulted in the recruitment of millions of people of peasant stock into the working class. They brought with them, along with their Soviet schooling and experience, residues of the traditional peasant mentality, including respect for personal authority, whether it emanated from the immediate boss or from the head of the party and state. The social condition of Russia at the time of the "great

46. Karl Marx, "The Eighteenth Brumaire of Louis Bonaparte," in Karl Marx and Friedrich Engels, *Selected Works* (Moscow: Foreign Languages Publishing House, 1950), vol. 1, pp. 302–3.

47. See above, p. 155–156.

turn" (1929–33) was, therefore, receptive to the cult of a deceased leader—or a living one."[48]

Similar arguments have been advanced to explain the cult of Mao Tse-tung. And one was once suggested by Mao himself. In late 1970, when Mao was engaged in "cooling" his "cult of personality," he candidly acknowledged that the cult had been a political necessity during the previous decade and also acknowledged that cult-worshipping had been overdone. The rituals of the cult could not easily be discarded, however, for Mao observed that it was difficult for people to overcome the habits of three thousand years of emperor-worshipping tradition.[49] That tradition, needless to say, was most widespread and most deeply ingrained among the peasantry.

The peasantry also looms large in more recent Chinese Communist explanations of the cult of Mao. The political and ideological leaders of the post-Mao regime now condemn the whole Cultural Revolution decade (1966–76) as a period of "feudal-fascism," one feature of which was the deification of the leader. Lin Piao and the "Gang of Four" are held responsible for the more horrendous evils of the era in general and for the Mao cult in particular: "They preached the theory that 'men of genius' decide everything and treated revolutionary leaders as omniscient and omnipotent deities."[50] The sociohistorical basis of the phenomenon of "feudal-fascism," in turn, is attributed to the persistence of feudalistic ideas in an economically and culturally backward land, and particularly to the "petty-bourgeois ideology" emanating from the lengthy dominance of a small-producers' economy in Chinese history. "The patriarchal system of the small producers has for a long time been predominant in the country," it is argued, "and this was the social and historical background for the prevalence of modern superstition for some time."[51] "Modern superstition," of course, is a euphemism for the cult of

48. Tucker, "The Rise of Stalin's Personality Cult," p. 347.

49. The comment was made during the course of a lengthy discussion with Edgar Snow on 18 December 1970. Edgar Snow, "A Conversation with Mao Tse-tung," *Life Magazine*, 30 April 1971, p. 46.

50. Yeh Chien-ying, speech of 29 September 1979 commemorating the thirtieth anniversary of the founding of the People's Republic. *Beijing Review*, 5 October 1979, pp. 17–22.

51. *Jen-min jih-pao* [People's daily], 30 October 1979.

Mao Tse-tung. And it was "Lin Piao and the gang of four [who] spread modern superstition by taking advantage of mistaken conceptions among the people and exploiting simple sentiments of respect for their leader."[52] The backward peasantry, needless to say, is the main social carrier of "petty-bourgeois ideology," which, it is alleged, is the root of the pernicious "ultraleftist" current which found its ultimate political expression in "feudal-fascism." It is thus that the responsibility for the deficiencies of the present, and the evils of the recent past, are shifted from the eminently urban leaders in Peking to the lingering "feudal remnants" of China's historic past, with the peasantry implicitly bearing the blame as the social source of backward ideas and ideologies.

If the cult of Mao Tse-tung grew out of a rural environment, and if Chinese peasants were the most ardent worshippers of the cult, the social function of the Mao cult was far different than the cults of Louis Bonaparte and Joseph Stalin, which also are usually attributed to the persistence of traditional peasant mentalities. Marx termed the Bonapartes "the dynasty of the peasants," but he also pointed out that the empire of Louis Bonaparte functionally served to preserve the existing capitalist order (albeit without the political participation of the bourgeoisie), and that the French peasants were being ruined under the twin exploitation of urban capital and state taxation.[53] Likewise if traditional peasant veneration of personal authority contributed to the growth of Stalin's "cult of personality," the Russian peasantry hardly benefited from Stalin's authority. Apart from the enormous human and economic costs exacted by Stalinist-style collectivization in the early 1930s, the whole Stalinist strategy of development rested on the general exploitation of the peasantry in order to finance rapid urban industrialization. The Mao cult, by contrast, was used by Mao to promote policies which mitigated the exploitation of the rural areas, policies which attempted to narrow the economic and cultural gap between the modern cities and the backward countryside, and policies which envisioned an agrarian road to socialism. The successes and the failures of those policies

52. "On the Role of the Individual in History," *Jen-min jih-pao* [People's daily], 4 July 1980.

53. Marx, "The Eighteenth Brumaire of Louis Bonaparte," pp. 305–7.

are matters of dispute, but few would dispute the attempt and the intent.

Yet if Mao spoke on behalf of the peasantry, he did so in archaic and alien political form. For the cult of Mao Tse-tung is one of the most extreme examples in modern history of the alienation of the social power of the people into fetishized political authority. The peasants not only bowed before the power of the state which stood above them, but willingly subordinated themselves to the deified authority of a single man, and worshipped him as the source of all wisdom and the embodiment of their collective will, just as they traditionally had subordinated themselves to and worshipped their self-created gods. Mao, who had contributed so greatly to the socioeconomic emancipation of the Chinese peasantry, became their political master in the process. The old shackles of economic oppression were thrown off, only to be replaced by a new form of political bondage. The once insurgent peasants who had given Mao his power in the first place, and who provided him with the mystique of "savior" and "genius," now bowed before plaster statues of their liberator. And thus for the Chinese people, Liberation was only partially liberating, for, as Marx once said, "only when man has recognised and organised his own powers as social forces, and consequently no longer separates social power from himself in the shape of political power, only then will human emancipation have been accomplished."[54]

54. Karl Marx, "On the Jewish Question," Karl Marx and Friedrich Engels, *Collected Works* (New York: International Publishers, 1975), vol. 3, p. 168.

7

Utopian and Dystopian Elements in the Maoist Vision of the Future

In the thought of Mao Tse-tung—and it is the thought of the most celebrated utopian prophet of our age—one encounters a vision of the future which contains both an *eutopia* ("the good place") and an *outopia* ("no place"). On the one hand, Mao prophesied the advent of socialism and communism, a vision derived from the ultimate goals set forth in Marxist theory. On the other hand, Mao's communist utopia appears as only a transient stage in what he envisioned as an endless process of change beyond communism which leads nowhere—or, more precisely, an ahistorical vision of a cosmic process which results in the end of history, the death of the human race, and indeed the destruction of the universe. In the Maoist vision one finds both a future and a nonfuture, both a utopian and a dystopian projection of the contradictions of the present into an almost theological vision of "the end of days." What, then, is "the Maoist vision"? And what is the significance of the utopian and dystopian strains present in that celebrated conception of the future?

I. The History of the Maoist Vision

During the revolutionary years, there is little that can be described as utopian about Maoist theory and practice or about Mao Tse-tung's vision of the future. Even with all the benefits of historical hindsight, there is no reason to question Benjamin Schwartz's 1951 assessment that Mao's innovations as a Marxist-Leninist resided less in the realm of theory than in the more mundane and practical realm of revolutionary strategy and tactics.[1] Nor is there anything in the history of the Chinese Communist revolution prior to 1949 to suggest that Mao, or Chinese Marxists in general, were more inspired than Marxists in other lands by utopian visions of a socialist future or that they envisioned the future that Marxism prophesies in any special chiliastic fashion.

Mao, to be sure, was not completely unconcerned with the question of the ultimate aims of the revolution he led. His political and intellectual commitment to Marxism-Leninism as the means of revolution implied of course a commitment to the socialist ends proclaimed in that theory. But in his pre-1949 writings, Mao said little about the postrevolutionary future, and on the rare occasions when he did refer to socialism and communism, he spoke only in the most vague and general terms. In discussing the relationship between the "bourgeois" and "socialist" stages of the revolution in 1939, for example, he was content to simply note that "the ultimate aim for which all communists strive is to bring about a socialist and communist society."[2] In 1940 he discussed the future in somewhat more enthusiastic terms. Communism, he then wrote, "is the most perfect, the most progressive, the most revolutionary, and the most rational system ever since human history began."[3] And in 1945 he proclaimed: "We Communists do not conceal our political views. Definitely and beyond all doubt, our future or maximum programme is to carry China forward to socialism and communism. Both the name of our Party and our Marxist world outlook unequivocally point to this supreme ideal of the future, a future of incomparable brightness and splendour."[4]

There is of course nothing exceptional about these passages. They

1. Benjamin Schwartz, *Chinese Communism and the Rise of Mao* (Cambridge, Mass.: Harvard University Press, 1952), pp. 189 ff.

2. Mao Tse-tung, "The Chinese Revolution and the Chinese Communist Party," in Mao Tse-tung, *The Selected Works of Mao Tse-tung* (Peking: Foreign Languages Press, 1961), vol. 1, p. 331.

3. Mao Tse-tung, *On New Democracy* (Peking: Foreign Languages Press, 1954), p. 43.

4. Mao Tse-tung, "On Coalition Government," in Mao Tse-tung, *The Selected Works of Mao Tse-tung* (Peking: Foreign Languages Press, 1967), vol. 3, p. 232.

are rather standard Marxist-Leninist statements about the socialist future and reflect the usual Marxist reluctance to discuss that future in any detail. Indeed, if there is anything at all noteworthy about Mao's pre-1949 "vision," it is its rather prosaic character, as in 1938 when he replied to an English correspondent's query about his conception of the new China: "Every man has food to eat and clothes to wear. Every man understands the rights and duties of citizenship and has a fair chance of education and amusement. The marriage customs are to be reformed, roads built, industry developed, a six-hour day established. There is no foreign aggression. No man oppresses another. There is equality and freedom and universal love. Together all [will] build the peace of the world."[5]

The Chinese Communist victory of 1949 itself was not accompanied by the same chiliastic revolutionary expectations and utopian visions which had marked the Russian Bolshevik Revolution of 1917. The anticlimactic consummation of a prolonged revolutionary struggle which had taken place in the rural hinterlands, the peculiarly insular character of the revolution and the mentality of its leaders, the long period of Chinese isolation from international revolutionary currents (indeed the absence of any international revolutionary situation), and the continued Maoist insistence on the "bourgeois" character of the revolution itself—all were factors which militated against utopian expectations that political victory portended the imminent advent of a perfect order of justice and equality. Mao Tse-tung, to be sure, celebrated the revolutionary triumph by reaffirming the eventual Marxist goal of a classless society, but he did so only to postpone the goal to a vaguely indefinite time in the future and to dampen such utopian hopes as the Communist victory may have aroused. Ultimate Marxist goals, as Mao put it at the time, merely were "mentioned in passing" and were to be seen only in terms of "the long-range perspective of human progress." In the meantime, and for the foreseeable future, energies were to be turned to more immediate, realistic, and tangible tasks—the building of a strong state and a strong economy.[6] "Three years of recovery, ten years of de-

5. *Times* (London), 25 July 1938.

6. Mao, Tse-tung, "On People's Democratic Dictatorship" (July 1949), in Mao Tse-tung, *The Selected Works of Mao Tse-tung* (Peking: Foreign Languages Press, 1961), vol. 4, especially pp. 411–12 and 418–22.

velopment," was the slogan with which the history of the People's Republic began, and it reflected the relatively sober temper of the time.

It was entirely in harmony with the presumably "pragmatic" character of Maoist revolutionary strategy that Mao and other Chinese Communist leaders formulated their strategy for postrevolutionary development. Unlike Lenin in 1917, Mao in 1949 was not burdened by any utopian expectations of a global revolutionary upheaval, and thus the postponement of socialist goals was easily accomplished—indeed, taken for granted from the beginning. Nor did Mao harbor any of Lenin's anguished doubts about the historical viability and moral validity of attempting to build a socialist society in conditions of economic and social backwardness. For Mao and the Chinese Communists, the overcoming of backwardness was viewed as an enormous practical task to be undertaken; it did not present them with any Marxist theoretical dilemmas to be resolved, partly because they were far less firmly tied than their Russian counterparts to orthodox Marxist assumptions on the economic, social, and cultural prerequisites for socialism. Moreover, the Soviet historical experience, it was believed at the time, provided the appropriate model to be adopted and emulated—the historical model which demonstrated how to industrialize an economically backward country under socialist political auspices and the model for a noncapitalist path to socialism. However much the Chinese Communists had come to distrust and defy Stalin's "guidance" during the revolutionary years, they apparently had no reservations about the validity of the Stalinist strategy of postrevolutionary development. Even though Mao long had warned against "the mechanical absorption of foreign material" (as he put it in 1940), he proved remarkably uncritical during the early 1950s in accepting and adopting the Stalinist strategy of economic development. Nor is there any evidence that he had any doubts at the time that Stalinist means of economic development led to the desired socialist ends. Although the Chinese Communists knew little about the nature of Soviet society other than what they had read in official Stalinist textbooks, it was then a prime article of the Maoist faith that Russia was "the land of socialism," and, as Mao proclaimed in 1949, "a great and glorious socialist state." "Learn from the Soviet Union" was the guiding Maoist slogan during the early years of the People's Republic as the Communists strove to revive an economy ravaged by decades of foreign invasion and civil war and to establish political order and national unity after a century of disintegration. At the end of 1952 the slogan was translated into China's First Five Year Plan (1953–57), a plan based on the almost wholesale adoption of Stalinist methods, techniques, and ideological assumptions.

It seems strange that the Chinese Communists should have embraced so ardently and uncritically the ready-made Soviet model. Having come to power through a revolutionary strategy that abandoned many Stalinist orthodoxies—indeed in direct defiance of Stalin's political authority—they now quickly and uncritically accepted Stalin's authority as an economic strategist and as the "builder of socialism." Having emerged from a rural revolutionary environment where they had worked out their own distinctive patterns of thought and organizaiton, they now turned their backs on their unique revolutionary heritage in favor of a program of rapid urban industrialization which demanded the subordination of agriculture to modern industry and the exploitation of the countryside for the benefit of the cities. And it was Mao, among the most unorthodox of Chinese Communists during the revolutionary years, who took the lead in promoting the orthodox Stalinist strategy of development during the early postrevolutionary years.

Since Chinese industrialization proceeded largely in accordance with Soviet-borrowed methods and techniques, it is hardly surprising that the process gave rise to similar social and ideological tendencies. The social results of China's First Five Year Plan are well known: the emergence of new administrative and technological elites; growing inequalities among the urban working class and the subjection of workers to an increasingly harsh and repressive labor discipline; a stronger and more oppressive state apparatus presided over by an increasingly bureaucratized Communist Party; and a widening economic and cultural gap between the modernizing cities and the backward countryside.

And, as in the Soviet case, the growth of new patterns of social inequality was accompanied by a familiar process of the indefinite postponement of Marxian social goals. To be sure, when the Communists formally launched the First Five Year Plan at the beginning of 1953 they also announced the inauguration of the era of "the transition to socialism." But though the pursuit of modern industrial development was clear enough, the meaning of socialism became increasingly ambiguous. Chinese society seemed to be moving further away from, rather than closer to, the socialist future that the revolution had promised to bring. Modern industrial development was conceived as the means to achieve socialist ends, but the logic of the process soon made industrialization itself the primary goal while socialist goals were postponed to an ever more distant future and tended to become ritualized into slogans to spur production. This eminently Stalinist pattern was also eminently Maoist at the time, for Mao then fully accepted the Marxist-Leninist orthodoxy that a high level of economic development was the essential precondition for the socialist transformation of society. Socialism and communism required a long and indefinite period of preparation, it was emphasized, and no one emphasized the point more strongly than Mao. He hardly could have been described as a utopian visionary at the time. Neither the theory nor the practice of the Chinese Communists in the early years of the People's Republic foreshadowed the utopian and apocalyptic impulses which eventually were to throw the postrevolutionary order into new revolutionary convulsions.

What is unique and extraordinary about the postrevolutionary history of China is the emergence of a powerful revolutionary utopianism long after the new order had become consolidated, routinized, and seemingly institutionalized. The contrast with Soviet history is, of course, striking. In Russia, the Bolsheviks had come to power with highly utopian expectations—hopes and expectations which soon faded and died as Soviet society underwent a familiar and presumably inevitable process of what Robert Tucker has termed "deradicalization." In China, by contrast, the Communists came to power as rather sobered realists, determined to achieve the mundane goals of political unity and modern economic development. And they found on hand—and quickly took into their hands—the ready-made Soviet model of development that was so eminently suited to the pursuit of these eminently nationalist goals. It was entirely in keeping with Chinese Communist theoretical perspectives of the time that the adopted foreign model came with built-in ideological rationalizations for the postponement of Marxist social goals. It was not until almost a decade after the revolutionary victory that what came to be known as "the Maoist vision" appeared on the historical scene to divert China from the Soviet path and to create a unique (and turbulent) Chinese pattern of postrevolutionary history. More precisely, it was only with the Great Leap Forward campaign of 1958–60 that observers of contemporary China discovered "the Maoist vision," and it was during that profoundly utopian episode that the vision received its fullest and most pristine expression.

The prehistory of the Great Leap—and the period crucial for the emergence of Mao as a utopian visionary—began with Mao's July 1955 speech on agricultural collectivization and concluded (after the conclusion of the Hundred Flowers era) in late 1957 with the triumph of distinctively Maoist socioeconomic policies. Without entering into the complex political struggles and policy conflicts which marked these years, it might be noted that the emerging Maoist vision involved a wholesale rejection of the Soviet developmental model and is closely bound up with the whole phenomenon of the cult of Mao, with its profoundly antibureaucratic and anti-Leninist implications.

Mao's July 1955 speech was more than an attempt to overcome economic stagnation in the countryside. It also was the first in a series of personal policy initiatives on the part of Mao which were to set him above the Communist Party as a supreme leader and utopian prophet. The speech marked not only the beginning of the Maoist abandonment of Stalinist orthodoxies (at least in the realm of socioeconomic change), but also the revival of socialism as an immediate goal to be actively striven for in the here and now. This was coupled with a newly revived faith in the peasantry as the main agency of the forthcoming socialist transformation, harkening back to the "Hunan Report" of 1927, which located the true sources of revolutionary creativity not in the Party, but in the spontaneous movement of the peasantry.[7] For in 1955 Mao again counterposed a revolutionary peasantry—a "mass movement [which] is in advance of the leadership"—to a Party that was insufficiently revolutionary:

7. Mao, "Report of an Investigation into the Peasant Movement in Hunan" (March 1927), in Mao Tse-tung, *The Selected Works of Mao Tse-tung* (London: Lawrence and Wishart, 1954), vol. 1, p. 22.

party officials who argued that collectivization was proceeding too rapidly and had gone beyond the understanding of the masses merely revealed their own lack of faith in the masses.[8] Here we find implicit the claim that only Mao himself, not the Party as such, best represented the desires and interests of the peasant masses. It was this claim which set the stage for the emergence of the Maoist vision as an active force in policy making and the emergence of Mao as the sole prophet of a new agrarian road to socialism.

The new Maoist formulae for economic development and socialist transformation were set forth in his 1956 speech "On the Ten Great Relationships," which implicitly repudiated both the Soviet model and China's own First Five Year Plan.[9] But Mao's proposals were opposed by most Party leaders and, as he later complained, largely ignored. They were to be accepted only in late 1957, after Mao had turned the Hundred Flowers campaign and its "antirightist" aftermath into a movement to break down the resistance of state and party bureaucrats to the radical socioeconomic policies he was advocating, and which he implemented with the launching of the Great Leap Forward campaign in 1958.

It was during the Great Leap that the Maoist vision of the future received its fullest theoretical expression. And it also was the time which saw the most ambitious attempt to realize that vision in social practice. It was an era marked by a positive utopianism and a highly optimistic vision of the future. Three years of struggle would be followed by a thousand years of happiness, a popular slogan promised, and it was envisioned that China would reach the economic levels of the advanced industrialized countries within fifteen years. But it was not simply a good material life that Maoists promised, for they conceived the Great Leap as more than a crash program for modernization. It was also proclaimed to be the period of the transition from socialism to communism. The ultimate goals of classical Marxism, hitherto postponed to an indefinite time in the future, now

8. Mao Tse-tung, "The Question of Agricultural Cooperation" (31 July 1955), in Robert Bowie and John K. Fairbank, eds., *Communist China 1955–1959: Policy Documents with Analysis* (Cambridge, Mass.: Harvard University Press, 1962).

9. Mao Tse-tung, "On the Ten Great Relationships" (25 April 1956), translated in Stuart R. Schram, ed., *Mao Tse-tung Unrehearsed: Talks and Letters 1956–71*, (Middlesex: Penguin Books, 1974), pp. 61–83.

became immediate goals to be undertaken in the here and now. The rural communes were to bring about not only economic miracles but a social miracle as well—the leap to a communist utopia based on the principle of "to each according to his needs." The communes were to abolish the distinctions between town and countryside, between mental and manual labor, and between workers, peasants, and intellectuals—and indeed even hasten the abolition of the internal functions of the state. These utopian socially revolutionary tasks were conceived and popularized not as distant ends dependent on the prior development of material forces of production but rather as immediate tasks of the day to be pursued and implemented (at least in embryonic form) in the very process of constructing the Marxian-defined material preconditions for their realization. Through combining industry and agriculture in what was perceived to be an ideologically and spiritually pure rural setting—and with a deep faith in the inherent socialist aspirations of the masses and in the powers of human consciousness to mold reality in accordance with its dictates—it was envisioned that the building of a communist society and the development of a modern economy could proceed simultaneously. The conditions of communism and its preconditions, it was assumed, would prove mutually reinforcing, and thus the ends and means of communism would be reconciled.

The Great Leap Forward vision of the future was derived from classical Marxist sources, and Maoists drew on the more utopian strains in the Marxist-Leninist tradition. Nothing was more frequently quoted in the theoretical and popular literature of the Great Leap era than the famous passage in *The German Ideology* where Marx took one of his rare glimpses into the future and saw a communist society "where nobody has one exclusive sphere of activity, but each can become accomplished in any branch he wishes," a society which "regulates the general production and thus makes it possible for me to do one thing today and another tomorrow, to hunt in the morning, fish in the afternoon, rear cattle in the evening, criticize after dinner, just as I have a mind, without ever becoming hunter, fisherman, shepherd or critic." This idyllic and almost pastoral vision of communism was entirely in harmony with the Maoist expectation of the time that "new men" of "all-round" abilities would soon produce a society where "everyone will be a mental laborer and at the same time a physical laborer. Everyone can be a philosopher, scientist, writer, or artist." Also widely propagated in the Great Leap literature were passages from Marx's *Civil War in France* and Lenin's *State and Revolution,* for the Marxian model of the Paris Commune was seen as relevant to the contemplated decentralization of state power to the rural communes which would integrate political and economic organization. The communes were envisioned as instruments of "the dictatorship of the proletariat," the agencies which would carry out the transition from socialism to communism and achieve a classless and stateless society.[10]

The social goals proclaimed in the Great Leap vision were Marxist-inspired, but the means to achieve them were not. There is of course nothing either Marxist or Leninist in the Maoist belief that the truly creative forces for revolutionary social change reside in the countryside rather than the cities, in the faith that the power of the human spirit is the decisive factor in bringing about the new society, or in the assumption that "the transition from socialism to communism" could be accomplished in conditions of economic scarcity. The Great Leap Forward campaign was a profoundly utopian historical episode, utopian in the chiliastic fervors and expectations which characterized the early stages of the movement—and perhaps even more "utopian" in the pejorative Marxist sense of that term.

Although the popular and public ideology of the Great Leap Forward promised the more or less imminent advent of a harmonious communist utopia, one cannot fail to note the appearance of a contradictory, and partially dystopian, strain in Mao's own vision of the future. In setting forth his peculiar version of "the theory of permanent revolution" in early 1958—a theory which served as the main ideological rationale for the policies of the Great Leap—Mao expounded as a universal and eternal law of historical development the notion that "disequilibrium is normal and absolute" whereas "equilibrium is temporary and relative."[11] Not only would the whole

10. "The integration of the *hsiang* with the commune," it was typically proclaimed, "will make the commune not very different from the Paris Commune, integrating the economic organization with the organization of state power." See Wu Chih-pu, "On People's Communes," *Chung-kuo ch'ing-nien pao* [China youth], 16 September 1958. See also Chapter 5 above.

11. Mao Tse-tung, "Sixty Points on Working Methods" (19 February 1958), translated in Jerome Ch'en, ed., *Mao Papers* (London: Oxford University Press, 1970), p. 66.

period of the "transition from socialism to communism" be characterized by a continuous series of social contradictions and class struggles, but communist society itself would be marked by a continuing process of ideological and political struggle.[12] Mao, in effect, proclaimed the permanence of conflict and denied the possibility of any definitive resolution.

The dystopian aspects of the Maoist law of "disequilibrium" and its implications for the Maoist vision of the future will be discussed shortly. Here it is sufficient to note that whereas the newly proclaimed doctrine of permanent revolution served to intensify the long-standing Maoist emphasis on the necessity and value of struggle—struggle in the social realm as well as the struggle to conquer nature—the vision of the future projected in the ideology of the Great Leap Forward era was not one of endless struggle. Struggle, to be sure, was ethically valued, but it was not an end in itself. Rather, struggle and sacrifice in the present were the means to realize a future communist utopia. "Three years of struggle, a thousand years of communist happiness" was the slogan that reflected the optimistic utopian temper of the time.

In the early phase of the Great Leap Forward campaign Mao had assumed the role of prophet, stimulating and articulating popular utopian expectations. It was a posture that he was able to maintain as long as the movement went well and promised success, but the posture was undermined and the bond between Mao and the masses was broken when the Great Leap ran into economic difficulties and faltered. The forced retreat from the radical Great Leap policies led to the reassertion of the power of state and Party bureaucracies, accompanied by widespread popular disillusionment and, on the part of Mao, a growing pessimism about the future. By the summer of 1959, Mao no longer spoke about the imminence of the transition to communism but now began to view China's modern economic and social transformation as a prolonged historical process: "About the people's communes, I said that they were a system of collective ownership. I said that for the transition to be completed from collective ownership to communist ownership by the whole people, two five-year plans was too short a period. Maybe it will take twenty

12. Ibid., p. 65.

five-year plans!" "The chaos caused was on a grand scale," he admitted, "and I take responsibility."[13] He even brooded over the possibility that the work of the revolution might be totally destroyed and that he might have to begin the revolution anew. Complaining that the media had been too free in reporting errors and failures, he commented that

> if we do ten things and nine are bad, and they are all published in the press, then we will certainly perish, and we will deserve to perish. In that case, I will go to the countryside to lead the peasants to overthrow the government. If those of you in the Liberation Army won't follow me, then I will go and find a Red Army, and organize another Liberation Army.[14]

The pessimism about the future which came with the disintegration of the Great Leap campaign deepened during the early 1960s, the "Thermidorian" years which saw the reestablishment of the power of regular bureaucratic organs and the pursuit of "revisionist" socioeconomic policies, Mao's withdrawal from day-to-day Party affairs, and a sharpening conflict between Maoists and Party bureaucrats. No longer was there any expectation of an imminent transition from socialism to communism. The vision of a "leap" from "the realm of necessity to the realm of freedom" was now described by Mao as a gradual process of indeterminate length.[15] The Great Leap Forward promise of an economic miracle was similarly postponed. Whereas in 1958 Mao announced that it would take only fifteen years for China to surpass the economic levels of the industrialized West, in 1962 he somberly concluded that "it will be impossible to develop our productive power so rapidly as to catch up with, and overtake, the most advanced capitalist countries in less than a hundred years."[16] He observed that capitalism had developed over a period of three

13. Mao Tse-tung, "Speech at the Lushan Conference" (23 July 1959), in Schram, ed., *Mao Unrehearsed,* pp. 145–46.

14. Ibid., p. 139.

15. Mao Tse-tung, "Talk at an Enlarged Central Work Conference" (30 January 1962), ibid., pp. 170–73.

16. Ibid., p. 175.

centuries and implied that perhaps the growth of socialism and communism would span an equally lengthy historical era.[17]

Not only did visions of communism fade, but so did confidence in the continued viability of the existing social system. Maoists became increasingly concerned with the possibility of historical regression. "In a socialist society, new bourgeois elements may still be produced," Mao declared in January 1962. "During the whole socialist stage there still exist classes and class struggle, and this class struggle is a protracted, complex, sometimes even violent affair."[18] And it was by no means assured that this protracted class struggle would have a favorable outcome. In the autumn of 1962 Mao raised the possibility of "the restoration of reactionary classes" and warned that "a country like ours can still move toward its opposite."[19] In the years preceding the Cultural Revolution the sense of historical indeterminacy that generally characterized the Maoist mentality assumed darkly pessimistic overtones and implications.

It was, of course, precisely the fear that the country was turning into its "opposite," the specter of China undergoing a "bourgeois restoration," that motivated the extraordinary events officially baptized as the Great Proletarian Cultural Revolution. In the course of that cataclysmic upheaval, Mao (as during the Great Leap era, but in more dramatic and extreme fashion) appeared on the political scene as the supreme utopian prophet issuing from above "directives" and "instructions" and "communications" to which his masses of loyal followers below were to respond and translate into revolutionary action. But if Mao again assumed the posture of utopian prophet, he was prophesying a far different vision of the future than he had during the time of the Great Leap. The Maoist message now no longer promised economic abundance, much less an imminent leap to a communist utopia, but rather emphasized the need to dismantle the very institutions which had been built to achieve communism, and especially the Chinese Communist Party itself. To be sure, ultimate Marxist goals were not entirely forgotten; the Cultural

17. Ibid., pp. 174–75.

18. Ibid., p. 168.

19. Mao Tse-tung, "Speech at the Tenth Plenum of the Eighth Central Committee" (24 September 1962), ibid., p. 189.

Revolution was depicted as part of a "proletarian" revolutionary process that eventually would abolish all forms of exploitation. But the utopian and chiliastic fervors which marked the upheaval were directed not to achieving great social ends but rather to a never-ending process of political and ideological conflict against the ever-threatening forces of "capitalist restoration" and "counterrevolution." "Destruction before construction" was the order of the day—and indeed the order of the future, for (as Mao soon proclaimed) China would require a "cultural revolution" every generation to stave off the deathly forces of revisionism and capitalism. Nor was it clear that the work of socialist construction, which presumably would follow the necessary acts of destruction, would necessarily result in any definitive Marxist resolution. For example, Liu Shao-ch'i, the principal villain and victim of the drama, was condemned (among other things) for envisioning the future communist society as one characterized by harmony and the absence of social conflict. The Cultural Revolution was dominated more by a fear of the resurrection of the forces of the past than by a positive vision of the future. And the revolutionary message Maoism now conveyed was a future of indefinite (and perhaps endless) political and ideological struggle.

II. The Nature and Components of the Maoist Vision

The Maoist vision of the future is not a fixed and integrated "goal structure" which Maoists pursued with unbending consistency over the years. The vision is composed of diverse and contradictory elements which have been combined and recombined in different ways in response to changing historical circumstances. Depending on which point in historical time one chooses to select, both Maoism and the vision of the future it projects can be characterized in significantly different ways. Yet it is possible to outline, albeit in rough and general fashion, the salient elements of "the Maoist vision," and ascertain its main philosophic assumptions and theoretical implications.

A central part of the vision is certainly a Marxist-inspired conception of a future communist utopia. Maoists consistently proclaimed their determination to achieve the classic Marxist goals of abolishing distinctions between mental and manual labor, between town and countryside, and between workers and peasants—and even the eventual "withering away" of the state. And these Marxist ends (or at least, the first three) were pursued vigorously in Maoist socioeconomic policies and programs—and not without significant historical consequences. Such distinctively Maoist policies as combining industrial with agricultural production, the emphasis on the development of the agrarian sector and the industrialization of the countryside, educational policies and various "work-study" schemes which stressed the combination of education with productive labor, the insistence that "brain workers" participate regularly in manual labor, and the vehement campaigns against bureaucracy hardly created a classless society or even a socialist one. But they did mitigate social inequality, did serve to narrow the economic and cultural gap between modern cities and a backward countryside, and did tend to forestall the entrenchment of privileged strata and the stratification of bureaucratic elites. It would be impossible to explain the course of postrevolutionary socioeconomic development in the People's Republic during the Maoist era without taking into account the Marxist components of the Maoist vision and the role they played in determining social and political action.

Yet if Maoists were committed to achieving the utopian goals prophesied by Marx, they departed profoundly from the premises of both Marxism and Leninism in the means they conceived to realize those goals. In place of the Marxian-defined economic and social prerequisites for socialism and communism, the Maoist faith in the future relied on the spiritual and moral transformation of people. "If you are not completely reborn," as Mao proclaimed, "you cannot enter the door of communism."[20] To be sure, both a communist consciousness and modern material conditions were to develop simultaneously in "uninterrupted" fashion; but it was the "transformation of the subjective world" that was regarded as the decisive factor in "transforming the objective world." Thus not only did

20. Mao Tse-tung, "Speech at the Enlarged Session of the Military Affairs Committee and the External Affairs Conference" (11 September 1959), ibid., p. 149.

Maoists relegate objective economic conditions to a secondary status, they celebrated the moral and ideological purity they perceived to be inherent in prevailing conditions of economic backwardness—a notion which received its most extreme formulation in Mao's thesis on the socialist virtues of being "poor and blank."

Moreover, the necessary and decisive processes of spiritual rebirth and social transformation were to take place in the countryside and not in the cities. This conviction was of course a wholesale inversion of the Marxist-Leninist view of the relationship between town and countryside in the making of modern revolutionary history. Just as Maoist revolutionary strategy rested on a faith in the revolutionary potential of the peasantry, so Maoism in the postrevolutionary era was characterized by a belief that the true sources for socialist construction resided in the countryside, a perception fortified by the powerful antiurban biases bred during the revolutionary years. When the Communists captured the cities of China in 1949, Mao warned against the moral and ideological impurities that urban life would likely foster.[21] Twenty years later, he complained that the occupation of the cities was "a bad thing because it caused our Party to deteriorate."[22]

Closely associated with the emphasis on spiritual transformation and the faith in the capacity of the peasantry to achieve socialist ends was, as noted earlier, a general Maoist belief in the revolutionary advantages of backwardness.[23] Though economic backwardness eventually was to be overcome, it nevertheless was perceived as the source of moral and revolutionary purity, in contrast to the economically advanced countries or the advanced areas of China where the revolutionary spirit tended to be stifled under the weight of moral decadence and political complacency. From this belief flowed that most extraordinary of Mao's revisions of Marx and Lenin, the thesis advanced in 1960 to the effect that "the more backward the econ-

21. See Mao Tse-tung, "Report to the Second Plenary Session of the Seventh Central Committee of the Communist Party of China," in Mao, *Selected Works,* (Peking), vol. 4, p. 374.

22. Mao Tse-tung, "Talk at the First Plenum of the Ninth Central Committee of the Chinese Communist Party" (28 April 1969), in Schram, ed., *Mao Unrehearsed,* p. 288.

23. See Chapter 3, pp. 101–3.

omy, the easier [is] the transition" to socialism.[24] It was a strain in the Maoist mentality that expressed itself in the worship of youth as the bearer of a socialist future and in a distrust of intellectuals as barriers to a socialist future. Just as the peasantry was seen as relatively ideologically pure by virtue of its very backwardness (in contrast to the inhabitants of the "advanced" cities), so youth were seen as potentially more revolutionary than their elders because their very youthfulness rendered them more amenable to moral and ideological transformation. "From ancient times the people who have created new schools of thought have always been young people without great learning," Mao declared, for "when young people grasp a truth they are invincible and old people cannot compete with them." For Mao it was a historical truism that young people have "the ability to recognize new things at a glance and having grasped them, they opened fire on the old fogeys. The old fogeys with learning always opposed them."[25]

This celebration of the creativity of youth was accompanied by a general Maoist distrust of intellectuals, of professionalism and expertise, and of formal education. "When the intellectuals had power, things were in a bad state [and] the country was in disorder," Mao observed, and thus "it is evident that to read too many books is harmful," for "Liu Hsiu [the founder of the Later Han dynasty who suppressed a peasant rebellion in A.D. 27] was an academician, whereas Liu Pang [the famed peasant rebel who founded the Han dynasty in 206 B.C.] was a country bumpkin."[26] Nor was Mao's evidence drawn only from Chinese history; to support his belief that "it is not absolutely necessary to attend school," Mao noted that such creative spirits as Benjamin Franklin and Maxim Gorky had little formal education.[27] And there were Maoist remedies to prevent the pernicious influences of intellectuals and intellectualism: "We must drive actors, poets, dramatists and writers out of the cities, and pack them

24. *Mao Tse-tung ssu-hsiang wan-sui* [Long live the thought of Mao Tse-tung] (Taipei: n.p., 1969), pp. 333–34.

25. Mao Tse-tung, "Talks at Chengtu" (22 March 1958) in Schram, ed., *Mao Unrehearsed,* pp. 118–19.

26. Mao Tse-tung, "Remarks at the Spring Festival" (13 February 1964), ibid., p. 204.

27. Mao, "Talks at Chengtu," pp. 119–20.

off to the countryside."[28] Moreover, "We shouldn't read too many books. We should read Marxist books, but not too many of them either. . . . If you read too many books, they petrify your mind in the end."[29] And Mao, if no longer young nor unread, nevertheless prided himself on being "a rough fellow, not cultured at all."[30]

In no area is the contrast between Maoism and Marxism more pronounced. Marx and indeed Lenin found the promise of a socialist future in the activity of the most advanced and modern social classes; they believed that socialism could be built only on the cultural as well as the material foundations of modern capitalism, and they took it for granted that the new society would inherit and appropriate all the historical and cultural accomplishments of the past. Mao and Maoists, by contrast, placed their faith in the future in the potentialities of backwardness and the backward, looked to the revolutionary spontaneity and the practical experience of the "uneducated" and the "uncultured," celebrated the virtues of being "poor and blank," and saw peasants and youth as the bearers of socialism and communism.

Moreover, as we have seen in Chapter 4, the Maoist road to socialism placed an enormous emphasis on the internalization of the ascetic values of struggle, self-sacrifice, and self-denial. It involved a generalization and idealization of the whole galaxy of ascetic values embodied in the model guerilla leader of the revolutionary years. In the extreme voluntarism that characterized the Maoist world view, it was men imbued with the proper revolutionary spirit and moral values who were crucial in the making of history and in the achievement of a communist future.

The Maoist departures from Marxism lay not simply in the "utopian" character of the means by which Maoists proposed to realize communist ends, but also—and more profoundly—in the normative value placed on those means and their partial conversion into ultimate ends. The means of Maoism were themselves components of the Maoist vision of the good society of the future. The moral transformation of the people was not only the prerequisite for communism

28. Mao, "Remarks at the Spring Festival," p. 207.
29. Ibid., pp. 210–11.
30. Mao, "Speech at the Lushan Conference," p. 140.

but part of a vision of a future that was as much a spiritual utopia as a social and material one. A collectivistic society based on common spiritual bonds and maintained through a ceaseless process of "ideological struggle" against the ever-present danger of the intrusion of incorrect thoughts was a central element in the Maoist vision of the future. The Maoist conception of the leap from "the realm of necessity" to "the realm of freedom" suggests not the Marxist image of a society conducive to the free realization of individual human potentialities but rather a society whose members are engaged in a constant struggle to internalize and practice prescribed collectivistic moral values and social norms.

Similarly, the belief that the truly creative sources of the future utopia reside primarily in the countryside rather than in the cities involved more than making a virtue out of necessity in a predominantly agrarian country. What were perceived as the virtues of peasants and rural traditions were ethically valued in themselves and projected into a conception of the good society of the future. The Maoist celebration of the rural traditions of "plain living and hard work" were seen not only as serving a utilitarian function in the present but also as components of an essentially rural utopian vision, a vision of a new society that would inherit the virtues of rural life and popular peasant cultural traditions.[31]

Moreover, the antitechnocratic bias in Maoism (the distrust of intellectuals in general and technological and bureaucratic expertise in particular) reflected not only the Maoist confrontation with the dilemma of the means and ends of socialism—the fear that the growth of bureaucratism and the emergence of a technological intelligentsia would preclude the realization of egalitarian social goals. The bias also was intimately connected with a positive image of "the new communist man," the layman "red and expert" who would be a politically conscious "jack of all trades," combining "brain work

31. The enormous Maoist celebration of popular folk culture—what Mao in the Yenan years praised as "the fine old culture of the people which has a more or less democratic and revolutionary character"—stands of course in striking contrast to the iconoclastic Maoist attitude toward both the Chinese Confucian tradition and the Western bourgeois tradition.

with brawn work" and mastering modern technology in the course of everyday work. The ideal "red and expert" of the present, modeled on the Yenan guerilla leader of the past, was the Maoist prototype for the "all-round" communist man of the future.

Finally, the value of struggle was seen not simply as a means to construct the socioeconomic foundations for a communist utopia, but received an absolute ethical sanction for all time. In the Maoist world view, struggles and contradictions were regarded as both infinite and good, and thus were themselves part of the vision of the utopia of the future.

In this conversion of the means to achieve communism into ultimate communist ends, one detects a partially dystopian strain in the Maoist mentality whereby the dominant values and tendencies of the present, and current conditions of economic backwardness, were projected into a vision of a spiritual and rural-based future utopia. Cultural backwardness gave rise to a celebration of the absolute virtues of youth and the eternal creativity of the uneducated masses, and the values of struggle and self-sacrifice to overcome backwardness themselves became absolute values and final ends. The imperatives of the present historical situation became, in effect, the goals to be realized more fully in the future.

The dystopian strain is especially pronounced in the Maoist belief in "the universality of contradiction." For Mao, contradictions and struggles were not simply the motive force of historical change in class society but universal and perpetual laws of nature and history which would persist under socialism and communism as well; they characterized not only the current historical epoch but would continue into eternity. Mao was opposed in principle (both political and philosophic) to any notion of a harmonious and united future society.

An enormous emphasis on contradiction and struggle was a characteristic feature of the Maoist mentality from the beginning, but it was not until his latter years that Mao set forth the view that contradictions were permanent and ceaseless features of human history. In his philosophic writings of the Yenan era, Mao equated "the law of the contradiction in things" with "the law of the unity of opposites" and predicted that contradictions would become "nonantagonistic" in a socialist society and disappear entirely with the realization of a communist society.[32] By the late 1950s he not only was insisting on the necessity and inevitability of the continuation of class struggle under socialism but also the permanence of contradiction and conflict in communist society as well. In 1956 there appeared the first hint that the future he envisioned would be one of ceaseless conflict: "For 10,000 years to come there will always be two sides. Each age has its two sides."[33] In 1957 Mao declared that class struggle in the "ideological field" will "never end."[34] In the following year he wrote that even after a classless society had been achieved, "ideological and political struggles between men and revolutions will continue to occur; they will never cease."[35] The law of "the unity of contradictions" no longer promised the overcoming of all contradictions in the communist future but rather dictated a future of unending struggle:

> In the communist era there will be many, many phases of development. The development from one phase to another must necessarily be a relationship between quantitative to qualitative changes. All mutations, all leaps forward are revolutions which must pass through struggles. The theory of cessation of struggles is sheer metaphysics.[36]

He later put the matter more explicitly: "When we reach Communism will there be no struggles? I don't believe that either. When we reach Communism there will still be struggles, but they will be between the new and the old, the correct and the incorrect, that is all. After tens of millennia have passed by, the incorrect will still be no good and will fail."[37]

32. Mao Tse-tung, "On Contradictions," in Mao Tse-tung, *The Selected Works of Mao Tse-tung* (London: Lawrence and Wishart, 1954), vol. 2, pp. 51–52.

33. Mao, "On the Ten Great Relationships," p. 81.

34. Mao Tse-tung, *On the Correct Handling of Contradictions Among the People* (Peking: Foreign Languages Press, 1957), p. 51.

35. Mao, "Sixty Points on Working Methods," p. 65.

36. Ibid.

37. "Summary of Chairman Mao's Talks with Responsible Comrades during His Provincial Tour" (August–September 1971), in Schram, ed., *Mao Unrehearsed,* pp. 297–98.

The Maoist notion of a future of inevitable and ceaseless contradictions and struggles did not deny a progressive historical development. Socialist and communist goals would be achieved, according to Mao, in a historical process that proceeded in what he described as a "wave-like advance" but "not as a continuously rising line,"[38] a conception that allowed for periods of historical regression as well as for Mao's oft-stated belief that China could as easily revert to capitalism as move forward to socialism and communism. In the Maoist view, the world of history as well as the world of nature was characterized by a perpetual dialectical interaction between "equilibrium" and "disequilibrium." As Mao put it: "The cycle, which is endless, evolves from disequilibrium to equilibrium and then to disequilibrium again. Each cycle, however, brings us to a higher level of development." Yet it was "disequilibrium [that] is normal and absolute whereas equilibrium is temporary and relative."[39] From this "general, objective rule" there logically followed the notion of the infinity of contradictions and struggles and the Maoist insistence that "one divides into two" was the principal law of dialectics.

Yet if these Maoist conceptions did not preclude historical progress, they did implicitly reject the Marxist vision of a historical process leading to a "total revolution" and a "final denouement" (as Marx characterized it) resulting in the definitive overcoming of all contradictions and antagonisms.[40] In the Maoist world view there could be no final resolution of contradictions and no possibility of any perfect social unity. There is a remarkable similarity here between Mao and Pierre Joseph Proudhon, the nineteenth-century theorist whose ideas Marx characterized as a form of "bourgeois socialism." Like Mao, Proudhon believed that contradiction was an absolute and eternal law—although, unlike Mao, his solution was to establish an equilibrium of contradictions and antagonisms. But like Mao, Proudhon (as Robert Tucker has observed) "was opposed in principle to a

38. Mao Tse-tung, "Talk at Seventh Plenum of the Eighth Central Committee of the Chinese Communist Party," translated in "Miscellany of Mao Tse-tung Thought (1949–1968)," in *JPRS* 61269-1:175.

39. Mao, "Sixty Points on Working Methods," p. 66.

40. Karl Marx, *The Poverty of Philosophy* (Moscow: Foreign Languages Publishing House, n.d.), p. 168.

search for unity in society."[41] Proudhon's "dialectics" revolved about a notion of an everlasting distinction between the "good" and the "bad," just as Mao foresaw an eternal battle between "the correct" and "the incorrect." It was, of course, precisely on these issues that Marx directed some of his most sarcastic criticisms against Proudhon. Marx accused Proudhon of failing to even pose the question of the basis of contradictions that Marx demanded be overthrown and overcome; instead, Proudhon simply accepted them as inherent in history and sought to reconcile them. Nor did Marx have a high opinion of Proudhon's understanding of dialectics: "M. Proudhon has nothing of Hegel's dialectics but the language. For him the dialectic movement is the dogmatic distinction between good and bad."[42] It would not be unfair to suggest that Marx might have viewed Mao in a similar light.

If the dystopian strain in the Maoist mentality reflected itself by projecting the contradictions and struggles of the present into the communist future (albeit in a more benign form), Mao was more profoundly dystopian in his philosophic speculations about the ultimate future of mankind. For Mao's ultimate vision extended far beyond the communist future. In accordance with the dictum, first set forth in 1956, that "everything which is produced by history will also be destroyed by history,"[43] one finds "the Maoist vision" taking the following form in 1958:

> Capitalism leads to socialism, socialism leads to communism, and communist society must still be transformed, it will also have a beginning and an end. . . . it cannot remain constant. . . . There is nothing in the world that does not arise, develop, and disappear. Monkeys turned into men, mankind arose; in the end, the whole human race will disappear, it may turn into something else [and] at that time the earth itself will also cease to exist. The earth must certainly be extinguished, the sun too will grow cold. . . . All things have a beginning and an end. Only two things are infinite: time and space.[44]

41. Robert C. Tucker, "Marx and Distributive Justice," in Robert C. Tucker, *The Marxian Revolutionary Idea* (New York: Norton, 1969), p. 52.

42. Marx, *The Poverty of Philosophy*, p. 108.

43. Mao, "On the Ten Great Relationships," p. 75.

44. Mao, "Talks at Chengtu," p. 110.

And in 1964 Mao once again peered into the "postcommunist" future:

> The life of dialectics is the continuous movement toward opposition. Mankind will also finally meet its doom. When theologians talk about doomsday, they are pessimistic and terrify people. We say that the end of mankind is something which will produce something more advanced than mankind. Mankind is still in its infancy.[45]

Here the Maoist "law of dialectics" is carried to its ultimately logical but historically absurd conclusion.

III. Functions of the Maoist Vision

The general role that Maoist utopianism has played in contemporary Chinese sociohistorical development might briefly be summarized. As is typically the case with activistic utopian mentalities, Maoism established a radical contrast between the ideal and the actually existent, an extraordinary sense of tension between a vision of what the world should be and what it actually is, and thus served to orient human activity to transform the world in accordance with the ideal future it portrayed. Insofar as Maoism projected a positive Marxist image of a socialist and communist future, it served (as suggested in Chapter 4) to ethically sanction ascetic values of struggle, self-sacrifice, frugality, self-discipline, and hard work conducive to promoting production and modern economic development, especially since these familiar virtues tended to be presented as ultimate values and ends in themselves.

The "modernizing" role of Maoism was reinforced by the extremely iconoclastic and strongly antitraditionalist thrust of the doctrine. As is typical of utopian mentalities, Maoism demanded the total renunciation of the values of the past in favor of a commitment to the new ethics and morality of the envisioned new society; it demanded a rejection of all the values associated with the Confucian preference for a harmonious adaptation to the world, a radical devaluation of traditional kinship ties and loyalties, and a repudiation of the Confucian disdain for manual labor. It sought instead, "rational

45. Mao Tse-tung, "Talk on Questions of Philosophy," in Schram, ed., *Mao Unrehearsed*, p. 228.

mastery over the world" and in doing so encouraged a spirit of experimentation and innovation favorable to modern economic development. The virulently iconoclastic stance of Maoism clashed with the Marxist view that the new society must be built on the foundations of the old society from whose womb it emerged, and that socialism presupposed inheriting and appropriating all the cultural as well as material accomplishments of the past; yet it was a stance well in keeping with the Weberian view that a decisive and fundamental break with the traditions and values of the past was an essential prerequisite for modern economic and political rationalization. And in the tradition-bound Chinese historical environment, a disciple of Weber might well view the utopian and prophetic element in Maoism as the necessary precondition to bring about that break.

Yet the Maoist utopian vision functioned as more than simply a means of "modernization." It had social results and political consequences largely antithetical to those posited in most theories of modernization. The messianic posture that Mao and Maoism assumed proved profoundly resistant to bureaucratic routinization, resistant to the new forms of social inequality which naturally accompany the modern economic development of a backward country, and resistant to the general institutionalization of the postrevolutionary order. The deeply egalitarian and antibureaucratic components of the Maoist vision, if not realized in social reality, nonetheless produced a continuous struggle against social, political, and ideological tendencies incongruous with that vision of the future. If the attempts to implement the Maoist vision have not resulted in anything resembling a classless society (or even a socialist one), they did succeed in limiting the degree of social inequality. If bureaucracy has not been (and perhaps cannot be) eliminated as Mao may have wished and as his vision promised, Maoist policies served to inhibit the stratification of bureaucratic elites operating on the basis of a vocational ethic separated from the Maoist political ethic. And perhaps most importantly, Maoist utopianism forestalled the ritualization of socialist and communist goals and eluded the presumably inevitable processes of "deradicalization."[46] Whether this resistance to routinization and

46. See Robert C. Tucker, "The Deradicalization of Marxist Movements," in Tucker, *Marxian Revolutionary Idea*, pp. 172–214.

institutionalization will survive into the post-Maoist era is of course highly problematic, for so much of what has been unique and distinctive about China's postrevolutionary history has been intimately tied to the vision and the cult of Mao, and both presuppose his person and presence.

If Mao's positive vision of a Marxist-prophesied future served to orient human action toward achieving the economic and social goals demanded by that vision, then what was the functional significance of the dystopian strains in the Maoist mentality—the idiosyncratic vision that projected a future of endless contradictions and struggles, the vision that looked not only to a communist utopia but to the supersession of communism, a vision that foresaw the end of history and the disintegration of the universe? It would seem to be the paradoxical case that Mao's dystopia played much the same social role as did his utopia. For the dystopian strains flowed from a philosophical world view that postulated the constancy of change as both inevitable and desirable, as both a cosmic law and a human need. It is a philosophy which taught that change is an absolute and objective law of history and nature, and at the same time placed an absolute normative value on change and the spirit of change as a way of life. Just as Mao's utopian vision of a future communist society demanded human action in the here and now to create that society, so his long-term dystopian vision and speculations supported a political and ethical demand to struggle and strive for change. Both his utopia and his dystopia served to activate men to transform themselves and the world in which they live. And if Mao's ultimate vision of the dialectical movement led out of history to the doom of mankind, to the end of time when the sun "will grow cold," then that prospect resided in a future far too distant to have any imaginable relationship to the present, far too distant and unrelated to human experience to contemplate. In the historical time before "the end of days," Mao's dystopian philosophy conveyed a message of the necessity and desirability of change in general and the ethical value of struggle to effect change in the present world.

The dystopian strain in the Maoist vision of the future—if not carried to its ultimate conclusion of the end of history and the extinction of the universe—has the perhaps paradoxical effect of making the Maoist utopia seem more historically realistic and humanly comprehensible than is generally the case with utopian visions of a future perfect order. For one of the most common and compelling objections to utopia is that it is a product of a sterile blueprint which portrays a society that is ultimately static, lifeless, and boring. Ralf Dahrendorf, for example, finds little difference between utopia and a cemetery, with the exception that "occasionally some things do happen in utopia." But what little happens is not very interesting because "all processes going on in utopian societies follow recurrent patterns and occur within, and as part of, the design of the whole," and thus utopia remains "a *perpetuum immobile*."[47] The problem is that most conceptions of utopia preclude the possibility, or at least the desirability, of change. As George Kateb has observed, the problem is "the apparent incompatibility between the intention of most utopian writers and the inevitability and moral desirability of change."

> It is right to say that almost all utopian designs do not reckon with change. The common assumption is that once the design is realized in the world—if it ever is—it will continue indefinitely in the form in which it began. Utopian thought is dominated by a "rage for order." A strong utopian impetus is to save the world from as much of its confusion and disorder as possible. Utopia is a dream of order, of quiet and calm. Its background is the nightmare of history. At the same time, the order, in each case, is thought to be either perfect or as close to perfect as human affairs can get. How, in truth, could a thinker possessed both of a rage for order and a sense that he commands a vision of perfection (or near perfection) comfortably allow for change? . . . by definition, change away from perfection must necessarily be for the worse. To build in the possibility for change in utopia, therefore, is to compromise the usual premises of utopian thought.[48]

Mao, by postulating the inevitability of change and the eternity of struggle, and incorporating them into his vision of the future, made his utopia immune to this critique. The Maoist utopian vision not only allowed for change but demanded it, and at the same time

47. Ralf Dahrendorf, "Out of Utopia: Toward a Reorientation of Sociological Analysis," in George Kateb, ed., *Utopia* (New York: Atherton Press, 1971), p. 106.

48. Kateb, ed., *Utopia*, p. 8.

envisioned a future utopia which remained tied to the struggles and sorrows of human experience in the present world, a future which remained fraught with risk and uncertainty and one which allowed a role for human heroism and courage. Indeed, in many respects, the Maoist vision of the future filled the prescription H. G. Wells once recommended to cure utopia of its historically inert and humanly confining character, a prescription to create a "Modern Utopia [which] must not be static but kinetic, must shape not as a permanent state but as a hopeful stage, leading to a long ascent of stages."[49]

49. H. G. Wells, *A Modern Utopia* (1905), quoted in Kateb, ed., *Utopia*, p. 9.

8

The Ritualization of Utopia: Chinese Marxism in the Post-Maoist Era

I. The Post-Revolutionary Era

"The socialists might conquer, but not socialism, which would perish in the moment of its adherents' triumph," Robert Michels wrote at the turn of the century.[1] The histories of twentieth-century socialist revolutions offer little evidence, and even less comfort, for those who might be inclined to dispute Michels' cynical prediction. However one may choose to judge the social and economic accomplishments of revolutions which have proceeded under Marxist political auspices—and judgments of course differ—few would judge that socialist revolutions have produced socialist societies. The Marxist promise of "a truly human life" remains unfulfilled, and there is nothing on the contemporary historical horizon to sustain a faith that the promise will be realized under any of the current Communist regimes which rule over what all too easily are labelled socialist societies.

The failure of revolutions to achieve the goals proclaimed by their leaders and ideologists is of course not a peculiarity of contemporary socialist revolutions. It has been the general historical case that great social revolutions have been inspired by great utopian visions of a future perfect social order—and it has been no less generally the case that such grand visions have perished in the postrevolutionary era. It

1. Robert Michels, *Political Parties* (Glencoe, Ill.: The Free Press, 1949), p. 391.

is not simply a matter of revolutionaries in power betraying their ideals and their hopes for a radically new and better society (although that is a common enough phenomenon), but rather that the political and economic conditions of postrevolutionary situations seem to impel revolutionaries-turned-rulers to compromise with existing realities and with the traditions of the past. The process of the postponement and ritualization of utopian social goals, and the manipulation of utopian symbols to ideologically rationalize new forms of social inequality and political oppression, is of course an all too familiar pattern in the history of revolutions, and there are familiar formulae which describe the process. Perhaps the most familiar is Crane Brinton's thesis of the "universality of the Thermidorian reaction," which Brinton defines as that point in the revolutionary process when there is a "convalescence from the fever of revolution," the decline of revolutionary utopianism, and a return to "normalcy."[2] A recent variant of Brinton's thesis is Robert Tucker's intriguing argument on the "deradicalization" of Marxist movements—the presumably inevitable willingness, sooner or later, of Marxist revolutionaries to come to terms with the existing order of things.[3]

It is no argument against revolution in general to acknowledge that the directions societies take in the wake of successful revolutionary upheavals are usually far different than those originally envisioned, and that the utopian visions essential to revolutionary endeavors are hopes which fade and die in postrevolutionary eras. Barrington Moore was perhaps too optimistic in drawing from his study of modern revolutions the generalization that "the utopian radical conceptions of one phase become the accepted institutions and philosophical platitudes of the next."[4] If utopian visions of the future survive successful revolutions, they do so only in distorted and disfigured form. They serve less as the foundations for new institutions than as ritualized ideological slogans manipulated to justify the institution-

2. Crane Brinton, *The Anatomy of Revolution*, rev. ed. (New York: Vintage, 1965), pp. 205–36.

3. Robert C. Tucker, "The Deradicalization of Marxist Movements," in Robert C. Tucker, *The Marxian Revolutionary Idea* (New York: Norton, 1969), pp. 172–214.

4. Barrington Moore, *Social Origins of Dictatorship and Democracy* (Boston: Beacon Press, 1966), p. 505.

alization of social orders which bear but faint resemblances to the original conceptions. Indeed, the tragedy of revolution resides precisely in the fact that utopian hopes do become transformed into philosophical platitudes rather than surviving as living sources of inspiration for social action. That such terms as "Thermidor," "Bonapartism," and "deradicalization" have become commonplace in descriptions of the life cycles of revolutions is itself testimony to the unhappy fate of utopian hopes and revolutionary ideals. They suggest not the simple failure of revolution but rather a process of degeneration which seems inherent in its very success. There is perhaps some measure of historical validity in the view that "the truth of all revolutions is not that they turn into counterrevolutions but that they become boring."[5]

The incongruity between utopian revolutionary ideals and postrevolutionary realities might best be understood less in terms of the personal limitations of revolutionaries than in light of the historical limitations imposed by the conditions of their times. For the utopian visions which inspire revolutions, and the even higher utopian hopes which periods of revolutionary upheaval arouse, always far outrun objective historical possibilities. The communitarian and egalitarian dreams of the Levellers and the Diggers in the English Civil War clashed with, and eventually were submerged by, the interests of the propertied classes in establishing an order favorable to the growth of modern capitalist commerce and industry. The social results of the French Revolution bore little resemblance to the great ideals of *liberté, égalité, fraternité*—and the radical intellectuals who proclaimed them and the radicalized plebeians who fought for them were soon swept off the historical stage once the destruction of the *ancien régime* was accomplished. As Isaac Deutscher observed: "The irrationality of the Puritan and Jacobin revolutions arose largely out of the clash between the high hopes of the insurgent masses and the bourgeois limitations of those revolutions."[6]

The clash between revolutionary utopian hopes and objective his-

5. Kenneth Allsop, *The Spectator* (March 1959), as quoted in James H. Meisel, *Counter-Revolution* (New York: Atherton, 1966), p. xii.

6. Isaac Deutscher, *The Unfinished Revolution: Russia 1917–1967* (London: Oxford University Press, 1967), p. 27.

torical limitations has been especially acute in the case of twentieth-century socialist revolutions. Karl Marx insisted that socialism presupposed a highly developed industrial economy and a large and politically mature proletariat, the products of modern capitalism. But it has been the great irony of the history of Marxism in the modern world that Marxist-led revolutions have succeeded not in the advanced industrialized countries which, Marxist theory taught, were prepared for a socialist reorganization of society, but rather in economically backward nations lacking the Marxian-defined material and social prerequisites for socialism. The postrevolutionary results of this incongruity are well known. Having achieved power in countries laboring under the burdens of agrarian backwardness, Marxist revolutionaries have been forced to turn their energies to industrializing the backward lands over which they have come to rule; in effect, they have been confronted with the task of building the preconditions for socialism rather than socialism itself. As Marxist rulers undertake the work of modern economic development which earlier and abortive capitalist regimes failed to accomplish, and create massive bureaucratic state structures to preside over the modernization process, socialist goals are postponed. Industrialization, originally conceived as the means to attain socialist ends, soon acquires a dynamic of its own and, indeed, tends to become an end in itself. And while the means and values of modern economic development remain lasting, the goals of socialism are relegated to an increasingly vague and indefinite future, and eventually degenerate into ritualized ideological slogans invoked to spur production and to provide a spurious political legitimacy. In the end, the subjective aims of the revolutionaries seem vanquished by the objective limitations of history and the socialist regime appears little more than "capitalism without capitalists," to borrow Adam Ulam's suggestive phrase.[7]

The Maoist era of the People's Republic seemed to promise a radical departure from these familiar processes of the postrevolutionary institutionalization of an industrializing order and the ritualization of utopian goals. Rather than declining after the political triumph

7. Adam Ulam, *The Unfinished Revolution* (New York: Random House, 1960), p. 45.

of 1949, the utopian impulse in Maoism grew stronger and the commitment to ultimate Marxian aims took on increasingly chiliastic overtones in the 1950s and 1960s, portending new and ever more radical revolutionary dramas which attempted to enact the prologue to a communist future. The backwardness of the Chinese economy, rather than serving as a reason to postpone the socialist reorganization of society, was converted into a socialist advantage in Maoist ideology. The proclaimed socialist virtues of being "poor and blank," though a startling inversion of Marxist and Leninist orthodoxies, by no means implied that Mao envisioned a communist society residing in perpetual conditions of material impoverishment. The modernization of China was no less highly placed on Mao's political agenda than it is on that of his successors. But modernization, during the Maoist era, was accompanied by a unique willingness to confront the dilemma of the means and ends of socialism in an economically backward land, by a demand to reconcile the means of industrialization with the goals and values of socialism and communism. Through a process of "permanent revolution" which demanded increasingly radical social and ideological transformations, the ultimate goals prophesied in Marxist theory were to be striven for (and realized in at least embryonic form) in the here and now, in the very process of constructing their Marxian-defined economic prerequisites. During the first quarter-century of the history of postrevolutionary China, at least during times when Mao and Maoists held sway, there were few signs of the presumably inevitable process of "deradicalization." The utopian spirit of the era was conveyed in one of Mao's last poems, *Reascending Chingkangshan:*

> We can clasp the moon in the ninth heaven
> And seize turtles deep down in the five seas.
> We'll return amid triumphant song and laughter.
> Nothing is hard in this world
> If you dare to scale the heights.[8]

Yet Maoist utopianism, it would now seem, has not survived the passing of Mao Tse-tung from the historical scene. It doubtless is

8. Mao Tse-tung, *Poems* (Peking: Foreign Languages Press, 1976), p. 5.

hazardous to predict the future of Chinese society on the basis of current Chinese political and ideological proclivities, much less on the basis of the historical experience of other postrevolutionary societies. The Chinese Revolution has taken a good many unanticipated radical turns over the decades, and it may yet produce new revolutionary dramas by actors who now wait in the wings. But from the vantage of the present it would appear that the Chinese Revolution, albeit more belatedly than most revolutions, has not eluded "the universality of the Thermidorian reaction." The depoliticization of socioeconomic life and the deradicalization of political life in the years since the death of Mao Tse-tung—or what most foreign observers celebrate as the "pragmatism" of the policies of the post-Mao leadership—has been accompanied by the emergence of a new version of Chinese Marxist theory which both reflects and promotes an accommodation to the existing social order. The doctrine that is still officially termed "Marxism-Leninism-Mao Tsetung Thought" now bears little resemblance to what it was during the Maoist era. It is above all a doctrine from which all utopian elements and impulses have been purged, and one in which new authors have rewritten or abandoned most of what was distinctively "Maoist" in the Chinese version of Marxism in favor of more orthodox Marxist-Leninist perspectives. Several of the more salient features of this recent process of ideological transformation might be briefly examined for what they reveal about the processes of the ritualization of utopian goals and visions.

II. Economic Determinism and the Objective Laws of Development

One of the most striking and pervasive characteristics of Chinese Marxism in the post-Mao era is a newly found faith in the existence of objective laws of historical and economic development. Whereas Maoism (during the Maoist era) was characterized by a highly voluntaristic faith in the ability of people armed with the proper will and consciousness to conquer all material barriers and mold social reality in accordance with their ideas and ideals, Chinese Marxist theoreticians now view history as a more or less natural process governed by immutable laws which operate independently of human wishes and desires. As typically stated: "The laws of development of social history are objective laws which cannot be changed at will. They should be treated the same as the laws of the process of natural history."[9]

Such objective social laws, it is believed, can be determined with a scientific accuracy approximating the precision of research in the natural sciences. Indeed, the tendency to equate the laws of nature and the laws of history gives an almost positivistic cast to the contemporary Chinese Marxist mentality. "The development of society," it is repeatedly proclaimed, "is just like the development of the material world and is determined by objective rules."[10]

Just as there are general objective laws of history whose dictates must be obeyed, so, it is believed, there are specific (but no less objective) economic laws which govern the development of a socialist society. Progress is therefore dependent on discovering what are termed "the objective laws of socialist economic development" and pursuing policies in accordance with them. To do otherwise invites disaster, for "objective economic laws are inviolable and [those] who violate them will be punished." The most flagrant violators of such laws were of course Lin Piao and the "Gang of Four" (and, by implication, Mao Tse-tung)—and the Chinese nation which was subjected to their ill-advised and nonscientific policies was duly "punished by the law of objectivity."[11]

The existence of objective laws of socialist economic development is taken for granted by post-Maoist theoreticians, yet the precise nature and content of such laws remains less than entirely clear. Here

9. Discussion at Institute of Philosophic Research, Chinese Academy of Social Sciences, Peking, 25 June 1980. The comment was made to a group of seven Western scholars, including this writer, who held talks with leading Chinese Marxist theoreticians and scholars in the People's Republic from 15 June to 15 July 1980. Further references to statements made during the course of these conversations will be entitled "Discussions" and will indicate the place, time and institution but not the individual speaker. The trip to China was made possible through the assistance of a research grant from the National Endowment for the Humanities.

10. *Che-hsüeh yen-chiu* [Philosophic research] 2 (February 1979) in *JPRS* 73710:13.

11. Xue Moqiao, "Study and Apply the Objective Laws of Socialist Economic Development," *Jingji Yanjiu* [Economic research] 6 (1979) in *JPRS* 74029:1–5.

the theoreticians have thus far largely contented themselves with repeating some of the more deterministic formulations of Karl Marx and Joseph Stalin. From Marx there is derived the familiar proposition that the economic "base" determines the sociopolitical "superstructure"; it was the inversion of the proper relationship between base and superstructure, it is charged, that was responsible for many of the most grievous errors of the past. (A much favored source of textual authority is Marx's well-known summary of the materialist conception of history in the preface to the *Critique of Political Economy,* a statement which easily lends itself to an economically deterministic interpretation.) Stalin is praised for his correct exposition of "the laws of economics under socialism," especially the law that the relations of production must conform to the character of productive forces, the law that the national economy must be developed according to a plan, and the continuance of "the law of value" in a socialist economy.[12]

The belief in objective historical and economic laws appears in the context of a new Chinese Marxist mentality characterized by an increasingly economically deterministic interpretation of the doctrine in general. This is especially apparent in prevailing views on the question of the material preconditions for socialism. Whereas Mao Tse-tung believed that a "continuous" process of the transformation of social relationships and popular consciousness must accompany (and indeed precede) the process of modern economic development in order to bring about a socialist historical outcome, his political and ideological successors emphasize the orthodox Marxist view that the prior development of productive forces to a very high level is the first and essential prerequisite for a socialist society. Marxism, it is stressed, teaches that "socialism can only be built on a foundation of highly developed socialized large-scale production."[13] And, it is further stressed, the process of constructing such necessary economic preconditions will span a lengthy historical era. As one leading theoretician recently speculated: "Perhaps by the year 2050 we

12. For example, ibid. pp. 7ff.

13. Li Yinha and Lin Chun, "Tentative Discussion on the Struggle Against Vestiges of Feudalism in China During the Period of Building Socialism," *Lishi Yanjiu* [Historical research] 9 (1979), in *JPRS* 74829:32.

shall accomplish our high degree of modernization, the developed stage of socialism."[14]

The emphasis on objective laws of history, at least as presented in post-Maoist Chinese Marxist literature, serves less to convey an optimistic faith in the historical inevitability of a socialist future than it does as a warning that objective reality imposes stringent limits on the possibilities for human action and social change. For, it is repeatedly emphasized, the laws which presumably determine the course of historical development "cannot be altered by the will of man," nor, for that matter, even by "the subjective will of the Party."[15] Men thus must recognize the restraints imposed by objective laws and obey their dictates. Indeed it is assumed that the economic failures and political turbulence of the Maoist era resulted from an exaggerated stress on the factors of human will and consciousness—and from premature changes in the social relations of production. The notion that the "superstructure" might play a decisive role in historical development is now condemned as a "reactionary theory" propagated by Lin Piao and the "Gang of Four."

By invoking objective historical and economic laws, and by making the socialist utopia dependent on their workings, post-Maoist Chinese Marxist theory both postpones socialism and communism to an indefinite time in the future and counsels that people can do little to hasten the arrival of the good society. For objective social laws, particularly when they are conceived as analogous to the laws of nature, work slowly and yield their presumably socialist results only gradually, and thus it would be "utopian" and "unscientific" to anticipate the hoped-for society in the foreseeable future. And since objective laws cannot be altered by human will and consciousness—and indeed since recent historical experience allegedly teaches that such intrusions are not only historically fruitless but politically pernicious—the socialist future is made ultimately dependent on the impersonal workings of such presumably objective historical and economic laws. Moreover, both the lengthy and impersonal nature

14. "Discussions," Marxism-Leninism-Mao Tsetung Thought Institute, Peking, 17 June 1980.

15. Xue, "Study and Apply the Objective Laws of Socialist Economic Development," p. 7.

of the process is underlined by the repeated insistence that the very highest level of the development of productive forces is the first and essential prerequisite for the emergence of a genuine socialist society. And as China is an impoverished and backward land, the road to be travelled is a long and arduous one, and thus the destination lies far in the distance. In the meantime, human energies are to be devoted almost exclusively to productive work, not to the building of socialism but rather to the task of constructing its necessary economic foundations.

What is therefore envisioned in the contemporary Chinese Marxist mentality is an essentially evolutionary rather than revolutionary process of historical development governed by the operation of objective laws rather than by human desires and visionary hopes. The radical aspects of the Maoist tradition which are incongruous with this evolutionary perspective are naturally eliminated from the reinterpreted body of orthodox doctrine which is still presented under the label of "Marxism-Leninism-Mao Tsetung Thought." Mao's theory of "permanent revolution," for example, is now denounced as non-Marxist,[16] or sometimes simply reinterpreted as meaning no more than a "technological revolution, identical in meaning with modernization."[17] And Mao's doctrine of the continuance of class struggle under socialism has been replaced by a doctrine which announces the withering away of class struggle. Just as Stalin announced the cessation of class struggle in the Soviet Union in 1936, so Chinese Communist leaders now proclaim that "class struggle has ceased to be the principal contradiction in our society,"[18] indeed sometimes dismissing it as no more than "a legacy from the past."[19] The notion that class conflict has all but ceased, the further implications of which will be discussed shortly, reinforces the image (if not necessarily the reality) of a harmonious and stable society developing in a smooth and evolutionary fashion. For the purpose of the present

16. *Jen-min jih-pao* [People's daily], 19 June 1980.

17. "Discussions," Institute of Philosophic Research, Chinese Academy of Social Sciences, Peking, 25 June 1980.

18. "Fundamental Change in China's Class Situation," *Beijing Review,* 23 November 1979, p. 17.

19. "Discussions," Marxism-Leninism-Mao Tsetung Thought Institute, 17 June 1980.

discussion, it will perhaps suffice to note that an evolutionary conception of social development largely excludes human purpose from the historical scheme of things and is certainly incongruous with any sort of visionary utopianism. "Were some utopian social order to emerge from processes of evolution," it has been observed, "it would be a long time coming, and essentially accidental."[20]

III. The Burdens of History

The postponement of radical social change, and the message that the socialist and communist utopia lies far in the distant historical future, are further conveyed by a new historical analysis which places an enormous emphasis on the persistence of China's "feudal" past.[21] Although it is maintained that China is a socialist society, it is a country that still suffers from the weight of its long history, a past which manifests itself in the present both in the form of a heritage of economic backwardness and in the persistence of a deeply ingrained "feudal consciousness." The economic and ideological burdens of the past, it is suggested, make the development of socialism a far more difficult and lengthy process than hitherto anticipated.

This pessimistic assessment of the effects of China's lingering "feudal backwardness" stands in striking contrast to the Maoist perception of the relationship between China's past, present, and future. Mao, inspired by a utopian impulse to escape history, converted China's heritage of backwardness into socialist advantages. Whereas the bourgeoisie had dominated the advanced industrialized countries of the West for nearly three centuries, thus making "the poisons of the bourgeoisie very powerful" and permeating "every nook and cranny" of Western societies, China, he argued, was fortunate to suffer only three generations of bourgeois class dominance. Whereas the capitalist regime in the West was firmly consolidated and thus resistant to radical social and ideological transformation, China, relatively unencumbered by capitalist influences, was amenable to con-

20. Wilbert E. Moore, "The Utility of Utopias," *American Sociological Review* 31 (1966):767.

21. For example, Li and Lin, "Tentative Discussion on the Struggle Against Vestiges of Feudalism," pp. 29–42.

tinuous processes of revolutionary transformation. And whereas the moral corruptions inherent in the overly mature and ossified capitalist countries had sapped the revolutionary spirit of their working classes, the Chinese people were characterized by the virtues of being "poor and blank"—and, as Mao so often proclaimed, poor people want change and revolution while blank sheets of paper offer the opportunity to write the newest revolutionary words. From these beliefs in the advantages of backwardness, Mao drew a strikingly optimistic conclusion: "Lenin said: 'The more backward the country, the more difficult its transition from capitalism to socialism.' Now it seems that this way of speaking is incorrect. As a matter of fact, the more backward the economy, the easier, not the more difficult, the transition from capitalism to socialism."[22] Backwardness, to be sure, was to be overcome, but it was the special moral and revolutionary potentialities inherent in that very condition which held the promise of China's future socialist greatness. Just as in the Biblical prophecy that the last shall be first, Mao believed that the backward were destined to soon overtake the advanced.

These eminently Maoist notions are now condemned as "utopian" and "reactionary," although the heresies are not always attributed directly to Mao who authored them, but rather to the author's evil associates. In post-Maoist Chinese Marxist ideology, there are no advantages, socialist or otherwise, to be found in China's economic, social, and cultural backwardness. Indeed, the absence of a full and genuine capitalist phase of development in modern Chinese history is regarded as a great historical tragedy, for it is now taken as an article of the Marxist faith that "capitalism is a necessary element in the victory over feudal relationships"; and, it is stressed, "Marxism holds that socialism is the outcome of basic production relationships when capitalism is at a high stage of development, and that socialism can only be built on a foundation of highly developed socialized large-scale production." But China was precluded from reaping the material and social benefits of capitalism due to the combination of foreign imperialism and domestic feudalism, a "mutual collusion"

22. Mao Tse-tung, "Reading Notes on the Soviet Union's 'Political Economy,' " *Mao Tse-tung ssu-hsiang wan-sui* [Long live the thought of Mao Tse-tung] (Taipei: n.p., 1969), pp. 333–34.

which inhibited the emergence of a genuine national bourgeoisie and instead gave rise to a "bureaucratic compradore bourgeoisie and its political domination." Under this regime, "the old feudal system never sustained total destruction."[23]

If China avoided many of the evils of capitalism, it suffered all the more because the abortiveness of capitalism facilitated the persistence of its pernicious feudal heritage. And that heritage survived into the postrevolutionary era, distorting the political and economic life of the new society: "In a country as backward as China, even following seizure of power by the proletariat, a restoration of feudalism continued to be the most important danger faced by the revolution. History is not severed by a single stroke of the knife. . . ."[24]

The persistence of "feudalism," and the continued danger of a "feudal restoration," are attributed not only to the objective conditions of the modern Chinese historical situation but also to the political and ideological failings of the Chinese Communist Party. If modern capitalism proved abortive in China, and if the indigenous bourgeoisie was too weak a social class to fulfill its historic mission, then the task of carrying out the "bourgeois-democratic" phase of the revolution fell to the Chinese Communist Party. But the Party's "new democratic" revolution, it is acknowledged, was less than completely successful,[25] partly because the Party gravely underestimated the vestiges of feudalism, and partly because of the Party's "metaphysical denial . . . of all positive results of the growth of capitalism."[26] Thus a "feudal consciousness," deeply-rooted in a two-thousand-year old tradition of an unchanging "small-scale peasant economy," persisted into the postrevolutionary era, there sustained by a relatively slow rate of modern economic growth and there finding its natural social base among a peasantry still mired in feudalistic habits, traditions, and ways of thought. Thus China re-

23. Li and Lin, "Tentative Discussion on the Struggle Against Vestiges of Feudalism," pp. 30–33.

24. Ibid., p. 33.

25. "On the Ideology of Feudalism," *Wen-hui pao*, 16 September 1979; *JPRS* 74526:11.

26. Li and Lin, "Tentative Discussion on the Struggle Against Vestiges of Feudalism," pp. 34 and 38.

mained not with the Maoist virtues of being "poor and blank" but in a deplorable "state of poverty and blankness."[27] And it was this state of affairs, it is argued, that was in large measure responsible for the political and economic errors which marked and marred the last years of the Maoist era.

It is interesting to note that this argument reveals not only the reappearance of orthodox Marxist views on the historically progressive character of capitalism but also the revival of orthodox Marxist judgments about the peasantry, frequently accompanied by conventionally pejorative Marxist imagery on "the idiocy of rural life." For Mao the sources of revolutionary creativity and social progress resided in the countryside, and the peasantry was the true revolutionary class. In post-Maoist Chinese Marxist theory, by contrast, peasants are portrayed as narrow in their thinking and conservative in their habits, and the countryside in general is seen as the repository of backwardness. Indeed, the peasantry is viewed as the social carrier of "feudalistic" ideas and "petty-bourgeois ideology," which, it is alleged, lie at the root of the pernicious "ultraleftist" current which manifested itself during the Great Leap Forward campaign and found its ultimate political expression in the "feudal-fascist" rule of Lin Piao and the "Gang of Four."

It is thus that the responsibility for the evils of the recent past and the problems of the present are shifted from the eminently urban-oriented leaders in Peking to the lingering "feudal remnants" of China's historic past, with the peasantry implictly bearing the blame as the social source of backward ideas and ideologies. As a leading Marxist theoretician recently remarked: "Our country is dominated by small producers who are accustomed to obey imperial paternalism and who cherish the dream of absolute equality. It will take a long time to change them."[28]

The stress on the survival of the evils of the past, and the emphasis on the need to overcome the burdens of the traditional heritage, is a way to deny that the problems which beset Chinese society may be contradictions inherent in the new society itself rather than remnants

27. "On the Ideology of Feudalism," p. 13.

28. "Discussions," Institute of Political Economy, Chinese Academy of Social Sciences, Shanghai, 12 July 1980.

inherited from the millennia. It is perhaps instructive to recall here that the enormous emphasis in Soviet ideology on the need to overcome the old Tsarist historical heritage long served as a means to ignore the contradictions of the new social order produced by the revolution.

If the persistence of "feudal consciousness"—which is regarded as the major barrier to modernization and thus to the development of socialism—is essentially an ideological problem, the agreed-upon solution is essentially economic. To be sure, educational efforts to "emancipate the mind" are necessary, but the ultimate remedy, it is stressed, is "the growth of productive forces" and the consequent rise in the cultural level of the populace.[29] "The ghost of feudal consciousness," it is proclaimed, "will in the end be disposed of by the thundering guns of modernization."[30] But modernization is of course a lengthy process. And thus the arrival of the good society must await the consummation of that process.

IV. The Stages of Socialism

China, contemporary Chinese Marxist theory claims, is a socialist society, and not merely a society in the process of "the transition to socialism." The claim rests on what is taken to be the defining feature of socialism, namely, the abolition of private property in the means of production and its replacement by a system of public ownership, a transformation essentially accomplished by the year 1956. Yet while China is socialist, it is acknowledged that it is a socialism of what is termed a "low" or "undeveloped" character: "Although we have established socialist public ownership, we still have a long way to go to establish a socialist society as described by Marx. . . . we remain in a stage of socialism not yet well developed. . . ."[31]

29. Li and Lin, "Tentative Discussion on the Struggle Against Vestiges of Feudalism," p. 30.

30. "On the Ideology of Feudalism," p. 16.

31. Su Shaozhi, "On the Principal Contradiction Facing Our Society Today," *Xue Shu Yue Kan* [Academic monthly], June 1979, in *JPRS* 74813:14. As put by another leading theoretician: "In the underdeveloped socialist stage, agricultural productivity remains low, ownership forms remain varied, and commodity production remains a fact. The system of distribution according to work does not function

For socialism, it is emphasized, is not a single stage in historical development but rather a process which proceeds through many stages, each of which is tied to, and essentially determined by, the level of economic development. Moreover, the procession through the various stages of socialism is of indeterminate historical length, and the time of the consummation of the process cannot be predicted in advance: "As to how long this period will last, we are not fortune tellers so we cannot guess. But owing to the backwardness of production in our country, it will undoubtedly be a very, very long period divided into numerous stages."[32]

There is of course nothing particularly novel about the view that socialism passes through various stages of development. The notion is present in original Marxist theory and, indeed, in the thought of Mao Tse-tung, who also spoke of the "stages" of development in postrevolutionary society. What is noteworthy about the post-Maoist view of "the stages of socialism" is that the process is conceived in essentially evolutionary terms, as a gradual and peaceful social progression from lower to higher stages, with each stage reflecting the growth of the productive forces. For Mao Tse-tung, by contrast, the whole process of development—from the transition to socialism to and through the realization of a communist utopia—was characterized by a continuous series of radical revolutionary ruptures with the past, by qualitative breaks with existing reality, and by changes in social relations and popular consciousness proceeding as rapidly as possible with, as Mao put it, "one revolution following another . . . without interruption."[33]

Whereas for Mao the socialist transformation of social relationships, forms of political organization, and especially the consciousness of the masses was more the precondition for modern economic development than its product, Mao's ideological successors believe that the development of material productive forces is the essential

---

in the same way Marx prophesized because productivity . . . is still underdeveloped." "Discussions," Institute of Economics, Nankai University, Tianjin, 28 June 1980.

32. Sun Shuping, "Tentative Discussion of Basic Contradictions in a Socialist Society," *Xue Shu Yue Kan* [Academic monthly], July 1977, in *JPRS* 74450:7.

33. Mao Tse-tung, "Speech to the Supreme State Conference," 28 January 1958, *Chinese Law and Government* 1.4:10–14.

prerequisite for social and intellectual change. Whereas Mao viewed "the stages of socialism" as a continuous process of revolutionary transformation, in which social contradictions and struggles would constitute the motive force of historical change, his successors look to a long-term and gradual process of evolutionary change, characterized by a relatively peaceful and socially harmonious course of economic and social development. These differences between the Maoist and post-Maoist versions of Chinese Marxism are particularly apparent in the treatment of the question of class struggle, an issue of enormous practical as well as theoretical significance.

In striking contrast to the enormous Maoist emphasis on social contradictions and class struggles as the necessary motive force of sociohistorical development, the evolutionary conception of the "stages of socialism" presented in post-Maoist ideology implies social harmony. It is thus hardly surprising that the Maoist doctrine of the continuance of class struggle in a socialist society has been condemned as erroneous in theory and harmful in practice.[34] It is acknowledged, to be sure, that certain social class differences remain and that a form of class struggle must still be waged—for it would otherwise be theoretically impossible to justify the continued existence of "the dictatorship of the proletariat"—but class struggle is now directed against what are termed "the remnants" of the old exploiting classes, their ideological residues, and "a handful of counterrevolutionaries." The exploiting classes themselves have been abolished, it is maintained, and under a "socialist system of public ownership of the means of production" it is impossible either for the old exploiting classes to reconstitute themselves or for new exploiting classes to emerge.[35] "Facts tell us," it is argued, "that the development of socialism has already passed through one stage and is currently in a second stage—the stage of two different kinds of public ownership of the means of production in which class and class struggle no longer persists."[36]

34. Wang Ruisun, Song Yangyan and Qin Yanshi, "A Chat About the Nature and Characteristics of a Socialist Society," *Jingji Yanjiu* [Economic research] 10 (1979), in *JPRS* 74866:2.

35. Jin Wen, "On Current Classes and Class Struggle, *Jiefang Ribao* [Liberation daily], 23 July 1979, in *JPRS* 74334:4–5.

36. Sun, "Tentative Discussion of Basic Contradictions," p. 9.

Thus the principal contradiction in Chinese society is no longer between antagonistic social classes but rather between the productive forces, which are relatively backward, and the relations of production, which are presumably socialist in character and therefore relatively advanced. And thus the obvious solution for the contradiction is to direct all energies to the building of a modern industrial economy. As the matter is typically formulated:

> Inasmuch as a fundamental transformation occurs in the class relationships of a socialist society, the principal contradiction in a socialist society is no longer between the proletariat and the bourgeoisie but rather the contradiction that socialist production is far from capable of satisfying the needs of society. If this contradiction is to be resolved, the priority must be to accelerate socialist construction and rapidly bring about the Four Modernizations. A look back at the previous period shows that because of confusion in demarcating the period of the transition [to socialism] and socialism itself, class struggle was seen as the paramount contradiction and the major efforts were devoted to political movements, which obstructed the shift to the emphasis on production and resulted in lost opportunities for socialist construction. We are determined not to follow this same old disastrous road again.[37]

All other social contradictions are of a secondary and nonantagonistic character, and can be resolved, it is confidently assumed, peacefully and gradually in accordance with the development of the productive forces.

The post-Maoist deemphasis on class struggle does more than simply lend support to an evolutionary conception of "the stages of socialism" which gradually unfold over a long historical era. It also serves as a way to mask the social contradictions of the present. One such contradiction—and one which loomed large in Maoist ideology—is the gap between town and countryside, and the resulting conflict of interests between workers and peasants. But that quite real social contradiction is largely ignored in a post-Maoist Chinese Marxist ideology which confines class struggle to a skirmish against "remnants" of the old exploiting classes and which propounds the new orthodoxy that there is "no basic conflict of interests among the

37. Wang, et al., "A Chat About the Nature and Characteristics of a Socialist Society," p. 11.

people."[38] The abolition of the distinction between town and countryside is, of course, still proclaimed as an ultimate goal, but its realization is postponed to a time when the growth of the productive forces have sufficiently ripened. And since social change can only follow in the wake of economic development, as is repeatedly emphasized, the goal of abolishing the distinctions between the urban and rural areas is severed from the social practice of the present, relegated to an unspecified time in the future, and safely ritualized.

A second, and perhaps more fundamental, socioeconomic contradiction which the present deemphasis on class struggle serves to mask is the conflict between rulers and ruled. In a society where private property and private ownership of the means of production largely have been abolished, and where the state has become the *de facto* economic manager of society, the principal social contradiction clearly is no longer primarily economic in nature but rather political, between those who hold political power in the state apparatus and those who do not; it is, in essence, the distinction between the rulers and the ruled. Mao early recognized this elemental fact, emphasizing in 1957 the contradiction between the "leadership and the led."[39] And from there he was driven inexorably to the conclusion that China's political and economic bureaucrats were becoming a new exploiting class, "bourgeois elements sucking the blood of the workers," he charged in 1965,[40] in effect, a functional (albeit propertyless) bourgeoisie able to exploit society and appropriate much of the fruits of social labor by virtue of the political power they wielded. When Mao and Maoists spoke of class struggle between "the bourgeoisie and the proletariat," the term "bourgeoisie" referred not to lingering remnants of an old and expropriated capitalist class but rather to those who occupied positions of privilege and authority in the postrevolutionary political and economic bureaucracies, and particularly in the higher echelons of the Chinese Communist Party. The

38. Wu Jiang, "Correct Handling of Contradictions Among the People is a General Subject," *Hung-ch'i* [Red flag] 2 (February 1979) in *JPRS* 73304:4.

39. Mao Tse-tung, *On the Correct Handling of Contradictions Among the People* (Peking: Foreign Languages Press, 1957), p. 49.

40. Mao Tse-tung, "Comment on Comrade Ch'en Cheng-jen's Stay in a Primary Unit" (29 January 1965), in *JPRS* 49826:23.

proposition that bureaucrats can constitute themselves as a new ruling class, a notion remarkably similar to Milovan Djilas' theory of "the new class," received abundant Maoist theoretical elaboration during the Cultural Revolution era.[41]

The Maoist theory of a bureaucratic ruling class has of course now vanished from Chinese Marxist writings, for it is obviously a notion profoundly unsettling to those in power and not one conducive to an ideology which insists on a diminishing role for class struggle in the development of a presumably socialist society. It is acknowledged, to be sure, that bureaucracy and bureaucratism remain problems in Chinese society, problems which are variously attributed to economic and cultural backwardness, the vestiges of feudalism, and the persistence of a "small producers' mentality." But the theory of a new bureaucratic class, with interests fundamentally opposed to the interests of the masses, is a matter now beyond the pale of acceptable political discussion. In its place has come the orthodox dogma that it is impossible for a new exploiting class to emerge in a society which has established a system of public ownership of the means of production. It is thus that the radical deemphasis on class struggle serves to obscure the social contradictions generated by the post-revolutionary order itself and instead directs attention to the problems inherited from the past, particularly the heritage of economic backwardness.

An evolutionary conception of "the stages of socialism," combined with the doctrine of the increasing diminution of class struggle, is an ideology which serves to support and rationalize the social status quo. Since it is assumed that social development must follow and reflect economic development—and since China is economically impoverished— it is an ideology that conveys the message that little or no social change can be anticipated in the foreseeable future. It is also an ideology which serves to dampen utopian hopes since it counsels that what people are able to achieve is bound to (and limited by) the stage of social development in which they find themselves, a

41. One of the more extensive theoretical discussions of the thesis appeared shortly before Mao's death in a treatise published under the acronym "Ma Yen-wen." See "The Bureaucratic Class and the Dictatorship of the Proletariat," *Pei-ching ta-hsüeh hsüeh-pao* [Peking University journal] 4 (1976).

stage which is determined, in turn, by the level of development of the productive forces. Thus the striving for socialist and communist goals is largely removed from the realm of human desires and volition and entrusted to the impersonal forces and objective laws of economic development.

V. Socialism and Modernization

The overwhelming emphasis on building the economic foundations for socialism and communism in post-Maoist Chinese Marxist theory provides—and is of course intended to provide—ideological support for the policy of "the Four Modernizations" pursued by Mao Tse-tung's successors. In contrast to Maoism, contemporary Chinese Marxism gives primacy to productive forces over productive relations, and assumes that economic development rather than class struggle is the motor of historical change. By thereby subordinating the transformation of social relationships to the development of the forces of production, post-Maoist theory serves to postpone the arrival of the communist utopia prophesied in Marxist theory to an unspecified time in the future, to a time when the level of economic development is sufficiently high to support further social change. The guiding theoretical notion which justifies the postponement is essentially the old Soviet assumption (which the Chinese Communists embraced in the early 1950s and which Mao Tse-tung abandoned in the late 1950s) that state ownership of the means of production combined with the rapid development of modern productive forces will more or less automatically produce a communist utopia.

While the economic results of the pursuit of "the Four Modernizations" remain to be seen, the social results are quite predictable—and it safely can be predicted that they will move China further away from, rather than closer to, the socialist goals which modernization presumably is intended to serve. It is above all a policy which will tend to increase and institutionalize socioeconomic inequalities in a society which already suffers from enormous and glaring inequality.

Socialism, by Marxist definition, does of course presuppose inequality. If the social product is to be distributed in accordance with the principle of "to each according to one's work," inequality necessarily will result for the simple reason that people are unequally endowed and their labor contributions will thus be uneven. But it is assumed in Marxist theory that the process of the transition to socialism and communism demands progressive reductions in social and economic inequalities.

Yet even the most cursory review of post-Maoist economic policies and ideological tendencies reveals an almost wholesale repudiation of egalitarian Maoist practices in favor of policies which may or may not produce a more rapid rate of economic growth but which will clearly produce greater social inequities. Growing wage differentials accompanied by a renewed stress on material incentives, piece-rate wages, and bonus payments obviously will increase economic differences among the urban working class. Strengthening the authority of factory managers and technological personnel, the borrowing of managerial methods from capitalist countries, and stringent demands for "labor discipline" can only widen the gap between managers and workers in factories. Higher wages and status for the technological intelligentsia, ideologically rationalized by the revival of the formula that "intellectuals are part of the working class," may yield short-term economic benefits but will certainly have the long-term result of promoting the stratification of bureaucratic and intellectual elites increasingly separated from the masses of workers and peasants. The adoption of profit-making criteria for the operation of economic enterprises is likely to increase already enormous regional economic differences. Agricultural policies which deemphasize collective work in favor of the expansion of individual family plots and market relations will surely result in greater socioeconomic inequality in the countryside. Finally, the abandonment of Maoist educational reforms in favor of the system which existed in the 1950s will promote and reinforce social differentiations in general. The educational system is of course a powerful force for fostering equality—or inequality—in any society, but particularly so in one where private ownership of the means of production has been abolished and where social status is based on income and function rather than property. The reintroduction of standardized examinations for admission to secondary schools and universities, the revival of traditional teaching methods and performance criteria, and the reopening of special schools for unusually talented youth are measures which obviously favor the children of bureaucrats and intellectuals over children from working class families, and favor urban over rural inhabitants.

These policies, which proceed under the slogan of "the Four Modernizations," are logically accompanied by increasingly strident condemnations of what is called "the fallacy of egalitarianism," an ideological drive reminiscent of Stalin's infamous campaigns against egalitarian strivings, which the old Soviet dictator once denounced as worthy only of "a primitive sect of ascetic monks." And the policies and ideology of Mao's successors are likely to yield social results similar to those brought about by their Soviet counterparts. If the degree of socioeconomic equality is one standard to measure whether a society is socialist, or one moving in a socialist direction, then it would seem that there is little socialist in the much-heralded program of "socialist modernization."

"If a socialist society does not promote socially collectivistic aims, then what of socialism still remains?" Mao Tse-tung once asked.[42] It is not a question that his political and ideological successors seem inclined to ponder.

An economically deterministic interpretation of Marxism which subordinates all to the over-riding task of developing productive forces in the most rapid possible fashion is not a version of Marxism conducive to confronting the dilemma of the means and ends of socialism. Whereas Maoism, in the Maoist era, was distinguished by its concern with reconciling the means of modern economic development with the ends of socialism, this concern is glaringly absent in the post-Maoist version of "Marxism-Leninism-Mao Tsetung Thought." The revised doctrine rests on a faith that modern technology is a universal panacea for all the ills and contradictions which afflict society. In the process, the means of economic development tend increasingly to be converted into final ends. Indeed, one of the more curious features of the current Chinese Marxist mentality is a proclivity to define socialism almost exclusively in terms of economic productivity. "The aim of the socialist revolution is to emancipate the productive forces," the Party theoretical journal *Red Flag* announced at the time of the inauguration of the policy of "the Four Modernizations."[43] "The ultimate goal of all our revolutionary struggle is to liberate and develop the productive forces, that is, to develop socialist economic construction to raise the material standards of all

42. Mao, "Reading Notes on the Soviet Union's 'Political Economy,' " p. 197.
43. *Hung-ch'i* [Red flag] 1 (January 1977).

the people," it is typically stated in the most prominent Marxist periodicals.[44] And high Party officials repeatedly declare that "the aim of our Party in leading the whole nation in making revolution and taking over political power is, in the final analysis, to develop the economy."[45]

The writings and speeches where such statements appear are remarkably unconcerned with the presumably Marxian socialist and communist goals of the revolution, save in the most ritualistic and passing fashion. "Socialism" is virtually equated with modernization and the rapid development of the productive forces. Indeed, it is often suggested that a socialist society is to be evaluated by its productive achievements. As China's leading economic journal rhetorically queries: "If the development of the socialist economy is permanently slower than that of the capitalist economy, where is the manifestation of the superiority of socialism?"[46] It might also be asked that if the aim of socialism is to "develop the productive forces," then wherein lies the difference between socialism and capitalism?

China's present political and ideological leaders believe that they are pursuing a path to a socialist and communist future, and there is no reason to doubt the sincerity of the belief. But one well might ask whether the means they are employing are consistent with the ends they proclaim to seek.

An economistic doctrine which subordinates social and ideological considerations to the task of building modern productive forces—and assumes that the desired social results will naturally flow from a developed economy—is a doctrine that not only ignores the dilemma of reconciling the means of modern industrialism with the goals of socialism, but also one which neglects the question of the nature of the human beings who presumably will construct the envisioned new society. It is most unlikely that a people schooled in the ideology and practice of "the Four Modernizations" will emerge from the

44. "The Great Transition and the Important Themes of Historical Materialism," *Che-hsüeh yen-chiu* [Philosophic research] 2 (February 1979), in *JPRS* 73710:14.

45. Han Guang, "On the Development of Modern Industry," *Beijing Review,* 23 March 1979, p. 9.

46. Xue, "Study and Apply the Objective Laws of Socialist Economic Development," p. 7.

process with socialist values and ideals—and the latter are no less necessary preconditions for socialism than its assumed material prerequisites. But the post-Maoist version of Chinese Marxist theory propagates the idea that one need only rely on the "vigorous development of productive forces and the gradual elevation of material life" to bring about a "gradual elevation of the socialist consciousness of the people."[47] It is a faith similar to, if not borrowed from, the longstanding Soviet ideological orthodoxy that raising the material standard of life will itself produce a popular socialist consciousness. And there is little reason to believe that the assumption, and the policies it rationalizes, will yield more salutary social results in China than it has in Russia.

By a deterministic reading of Marx's proposition that "being determines consciousness," with "being" often narrowly interpreted as the level of economic development, contemporary Chinese Marxists present a mechanistic version of Marxist theory which distorts the writings of Marx as well as abandons the teachings of Mao. Marx, for one, did not assume that socialism was simply the product of modern economic development, or even, for that matter, the transformation of social relationships. No less important was the socialist transformation of human beings through what Marx called "revolutionizing practice," whereby people would change themselves in the course of changing their social world. "The materialist doctrine that men are products of circumstances and upbringing, and that therefore changed men are the product of other circumstances and changed upbringing," Marx wrote, "forgets that it is men who change circumstances and that the educator must himself be educated. . . . The coincidence of the changing of circumstances and human activity can be conceived and rationally understood only as revolutionizing practice."[48] For Marx the new society presupposed, among other preconditions, the emergence of "new men."

Mao Tse-tung was very much in accord with this strand in the Marxist tradition in his repeated insistence on the importance of

47. Sun, "Tentative Discussion of Basic Contradictions in a Socialist Society," p. 10.

48. Karl Marx, "Theses on Feuerbach," Karl Marx and Friedrich Engels, *Collected Works* (New York: International Publishers, 1976), vol. 5, p. 7.

"remolding people."[49] And Mao shared with Martin Buber the "utopian" belief that the achievement of socialism "depends not on the technological state of things" but rather "on people and their spirit."[50] In the post-Maoist version of Chinese Marxism, however, it is precisely "the technological state of things" that is taken as decisive. And while the appropriate technological state is being built, the socialist and communist goals which modern technology presumably is to serve are postponed to an ever more remote future, and tend to become empty rituals increasingly divorced from social reality and political practice.

"History," Karl Marx wrote, "is nothing but the activity of men in pursuit of their ends."[51] What ends do Chinese Communists pursue in the post-Maoist era of the People's Republic? They claim to seek the communist utopia prophesied in Marxist theory, but they propagate a version of Marxism which relegates that utopia to a historical time so far in the future that it no longer bears any imaginable relationship to the present. Post-Maoist Chinese Marxism is an ideology that sets forth a gradual and evolutionary scheme of social development governed by impersonal and objective economic and historical laws, and thus one which provides little place for human will, wishes, and consciousness in the making of history. It is an ideology whose authors are preoccupied more with the burdens of the past than with visions of the future, who dwell more on the limitations imposed by historical reality than on the potentialities history offers. To be sure, it is an ideology which assumes that "modernization" eventually will produce communism, but also one which counsels that people can do little in the here and now to bring about the good society of the future, save to construct its economic foundations. Post-Maoist Chinese Marxism, in essence, is primarily

49. In Soviet ideology, Mao observed, "the emphasis is on the role played by machines in socialist transformation. However, if we do not raise the consciousness of the peasants and remold the ideology of man, how is it possible to rely on machines alone?" "Reading Notes on the Soviet Union's 'Political Economy,' " p. 336.

50. Martin Buber, *Paths in Utopia* (Boston: Beacon Press, 1958), pp. 46–47.

51. Karl Marx, *Selected Writings in Sociology and Social Philosophy*, T. B. Bottomore and Maxmilian Rubel, eds., (London: Watts, 1956), p. 63.

an ideology of modern economic development which promises, at least for the foreseeable future, no more than a slowly improving material standard of life.

If Chinese Marxist theoreticians have purged Maoism of its utopian elements, Chinese Communist political leaders have shorn socialism of its socialist meaning. "The purpose of socialism," Teng Hsiao-p'ing says, "is to make the country rich and strong."[52] That, of course, has been the purpose of Chinese modernizers and nationalists of all political and ideological persuasions for the past century—and indeed is the aim of nationalist leaders of all modern nations. While the goals of making the country "rich and strong" may satisfy Chinese nationalist impulses, it is not likely to inspire socially utopian aspirations. Nor are many likely to be moved to strive for Marxian utopian ends when Chinese Communist leaders repeatedly insist that the basic principle of Marxism is the vapid truism that "practice is the sole criterion of truth."

The official press now complains that China suffers from "a crisis of faith in Marxism."[53] And a foreign journalist observes that "the idealism, the drive, the almost religious fervor that marked Communism's early years and lasted until the Cultural Revolution have largely vanished."[54] And well might there be a "crisis of faith" and a vanishing of idealism when Marxism is reduced to an ideology of modernization, when the essence of the doctrine is redefined by the banal injunction "to seek truth from facts," when utopian goals are ritualized by being put off to a remote future, and when socialism itself is virtually equated with modern economic development.

Revolutions die not from failures to achieve utopian dreams, but when the goals, if not entirely forgotten, are lodged in a future so distant that they are severed from what is foreseeably possible and removed from the realm of what can be striven for in the here and now. It is precisely that function which is performed by the pro-

52. In remarks made to a visiting Rumanian delegation in November 1980. *New York Times*, 30 December 1980, p. 2.

53. Guo Luoji, "Commenting on the So-Called 'Confidence Crisis'" Shanghai *Wen Hui Bao*, 13 January 1980, *FBIS* (30 January 1980), pp. 9–11.

54. Fox Butterfield, "Apathy Replaces Idealism among Chinese," *New York Times*, 30 December 1980, p. 1.

foundly antiutopian character of Chinese Marxism in the post-Maoist era.

In pondering the fate of the Chinese Revolution in a conversation with an American writer in the mid-1960s, Mao Tse-tung wondered: "Is Communism only the piling of brick on brick? Is there no work to be done with man?"[55] Mao's successors are busily at work piling bricks, and no doubt they will eventually construct a huge edifice. But it seems doubtful that there will be anything socialist or communist about the structure and its inhabitants.

55. Anna Louise Strong, transcript of "Talk with Mao," 17 January 1964. Anna Louise Strong papers, Peking Municipal Library.

BIBLIOGRAPHIC NOTE

INDEX

Bibliographic Note

There are enormous bodies of literature on the topics of "Marxism," "Maoism," and "utopianism"—but very little has been written on the interrelationships between the three. The titles listed below constitute only a brief personal selection of writings relevant to the themes of the present volume, offered as suggestions for reading for those who might wish to pursue in greater depth the utopian aspects of the Maoist version of Marxism or who seek interpretations differing from those presented in the preceding pages.

The Writings of Mao Tse-tung

The official five volume edition of the *Selected Works of Mao Tse-tung*, covering the years 1926–1957, is published in English translation by the Foreign Languages Press in Peking (1965 and 1977). Besides excluding Mao's early writings and his more important post–1957 writings, the official edition excludes many works from the 1926–1957 period and alters the original texts of many of the writings it does include. The exclusions and alterations serve to obscure the more utopian aspects of Mao's thought. At present, there are no plans in the People's Republic of China to publish Mao's complete works, and it seems unlikely that a sixth volume of the *Selected Works* on the post–1957 period will appear at any time in the foreseeable future. It is in the post–1957 writings that the utopian character of the Maoist mentality is most fully apparent.

The deficiencies of the official *Selected Works* are compensated, in part, by several volumes published outside of China. About three hundred pages of extracts of Mao's writings from 1917 to the mid–1960s, translated from the original texts, are included in Stuart R. Schram, *The Political Thought of Mao Tse-tung*, revised and enlarged edition (New York: Praeger, 1969). A number of important post–1957 writings and speeches have been compiled by Jerome Ch'en in *Mao Papers* (London: Oxford University Press, 1970). Twenty-six texts dating from 1956 to 1971 are translated in Stuart Schram, ed., *Chairman Mao Talks to the*

People (New York: Pantheon, 1975). (The latter was originally published in England under the title *Mao Tse-tung Unrehearsed: Talks and Letters: 1956–71*, Penguin, 1974.)

Officially unauthorized writings of Mao which became available during the Cultural Revolution were reprinted in Taipei in 1967 and 1969 under the title *Mao Tse-tung ssu-hsiang wan-sui* [Long live the thought of Mao Tse-tung]. English translations of some of these texts can be found in the series "Translations on Communist China," *Joint Publications Research Service* (Washington, D.C.: U.S. Department of Commerce), *Current Background* (U.S. Consulate General, Hong Kong), and various issues of *Chinese Law and Government* (White Plains, N.Y.: International Arts and Sciences Press). Of special interest is Mao's 1961 treatise "Reading Notes on the Soviet Union's 'Political Economy,' " translated in *Joint Publications Research Service* 61269–2: 247–313.

A highly useful bibliographic guide to English-language translations of Mao's post–1949 writings has been compiled by John B. Starr and Nancy A. Dyer in *Post–Liberation Works of Mao Zedong: A Bibliography and Index* (Berkeley: University of California, Center for Chinese Studies, 1976).

A relatively complete edition of Mao's pre–1949 writings in Chinese was published in Japan in 1970 under the title *Mao Tse-tung Chi* [Collected works of Mao Tse-tung] (Tokyo: Mo Takuto Bunken Shiryo Kenyukai, 1970). A project to publish a complete edition of Mao's works in both Chinese and English is currently in progress under the editorship of Professor Kau Ying-mao at Brown University.

Maoism

Several of the best biographies of Mao analyze his thought as well as his life: Stuart R. Schram, *Mao Tse-tung* (New York: Simon and Schuster, 1967); Jerome Ch'en, *Mao and the Chinese Revolution* (London: Oxford University Press, 1965); and Ross Terrill, *Mao* (New York: Harper & Row, 1980).

Among the major works on the nature of Maoism and its relationship to the Marxist-Leninist tradition are: Benjamin I. Schwartz, *Chinese Communism and the Rise of Mao* (Cambridge, Mass.: Harvard University Press, 1951); Stuart R. Schram, *The Political Thought of Mao Tse-tung* (New York: Praeger, 1969); Stuart R. Schram, *Mao Tse-tung*; Frederic Wakeman, *History and Will: Philosophical Perspectives of Mao Tse-tung's*

Thought (Berkeley: University of California Press, 1973); John B. Starr, *Continuing the Revolution: The Political Thought of Mao* (Princeton, N.J.: Princeton University Press, 1979); Maurice Meisner, *Mao's China: A History of the People's Republic* (New York: The Free Press, 1977); Benjamin I. Schwartz, *Communism and China: Ideology in Flux* (Cambridge, Mass.: Harvard University Press, 1968); Franz Schurmann, *Ideology and Organization in Communist China* (Berkeley: University of California Press, 1968); James Peck and Victor Nee, eds., *China's Uninterrupted Revolution* (New York: Pantheon, 1975); Stuart Schram, *La "révolution permanente" en Chine* (Paris: Mouton, 1963); Helene Carrere d'Encausse and Stuart R. Schram, *Marxism and Asia* (London: Allen Lane, 1969); K. S. Karol, *China: The Other Communism* (New York: Hill & Wang, 1967); Paul M. Sweezy and Charles Bettelheim, *On the Transition to Socialism* (New York: Monthly Review Press, 1971); Raya Dunayevskaya, *Philosophy and Revolution* (New York: Dell, 1973); Stuart R. Schram, "The Cultural Revolution in Historical Perspective" in Schram, ed., *Authority, Participation and Cultural Change in China* (Cambridge: Cambridge University Press, 1973); James C. Hsiung, ed., *The Logic of "Maoism"* (New York: Praeger, 1974); and Dick Wilson, ed., *Mao Tse-tung in the Scales of History* (Cambridge: Cambridge University Press, 1977).

For a sampling of the diversity of Western views and interpretations, see the "Symposium on Mao and Marx," *Modern China,* 2.4 (October 1976) and 3.1, 2, and 4 (January, April, and October, 1977). The post-Maoist Chinese assessment of Mao and the redefinition of "Mao Tsetung Thought" is officially set forth in "Resolution on Certain Questions in the History of Our Party Since the Founding of the People's Republic of China," Sixth Plenary Session of the Eleventh Central Committee of the Communist Party of China, 27 June 1981, *Beijing Review,* 27 (July 6, 1981): 10–39. A typical Soviet view of Maoism is that of F. V. Konstantinov et al., *A Critique of Mao Tse-tung's Theoretical Conceptions* (Moscow: Progress Publishers, 1972).

On the early intellectual development of the young Mao Tse-tung see: Angus W. McDonald, *Urban Origins of Rural Revolution* (Berkeley: University of California Press, 1978); Jerome Ch'en, *Mao and the Chinese Revolution;* Stuart R. Schram, *Mao Tse-tung;* and Frederic Wakeman, *History and Will.* The latter three volumes also explore the influence of traditional Chinese thought on the evolution of Maoism, a theme emphasized in Wolfgang Bauer, *China and the Search for Happiness* (New York: The Seabury Press, 1976).

Utopianism

There is a long and continuing tradition of the scholarly study of utopias and utopian modes of thought. One hardly can do better, however, than the recently published volume, rich in quality as well as quantity, by Frank E. Manuel and Fritzie P. Manuel, *Utopian Thought in the Western World* (Cambridge, Mass.: Harvard University Press, 1979). For a representative sampling of the diversity of scholarly approaches to the study of utopianism, see Frank E. Manuel, ed., *Utopias and Utopian Thought* (Boston: Beacon Press, 1963). Other influential works include: Lewis Mumford, *The Story of Utopias* (New York: Viking Press, 1962); Joyce O. Hertzler, *The History of Utopian Thought* (New York: Macmillan, 1923); Norman Cohn, *The Pursuit of the Millennium* (New York: Harper & Row, 1961); J. L. Talmon, *The Origins of Totalitarian Democracy* (New York: Praeger, 1965) and *Political Messianism* (New York: Praeger, 1960); George Kateb, ed., *Utopia* (New York: Atherton, 1971); Peter Worsley, *The Trumphet Shall Sound* (New York: Schocken Books, 1969); Michael Walzer, *The Revolution of the Saints* (Cambridge, Mass.: Harvard University Press, 1965); and Wilbert E. Moore, "The Utility of Utopias," *American Sociological Review,* 31 (1966): 765–72.

For fruitful theoretical perspectives on utopian modes of thought, see Max Weber, *The Sociology of Religion* (Boston: Beacon Press, 1963); Karl Mannheim, *Ideology and Utopia* (New York: Harcourt Brace, 1952); and Sheldon S. Wolin, *Politics and Vision* (Boston: Little, Brown & Co., 1960).

Works on utopian strains in the Chinese tradition include: Wolfgang Bauer, *China and the Search for Happiness* (New York: The Seabury Press, 1976); Frederic Wakeman, *History and Will;* Vincent Shih, *The Taiping Ideology: Its Sources, Interpretations and Influences* (Seattle: University of Washington Press, 1967); Hsiao Kung-chuan, *In and Out of Utopia: K'ang Yu-wei's Social Thought* (Seattle: Far Eastern and Russian Institute, University of Washington, 1968); and Jean Chesneaux, "Egalitarian and Utopian Traditions in the East," *Diogenes,* 62 (1968): 76–102. On the relative absence of utopianism in traditional Chinese thought see Max Weber, *The Religion of China,* translated and edited by Hans H. Gerth (Glencoe, Ill.: The Free Press, 1951).

Marxism and Utopianism

The principal statements of Marx and Engels on utopian modes of thought are: Karl Marx and Frederick Engels, "The Manifesto of the

Communist Party," Part III, in Marx and Engels, *Selected Works* (Moscow: Foreign Languages Publishing House, 1950), vol. 1, and Engels, "Socialism: Utopian and Scientific" in Marx and Engels, *Selected Works*, vol. 2. For an orthodox Marxist treatment of the first modern utopian thinker, see Karl Kautsky, *Thomas More and His Utopia* (New York: International Publishers, 1927).

The significant interpretative works on the place of utopianism in Marxist theory include: George Lichtheim, *Marxism: An Historical and Critical Study* (New York: Praeger, 1961); Shlomo Avineri, *The Social and Political Thought of Karl Marx* (Cambridge: Cambridge University Press, 1968); Robert C. Tucker, *Philosophy and Myth in Karl Marx* (Cambridge: Cambridge University Press, 1961) and *The Marxian Revolutionary Idea* (New York: Norton, 1969) especially chapters 1 and 7; Erich Fromm, *Marx's Concept of Man* (New York: Frederick Ungar, 1961); Ernst Bloch, *Das Prinzip Hoffnung*, 3 vols. (Frankfort am Main: Suhrkamp, 1968); Herbert Marcuse, *Five Lectures: Psychoanalysis, Politics and Utopia* (Boston: Beacon Press, 1970); Bertell Ollman, "Marx's Vision of Communism: A Reconstruction," in Seweryn Bialer, ed., *Radical Visions of the Future* (Boulder, Colo.: Westview Press, 1977), pp. 35–83; Adam Ulam, "Socialism and Utopia," *Daedalus* 94 (Spring, 1965): 382–400; and Stanley Moore, "Utopian Themes in Marx and Mao," *Monthly Review* 21.2 (June, 1969): 33–44.

Utopian Socialism and Populism

On the history of utopian socialism and its relationship to Marxism see: G. D. H. Cole, *Socialist Thought: The Forerunners 1789–1850* (London: Macmillan, 1953); George Lichtheim, *The Origins of Socialism* (New York: Praeger, 1969); and Martin Buber, *Paths in Utopia* (Boston: Beacon Press, 1958), an eloquent modern statement of the utopian socialist tradition.

Works on Russian Populism include: Franco Venturi, *Roots of Revolution* (New York: Grosset & Dunlap, 1966); Leopold Haimson, *The Russian Marxists and the Origins of Bolshevism* (Cambridge, Mass.: Harvard University Press, 1955); and Richard Wortman, *The Crisis of Russian Populism* (London: Cambridge University Press, 1967). On the interaction between Marxist and Populist ideas see A. Walicki, *The Controversy Over Capitalism* (Oxford: Clarendon Press, 1969). Two important works on the varieties of Populism are: Ghita Ionescu and Ernest Gellner, eds., *Populism* (New York: Macmillan, 1969) and Peter Worsley, *The Third World* (Chicago: University of Chicago Press, 1970).

For Lenin's critique of Populist ideology see: "The Economic Content of Narodism," V. I. Lenin, *Collected Works* (Moscow: Foreign Languages Publishing House, 1960), vol. 1, pp. 333–507; "A Characterisation of Economic Romanticism" and "The Heritage We Renounce," *Collected Works*, vol. 2, pp. 129–265 and 491–534.

Marxism, Maoism, and Modernization

The relevant theoretical literature includes: Adam Ulam, *The Unfinished Revolution* (New York: Random House, 1960); Alexander Gerschenkron, *Economic Backwardness in Historical Perspective* (New York: Praeger, 1965); Herbert Marcuse, *Soviet Marxism* (New York: Columbia University Press, 1958); Barrington Moore, *Soviet Politics—The Dilemma of Power* (Cambridge, Mass.: Harvard University Press, 1950); Robert C. Tucker, *The Marxian Revolutionary Idea*, chapter 4; Charles Bettelheim, *Class Struggles in the U.S.S.R.: First Phase, 1917–1923* (New York: Monthly Review Press, 1976); Paul Baran, *The Political Economy of Growth* (New York: Marzani and Munsell, 1957); John G. Gurley, *Challengers to Capitalism: Marx, Lenin, and Mao* (San Francisco: San Francisco Book Co., 1976); Stephen Andors, *China's Industrial Revolution* (New York: Pantheon, 1977); Benjamin Schwartz, "Modernization and the Maoist Vision," *China Quarterly* 21 (January–March, 1965): 3–19; James Peck, "Revolution versus Modernization and Revisionism" in Victor Nee and James Peck, eds., *China's Uninterrupted Revolution* (New York: Pantheon, 1975), pp. 57–217; and Carl Riskin, "Maoism and Motivation" in Nee and Peck, eds., *China's Uninterrupted Revolution*, pp. 415–61.

On Personality Cults

For classic Marxist views, see: Karl Marx, "The Eighteenth Brumaire of Louis Bonaparte," Marx and Engels, *Selected Works*, vol. 1, pp. 221–311; George Plekhanov, *The Role of the Individual in History* (New York: International Publishers, 1940); Antonio Gramsci, "The Modern Prince" and "State and Civil Society" in *Selections from the Prison Notebooks of Antonio Gramsci* (New York: International Publishers, 1971), pp. 123–276.

Other relevant writings and documents include: Max Weber, *The Sociology of Religion;* Geoffrey Nelson, "The Concept of Cult, *The Sociological Review* 16.3 (1968): 351–62: Isaac Deutscher, *Stalin: A Political*

Biography (New York: Oxford University Press, 1949); Nikita Khrushchev, "Speech at the Twentieth Congress of the Soviet Communist Party" (1956), English translation in *The Anti-Stalin Campaign and International Communism,* edited by the Russian Institute, Columbia University (New York: Columbia University Press, 1956), pp. 1–89; Isaac Deutscher, "Khrushchev on Stalin" in Deutscher, *Ironies of History* (London: Oxford University Press, 1966), pp. 3–17; *On the Historical Experience of the Dictatorship of the Proletariat* (Peking: Foreign Languages Press, 1961); Frederic Wakeman, *History and Will,* chapters 1–6; Adrian Hsia, *The Chinese Cultural Revolution* (New York: The Seabury Press, 1972); Robert C. Tucker, "The Rise of Stalin's Personality Cult," *American Historical Review* 84.2 (April 1979): 114–45; Leonard Schapiro and John W. Lewis, "The Roles of the Monolithic Party under the Totalitarian Leader," in John W. Lewis, ed., *Party Leadership and Revolutionary Power in China* (Cambridge: Cambridge University Press, 1970), pp. 114–45; Edgar Snow, *The Long Revolution* (New York: Random House, 1972); Robert Jay Lifton, *Revolutionary Immortality* (New York: Random House, 1968); David Milton and Nancy Dall Milton, *The Wind Will Not Subside: Years in Revolutionary China—1964–1969* (New York: Pantheon, 1976); Stuart R. Schram, "The Party in Chinese Communist Ideology," *China Quarterly* 38 (April–June, 1969): 1–26; Benjamin Schwartz, "The Reign of Virtue: Some Broad Perspectives on Leader and Party in the Cultural Revolution," *China Quarterly* 35 (July–September, 1968): 1–17; and Central Committee of the Communist Party of China, "Resolution on Certain Questions in the History of Our Party Since the Founding of the People's Republic of China" (27 June 1981).

Ritualization and Deradicalization

Among the significant theoretical and historical works are: Crane Brinton, *The Anatomy of Revolution,* revised edition (New York: Vintage, 1965); Robert Michels, *Political Parties* (Glencoe, Ill.: The Free Press, 1949); Adam Ulam, *The Unfinished Revolution;* Robert C. Tucker, *The Marxian Revolutionary Idea,* especially chapter 6; James H. Meisel, *Counter–Revolution* (New York: Atherton, 1966); Paul M. Sweezy, *Post–Revolutionary Society* (New York: Monthly Review Press, 1980); Leon Trotsky, *The Revolution Betrayed* (New York: Merit Publications, 1937); Isaac Deutscher, *The Prophet Unarmed: Trotsky, 1921–1929* (New York: Vintage, 1965) and *The Unfinished Revolution, Russia 1917–1967* (London: Oxford University Press, 1967); Barrington Moore, *Soviet Politics—The Dilemma of Power;* Moshe Lewin, *Lenin's Last Struggle* (New York:

Index

TEXT DESIGNED BY DESIGN FOR PUBLISHING, BOB NANCE
JACKET DESIGNED BY RON FENDEL
COMPOSED BY WEIMER TYPESETTING CO., INC.
INDIANAPOLIS, INDIANA
MANUFACTURED BY BANTA COMPANY, MENASHA, WISCONSIN
TEXT IS SET IN TIMES ROMAN
DISPLAY LINES IN MELIOR AND TIMES ROMAN

Library of Congress Cataloging in Publication Data
Meisner, Maurice J., 1931–
Marxism, Maoism, and utopianism.
Bibliography: pp. 243–250.
Includes index.
1. Mao, Tse-tung, 1893–1976—Addresses, essays, lectures. 2. Marx, Karl, 1818–1883—Addresses, essays, lectures. 3. Communism—Addresses, essays, lectures. 4. Communism—China—Addresses, essays, lectures. 5. Utopias—Addresses, essays, lectures. I. Title.
HX418.5.M33M44 1982 335′.02 81-69825
ISBN 0-299-08420-5